TRADING LOCOMOTIVES

NAOFUMI NAKAMURA

TRADING LOCOMOTIVES

The Global Economy and the Development of

Japan's Railroads, 1869–1914

Columbia University Press / *New York*

This book was supported in part by a publication grant
from the Harvard-Yenching Institute.

Columbia University Press
Publishers Since 1893
New York   Chichester, West Sussex

Copyright © 2025 Columbia University Press
All rights reserved

Library of Congress Cataloging-in-Publication Data
Names: Nakamura, Naofumi, 1966– author
Title: Trading locomotives : the global economy and the development of Japan's railroads, 1869–1914 / Naofumi Nakamura.
Description: New York : Columbia University Press, [2025] | Includes bibliographical references and index.
Identifiers: LCCN 2024042496 (print) | LCCN 2024042497 (ebook) | ISBN 9780231218450 hardback | ISBN 9780231218467 trade paperback | ISBN 9780231562263 ebook
Subjects: LCSH: Railroads—Japan—History—19th century | Railroads—Japan—History—20th century | Railroads—History | Locomotive industry—Japan—History—19th century | Locomotive industry—Japan—History—20th century | Locomotive industry—History | Industrial revolution—Japan
Classification: LCC HE3358 .N328 2025 (print) | LCC HE3358 (ebook) | DDC 385.0952—dc23/eng/20241218

GPSR Authorized Representative: Easy Access System Europe, Mustamäe tee 50, 10621 Tallinn, Estonia, gpsr.requests@easproject.com

Cover design: Chang Jae Lee
Cover image: Utagawa Hiroshige III, *Tokyo Shiodome tetsudōkan jōkisha machiai no zu* [A Waiting Room for Locomotives at the Shiodome Station in Tokyo] (Tokyo: Iseya Kisaburō, 1873). Courtesy of the National Diet Library, Japan.

CONTENTS

Acknowledgments vii

Introduction 1

1 International Competition in the Global Locomotive Market 25

2 Technological Transfer and British Monopolization 53

3 Japan's Industrial Revolution and American Locomotives 77

4 The Rise of Japanese Trading Companies 115

5 War, Empire Building, and the Locomotive Trade 135

6 Localizing Locomotive Production in Japan 165

Conclusion 197

Notes 207
Bibliography 239
Index 251

ACKNOWLEDGMENTS

I am profoundly grateful to the numerous individuals and organizations whose support, guidance, and contributions made this book a reality.

First and foremost, I extend my heartfelt thanks to my parents, Seishi and Shizuyo, for their unwavering encouragement and support. I deeply regret that I was unable to complete this book before their passing. I am also immensely thankful to my wife, Saeko, for her patience, understanding, and unflagging belief in my work.

This book would not have reached fruition without the expertise and commitment of many dedicated professionals. I wish to extend my sincere gratitude to the following individuals: Shi-Lin Lo, my editor, for her insightful feedback and meticulous attention to detail; James Babb, Senior Editor at the International Publication Initiative of the University of Tokyo, for his exceptional support in the publication of this book; Caelyn Cobb, Senior Editor at Columbia University Press, for her invaluable guidance throughout the publication process; Marisa Lastres, Production Editor, for their exceptional and thorough production work; and Emily E. Simon and Ryan Perks for their essential contributions in advancing the book's progress. I also owe thanks to the three anonymous reviewers,

ACKNOWLEDGMENTS

whose constructive critiques significantly enhanced this work. Additionally, Jesus Solis helped me improve my English manuscript.

I would like to express my heartfelt gratitude to the following scholars for their invaluable intellectual support, advice, and encouragement: Professors Andrew Gordon, Steven J. Ericson, Geoffrey Jones, Takeshi Yuzawa, and Minoru Sawai, each of whom took the time to read the draft of this book and offer insightful feedback. In particular, I am incredibly grateful for Professor Ericson's thoughtful guidance, which has left a lasting impression on me. Professor Gordon offered me valuable advice and warm support for the publication of this book. Professors Victor Seow, Christopher Gerteis, Robert Hellyer, and Masaki Nakabayashi served as trusted confidants and were instrumental in my efforts to publish this book.

This research has been greatly enhanced by the resources and intellectual atmosphere at Harvard University and the Institute of Social Science at the University of Tokyo, for which I am deeply grateful. My experience as a visiting scholar at the Harvard-Yenching Institute was especially significant in completing this book. This study and its publication would not have been possible without the generous financial support from the Harvard-Yenching Institute and the Japan Society for the Promotion of Science (JSPS KAKENHI Grant Number 20H01521 and 24K04979).

I would like to express my gratitude to Yoshikawa Kōbunkan, Springer Nature, Cambridge University Press, the Journal of the Royal Asiatic Society, and the Business History Society of Japan for allowing the use of my previously published works in this book. Additionally, I want to thank the DeGolyer Library at Southern Methodist University, the Harvard University Asia Center, Professor Ellen Widmer, and the Railway Museum in Japan, for granting me permission to incorporate their essential materials into this publication.

To all who have contributed directly and indirectly, I extend my sincerest appreciation for your support and encouragement in bringing this work to fruition.

TRADING LOCOMOTIVES

INTRODUCTION

ROLLING STOCK AND THE GLOBAL ECONOMY

In June 2005, Hitachi Ltd. entered into a contract with the Government of the United Kingdom and a British rolling stock lease company to supply and maintain high-speed trains manufactured in Japan.[1] The contract, worth sixty-five billion yen, marked the first export of such trains to Europe.[2] The first of these trains arrived on UK shores in August 2007 and began test operations the following October.[3] More than a century years after Japan's first railroad commenced operations with technology imported from the United Kingdom, Japanese high-speed trains were running in the motherland of railroads for the very first time.

Japanese rolling stock manufacturers such as Kawasaki Heavy Industries and Nippon Sharyō started making inroads into overseas markets in the 1980s. At that time, their main targets were the United States and East Asia, the regions to which they exported commuter rail and subway trains.[4] Even Hitachi, which had traditionally focused on the domestic market, began to build factories in the United Kingdom for regular and high-speed trains that coordinated with mother factories in Japan during the early 2000s. And

INTRODUCTION

at present, railroad operators such as the East Japan Railway Company and the Central Japan Railway Company are intensifying international marketing efforts to export their technology, including bullet trains (*Shinkansen*) and urban transport systems.

Japan's exports of rolling stocks and railroad systems are proceeding in tandem with the globalization of societies and economies, which continues to accelerate the international movement of people, goods, money, and information. This has moved the capital, materials, human resources, and systems required for building railroads freely and quickly across oceans and national borders. International competition to supply railroad systems, of which rolling stock is a central component, has intensified and facilitated the rapid spread of high-speed rail technology and urban transport systems to both developed and developing countries. But the proliferation of railroad systems in a global economic context is not unique to the twenty-first century. A similar phenomenon occurred during the latter half of the nineteenth century until the outbreak of World War I. Geoffrey Jones, who has researched the history of multinational enterprises from a long-term perspective, terms the extraordinary scale of integration that the world economy experienced from the late nineteenth to the early twentieth centuries as "the first global economy."[5] Railroads, introduced to Japan from the United Kingdom in this period, rapidly developed through technological diversification and convergence.

In this book I examine the history of Japan's railroads, focusing on locomotive trade and technological development from a global perspective.[6] As railroads were a key industry of the Industrial Revolution, their worldwide proliferation proved integral to the emergence of a market-based global economy at the turn of the twentieth century. Japan's railroads played an essential part in that story, and the following chapters elucidate the international momentum that enabled the development of this industry by reconsidering the connections between the first global economy and the Industrial Revolution in Japan. In addition, I rethink the relationship between global and local events by focusing on how attempts at localization by Japan, a relatively underdeveloped country in this period, sought to counter the momentum of globalization.

2

INTRODUCTION

When thinking about the development of railroads in Japan, we have to ask who supplied the materials necessary to reproduce the industry and how. Of particular note here is that Japan struggled to achieve self-sufficiency in terms of steam locomotives until World War I. Accordingly, the above inquiry can be reformulated to ask what enabled the smooth importation of steam locomotives and their components. Answering this question requires understanding the global rolling stock market and the nature of rolling stock–related business transactions at the time.

To that end, we must examine three elements: the activities of the foreign manufacturers that supplied rolling stock, the domestic railroad operators that received these products, and the foreign and domestic trading companies that mediated these transactions. Moreover, to reconsider the growth of Japan's railroads amid the dueling forces of globalization and localization, it is important to examine the government's role in building a national economy in response to globalization. Taking a global perspective on the procurement of railroad materials at the start of Japan's modern era and cross-checking this with extant studies that emphasize domestic factors clarifies the overall picture of how Japan's railroads developed.

This book thus investigates the structure of steam locomotive manufacturing, distribution, and localization during the first global economy, concentrating on Japan and, where relevant, the broader East Asian region. In this regard, I first zoom in on the relationships between the providers of locomotives (manufacturers), recipients (railroad operators), and mediators (trading companies) involved in Japanese railroads' procurement of locomotives. I then outline the path to localizing locomotive production, focusing on the role of government officials and technical bureaucrats in particular.

Furthermore, I investigate the technological aspect of railroad development by focusing on Japanese society's capacity to adopt and adapt locomotives. Even in a context when people, goods, money, and information freely circulated within a global economy, only some countries and regions capitalized on this bountiful environment to achieve industrialization. A deciding factor here is what Japanese scholars call the "social capabilities for industrialization," which refer to a society's ability to effectively receive

INTRODUCTION

and assimilate new technology.[7] During the first wave of the global economy, the free choice of the most advanced railroad systems worldwide contributed to technological diversification and the accumulation of experience associated with exposure to these technologies. In Japan's case, the convergence of these systems and expertise bore fruit in the government-supported development of original technology, and the social capabilities for industrialization it formed during the Meiji era (1868–1912) were crucial to this achievement.[8]

My analysis covers the forty-five years from 1869, when the Japanese government first decided to introduce railroads, until the eve of World War I in 1913, when Japan stopped importing large-scale locomotives and started engaging in full-fledged domestic locomotive production. However, it deliberately excludes an examination of further structural changes in East Asia after the war, especially the emergence of the Chinese railroad market.[9] From 1914 onward, the East Asian railroad trade changed dramatically amid wars and Japanese manufacturers' rising dominance.[10] I therefore treat post–World War I developments as part of a distinctive era and limit the current study to the period under consideration. As these decades also marked the beginning of Japan's imperial expansion while advancing its national formation in response to globalization, this book also examines the links between nation-state and empire building in terms of railroad development. The circulation of locomotives connected topics in nation-state building, such as the introduction of modern industrial technology and the Industrial Revolution, to Japan's empire building, which was triggered by two international wars.

SIGNIFICANCE AND CONTRIBUTIONS

How did Japanese railroads successfully procure locomotives and railroad materials to rapidly develop during the intense competition of the first global economy? The question appears simple, but it implicates milestones in the histories of economics, international relations, and technology. Firstly, in terms of Japanese economic history, it is worth reexamining the global

INTRODUCTION

momentum that propelled Japan's Meiji-era Industrial Revolution. Research in this area has focused on light industries, such as cotton and silk reeling, and consequently overemphasizes imports of raw cotton and exports of raw silk. In contrast, this book takes up the import of a critical heavy industrial good—steam locomotives—and turns the spotlight onto how the formation and intensification of competition in that world market stimulated Japanese industry. This makes it possible to see the global economy as the key to Japan's rapid economic catch-up despite its late-developing status at the time.

Previous studies on the history of Japanese railroads, introduced below, emphasize domestic factors in this industry's development. However, because this book argues that Japan's railroads grew in close relation to an expanding global economy, its analysis focuses on the multinational activities of Japanese trading companies in the locomotive business.[11] Here it sheds new light on the role of former *oyatoi*, or hired foreign experts, as consulting engineers, and the relationship between manufacturers' representatives and agents. Both elements underpinned the international expansion of trading companies, and this study demonstrates their key contributions to business history in how they spurred Japanese trading companies' evolution into multinational corporations.

In regard to the history of international relations, this book explains the structure underlying competition among British, U.S., and German locomotive manufacturers that traded locomotives in the East Asian market centered on Japan. At the same time, it attends to changes in this market's global position and interactions between its key actors. In doing so, it illuminates the multilateral relations and commodity chains created by a network of suppliers, purchasers, and intermediaries in numerous countries and regions, in contrast to conventional histories that focus on bilateral economic ties such as those between the United Kingdom and Japan. In this regard, it focuses on trading companies as manufacturers' agents and sales engineers or sales reps as manufacturers' representatives because they played significant roles as intermediaries.[12] Spotlighting these players in the world locomotive market provides a new perspective on the history of international economic relations.[13]

INTRODUCTION

To understand the relationship between globalization and modern Japan, recent studies by Andrew Gordon and Robert Hellyer on individual commodities provide essential precedents.[14] Gordon uses the case of the sewing machine to discuss the relationship between the overseas expansion of global capitalism and local Japanese responses; Hellyer discusses the development and decline of green tea exports from Japan to the United States and the long-term impact of this trade on Japanese and U.S. culture, focusing on the interrelatedness of production, distribution, and consumption within a commodity chain at global scale.[15] In contrast, this book examines the commodity chain of locomotives in relation to the history of technology and management.[16] It emphasizes that behind the industrialization of Japan, a latecomer to the market, lay an aggressive attempt to localize in response to globalization. This point connects to Gordon's argument that localization as a reaction to globalization is characteristic of Japanese industrialization, and it once again highlights the state's role in developing Japan's railroads that Steven Ericson identifies as the driver of localization.[17]

Finally, this book also concerns itself with the history of technology that underpins Japanese locomotive manufacturing. Specifically, it examines technological diversification and convergence through Japan's cultivation of mechanical engineers, the accumulation of design skills, and the fostering of locomotive production capability. National development from imitator to designer involved training Japanese engineers and acquiring manufacturing expertise by copying a wide variety of model locomotives from the United Kingdom, the United States, and Germany. Instead of rapidly transferring Western technology and importing turnkey manufacturing facilities, Japan relied on locomotive imports for over four decades and spent that time steadily developing the technological capability for independent locomotive production. This diverges from the standard focus on developing countries' drive to end reliance on imported technology and gain self-sufficiency as soon as possible.[18] Such generalization underplays the importance of the era, and the episodes discussed in this book. In fact, as I later show, Japanese engineers developed high-performance locomotives that were smaller and lighter than their Western role models, and the skill to accurately imitate advanced technology played a critical role in this success. In short, rather than seeking simple technological advancement, they gradually localized by adapting existing technology to the terrain and social environment in specific regions of Japan through repeated imitation. This perspective on the importance of incremental innovation in technology, as in Japan's case, deserves further highlighting within the history of technical evolution in developing countries.[19]

Considering the localization of railroad technology also necessitates a focus on technology and national identity. On these issues, Jessamyn Abel argues that the *Shinkansen* played an essential role in foreign policy as a symbol of postwar Japanese progress.[20] As state-of-the-art railroad technology, despite its domestic problems, it externally embodied Japan's postwar reemergence as an industrialized democracy. Within the context of this book, the decision to replace imported locomotives with domestically manufactured ones was no mere technological shift but a conscious government policy that recognized the railroad's role in shaping national identity and mirrored the former's social and political impact. Furthermore, considering the relationship between railroads and national identity, it is crucial to comprehend the motivations that led the British and German governments to sell locomotives to Japan in the late nineteenth and early twentieth centuries, and the analysis here adds a vital comparative perspective to Abel's study.

GLOBALIZATION'S IMPACT ON JAPAN'S RAILROADS

In 1872, Japan's first railroad began running between Shinbashi in Tokyo and Yokohama. Remarkably, despite starting nearly a half century after Britain, Japan made great strides in developing its railroads from the 1890s to the 1900s. By 1913, it operated approximately ten thousand kilometers of railroads (figure 0.1) that carried twenty million passengers and four million tons of freight a year. Globally, Japan ranked fifteenth in length of railroad lines, eighth in passenger numbers, and twelfth in freight volume in

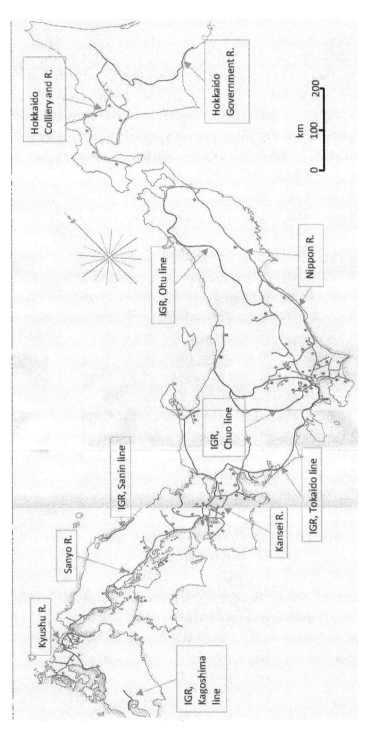

FIGURE 0.1 Japanese railroad network in 1907. (IGR is the abbreviation for Imperial Government Railways Japan).

Source: Tetsudō Kyoku [Railway Bureau], ed., *Meiji 40-nendo Tetsudō Kyoku nempō* [1907 annual report of the Railway Bureau] (Tokyo: Tetsudō In, 1909), appendix map.

this period.[21] And despite its relatively short length of railroad lines, which reflected its small land area, it placed third in passengers per kilometer of rail with regards to transportation density, behind the United Kingdom and Germany,[22] and fifth in freight per kilometer of rail, behind the United Kingdom, Germany, the United States, and France.[23] In just four decades since their inauguration, Japan's railroads grew to one of the largest in the world.

Railroads' rapid development in Japan is partly explained by Alexander Gerschenkron's hypothesis of economic backwardness as beneficial.[24] Gerschenkron attributed the relatively faster industrialization of late-adopter countries to the transfer of technology, institutions, and capital from more advanced countries. This, he argued, constitutes an "advantage of backwardness" that substantially reduces the time and money required to develop technology and accumulate capital.[25]

Yet it is not a foregone conclusion that this advantage enables latecomer countries to catch up to developed countries. Not all countries seek new and innovative developments that transcend imported technologies. A key characteristic of Japan's railroad development during the Meiji era, as this book argues, was to imitate imported technologies wholesale for subsequent adaptation and modified efficient use in local conditions long-term, which differs from Gerschenkron's classic story of the drive to achieve self-sufficiency. In addition, for latecomer countries to leverage the advantage of backwardness, they must possess not only the capacity for catch-up but also an international environment conducive to transferring technology from developed countries. Japan's railroads relied on the existence of engineers, business management, workers, and investors capable of constructing and operating them. They further required the establishment of business organizations and institutions, as well as the procurement of rails, bridge materials, rolling stock (including locomotives), signals, and other railroad supplies.

Steam locomotives, like steamships, represented the cutting edge of nineteenth-century transportation technology. But the use of steam power in land transportation severely restricted engine size and posed a greater technological challenge than in marine transportation.[26] With the exception

INTRODUCTION

of a few prototypes, Japan continued to depend on imported steam loco-motives until around 1913.[27] The smooth importation of steam technology thus proved essential to the railroad industry's success, which is another reason why I focus on the international trade of locomotives.

Around the turn of the twentieth century, under an imperialistic inter-national order centered on British hegemony, the world experienced its first period of global economy.[28] National governments, locomotive manufac-turers, and trading companies fiercely competed to export railroad materi-als and supplies. As table 0.1 shows, the annual production of locomotives in the 1880s reached 496 in the United Kingdom (1860–1889), 1,720 in the United States, 921 in Germany, and 174 in France, or an annual production of 3,300 locomotives by manufacturers in these four leading countries.[29] Of this total production, 1,300 locomotives were intended for export. At this stage, exports from the United States and Germany already far exceeded those from the United Kingdom. Nonetheless, UK manufacturing had yet to plateau, and it continuously increased locomotive production and exports from the 1890s to the 1990s. However, the magnitude of this growth trailed that of the United States, especially in terms of exports, where American sales more than doubled British ones. France, meanwhile, manufactured the majority of its locomotives for domestic use.

As the foregoing analysis makes evident, British, American, and Ger-man locomotive manufacturers expanded production and jousted to increase their respective shares of the global locomotive market as the twentieth cen-tury began. Table 0.2 demonstrates the shifting center of this trade: from Europe and South America in the 1880s and 1890s, to Asia in the late 1890s, and to British colonies in the 1900s. The Asian market gained importance for both British and American manufacturers in the 1890s.

Intensified competition worldwide likely enabled Japanese railroad com-panies to procure supplies with lower costs, shorter lead times, and an expanded breadth of technological choices. In this sense, the rapid devel-opment of Japan's railroads relied on a global environment and procurement system capable of supplying key materials such as rails and locomotives stably and economically. As illustrated above, we cannot discuss the development of railroads in a single country without considering contemporaneous international influences.

10

TABLE 0.1 Average annual production of locomotive manufacturers by nationality

	YEAR	AVERAGE OUTPUT (# OF CARS)	FOR DOMESTIC MARKET (# OF CARS)	FOR EXPORT MARKET (# OF CARS)	NOTES
United Kingdom	1860–1889	496	196	300	Major nine companies
	1890–1913	733	155	578	Major ten companies
United States	1880–1889	1,720	1,350	422	
	1890–1909	3,065	1,381	1,684	
Germany	1881–1893	921	381	540	Major twelve companies with maximum annual output of 1,441 cars
France	1881–1890	174	158	16	Major five companies*
	1891–1910	200	171	30	Major five companies

Source: Nakamura Naofumi, *Umi wo wataru kikansha* [Locomotives from across the sea] (Tokyo: Yoshikawa kōbunkan, 2016), 16.

Original sources: United Kingdom: S. B. Soul, "The Engineering Industry," in *The Development of British Industry and Foreign Competition, 1875–1914*, ed. D. H. Aldcroft (Toronto: University of Toronto Press, 1968), 200. United States: S. B. Carter, S. S. Gartner, M. R. Haines, A. L. Olmstead, R. Sutch, and G. Wright, eds., *Historical Statistics of the United States, Millennial Edition Online* (Cambridge: Cambridge University Press, 2006), https://hsus.cambridge.org/HSUSWeb /HSUSEntryServlet. Germany: R. Helmholtz and W. Staby, eds., *Die Entwicklung der Lokomotive 1 Band* (Munich: Georg D. W. Callwey, 1981), 441; Eisenbahnjahr Ausstellungsgesellschaft, ed., *Zug der Zeit, Zeit der Zuge: Deutsche Eisenbahn 1835–1985* (Berlin: Siedler, 1985), 135; R. Fremdling, R. Federspiel, and A. Kunz, eds., *Statistik der Eisenbahnen in Deutsceland 1835–1989* (St. Katharinen: Scripta Mercaturae Verlag, 1995). France: François Crouzet, "Essor, déclin et renaissance de l'industrie française des locomotives," *Revue d'Histoire Economique et Sociale* 55, nos. 1–2 (1977): 205–207.

Note: The number of American and German exports is estimated by the following formula: exports = products - increase of domestic locomotives.

* Schneider (1839–), Batignolles (1847–), Cail-SFCM (1845–), Five-Lille (1860–), SACM-Belfort (1880–).

INTRODUCTION

TABLE 0.2 Overseas exports of locomotives by the
United Kingdom and the United States

	YEAR	TO EUROPE (GBP)	TO SOUTH AMERICA (GBP)	TO ASIA (GBP)	TO NORTH AMERICA (GBP)	TOTAL (GBP)
United Kingdom	1888–1890	209,149	598,134	99,459	26,222	932,964
	1891–1893	206,728	257,520	49,083	27,902	541,233
	1894–1896	107,708	200,053	129,706	21,202	458,669
	1897–1899	118,232	135,809	169,375	7,755	431,171
	1900–1902	203,521	243,238	122,728	18,866	588,353

	YEAR	TO EUROPE (USD)	TO SOUTH AMERICA (USD)	TO ASIA (USD)	TO BRITISH COLONIES (USD)	TOTAL (USD)
United States	1890–1892	8,500	177,130	6,053	62,528	254,211
	1894–1896	63,170	217,708	83,579	15,685	380,142
	1897–1899	144,380	65,601	293,568	104,506	608,055
	1900–1902	142,307	57,333	66,699	235,814	502,153

Source: Nakamura Naofumi, *Umi wo wataru kikansha* [Locomotives from across the sea] (Tokyo: Yoshikawa kōbunkan, 2016), 17.

Original source: W. Pollard Digby, "The British and American locomotive export trade," *The Engineer*, December 16, 1904, 587–588, tabs. 3, 10, and 12.

Note: American data for 1893 is unavailable.

JAPAN'S RAILROAD HISTORY DURING THE FIRST GLOBAL ECONOMY

The starting point of this study, 1869, marked an important year for the transportation revolution that occurred in the latter half of the nineteenth century.[30] May 1869 saw the completion of the first American transcontinental railroad, and the Suez Canal opened in November of the same year, substantially shortening travel times between Europe and Asia.[31] Moreover, the 1871 laying of underwater cables that connected Nagasaki to both Shanghai and Vladivostok brought Japan into the global telegraph network. In addition to these advances in transportation and communications

INTRODUCTION

networks, the United Kingdom played a central role in establishing the international gold standard and a multilateral settlement system.[32] Together with the development of a shipping exchange and maritime insurance in London, these revolutionary factors led to the emergence of a tight-knit world trade network under the Pax Britannica. The first global economy emerged through the forging of close ties between international economies.[33] The market environment from the 1870s to the early 1910s fostered the growth of developing countries' railroad industries, including Japan's, by facilitating the procurement of railroad technology and materials. Against this background, I divide the history of Japan's railroads into stages based on trends in rolling stock supply and examine each in detail throughout this book.

From figure 0.2, which shows trends in the importation of rolling stock to Japan during this period, it is evident that imports peaked five times: during the first railroad boom (1887–1890), the second railroad boom (1893–1894 and 1896–1899), the Russo-Japanese War (1904–1905), the nationalization of railroad networks (1906–1907), and after the tariff reform of 1911, with the largest spike occurring amid the second railroad boom. Moreover, as shown in figure 0.3, railroad lines in Japan lengthened dramatically across the 1896–1898 period, while the quantity of rolling stock, primarily operated by private railroad companies, increased rapidly between 1897 and 1899.

Table 0.3, which presents trends in countries supplying locomotives to Japan, shows four distinct stages: (1) the British monopoly from 1872 to 1887; (2) the emergence of American manufacturers between 1893 and 1902; (3) American dominance and the emergence of German manufacturers lasting from 1903 to 1907; and (4) the decline of British manufacturers and an increase in the share of Japanese manufacturers from 1908 to 1913. In stage 1, which coincides with the inauguration of Japan's railroads, the vast majority of locomotives in Japan were imported from the United Kingdom. American manufacturers dominated in stage 2, which included the second railroad boom, as evidenced by the rise in new locomotives imported from the United States between 1893 and 1897. However, during this same period, UK locomotives still accounted for more than 50 percent of all locomotives imported. In addition, Switzerland exported several locomotives to Japan in this period, which were imported by small and medium private railroads

13

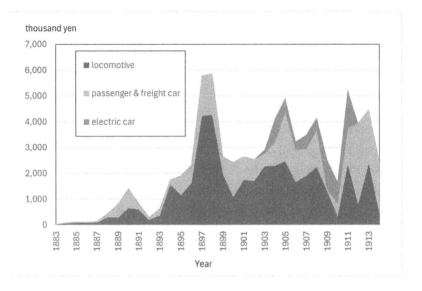

FIGURE 0.2 Trends in the importation of rolling stocks in Japan. The value of imported electric cars is included in the value of the passenger and freight cars after 1912.

Source: Sawai Minoru, *Nihon tetsudō sharyō kōgyō shi* [A history of Japan's railcar industry] (Tokyo: Nihon keizai hyōron sha, 1998), 26.

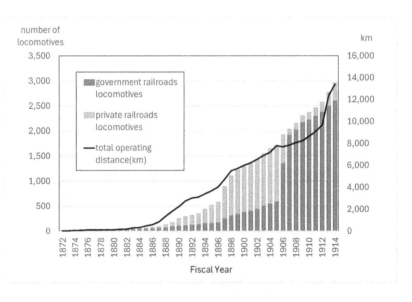

FIGURE 0.3 Expansion of railroads during the Meiji era.

Source: Minoru, *Nihon tetsudō sharyō kōgyō shi*, 6, 16.

INTRODUCTION

TABLE 0.3 Number of locomotives in use in Japan by country of manufacture.

YEAR	UNITED KINGDOM	UNITED STATES	GERMANY	SWITZERLAND	JAPAN	TOTAL
1872	10	–	–	–	–	10
1877	36	–	–	–	–	36
1882	47	–	–	–	–	47
1887	95	2	–	–	–	97
1892	240	26	28	–	–	294
1897	484	282	55	3	11	835
1902	684	524	70	11	30	1,319
1907	966	908	160	11	95	2,140
1912	983	995	226	11	162	2,377

Source: Sawai Minoru, *Nihon tetsudō sharyō kōgyō shi* [A history of Japan's railcar industry] (Tokyo: Nihon keizai hyōron sha, 1998), 27.

Note: Cumulative number of cars in use.

such as Nara Railway.[34] Stage 3 saw almost a hundred more American-made locomotives than British-made ones imported in the 1903–1907 period, and a swift increase in the share of German-made locomotives. Finally, in stage 4, the share of British-made cars plunged, signaling the decline of UK manufacturers after railroad nationalization in 1906–1907.[35] In contrast, the share of German- and Japanese-made locomotives gradually increased during this period, with Japanese railroad companies accelerating domestic production using German models.

The above shifts in locomotive supply stemmed from the evolution of national dominance in global locomotive manufacturing. Railroad manufacturing, which started in the United Kingdom in the 1820s, expanded to the United States and Germany in the 1830s. These latter countries achieved self-reliance in making rolling stock by the 1840s and rapidly developed this industry from the 1850s onward, supported by domestic railroad booms. In the United States, as chapter 1 details, a locomotive production method known as the American system emerged in the 1860s consisting of standardized types that used interchangeable parts. This manufacturing process, which involved railroad companies as end users, developed dramatically in the 1870s and 1880s and greatly increased American locomotive production.[36]

15

INTRODUCTION

In the 1890s, Baldwin Locomotive Works and other American manufactures, brandishing low prices and short lead times, began to erode the United Kingdom's monopoly in the global locomotive market. Germany introduced the American system into machine manufacturing and other industries in the late 1890s;[37] German locomotive manufacturers quickly adopted it to achieve a manufacturing process with costs and lead times on par with their American counterparts. And in the 1900s, as chapter 6 discusses, Germany and the United States developed superheated steam locomotives that improved locomotive fuel efficiency. Meanwhile, the United Kingdom, which had fallen behind in technological innovation, continued losing ground in the global locomotive market. These trends in manufacturing explain why the primary source of Japanese locomotives shifted from the United Kingdom to the United States and Germany, and recall the argument that late-adopter countries industrialize by leveraging the "advantages of backwardness."

A comprehensive consideration of the above three aspects allows us to divide the relationship between the global and Japanese locomotive markets into the following four stages: British hegemony and Japanese nascence lasting from 1869 to 1889; American advance and Japanese development from 1890 to 1903; German emergence and Japanese reorganization from 1904 to 1908; and British decline and Japanese domestic manufacturing from 1909 to 1914. With these stages in mind, I will examine the relationships between the locomotive manufactures, railroad operators, trading companies, and technical bureaucrats involved in procuring and producing locomotives in Japan.

BEYOND NATIONAL HISTORIES: A HISTORIOGRAPHICAL REVIEW

Japanese scholars have laid a foundation for examining the history of Japanese railroads from the perspective of international relations. Tanaka Tokihiko's classic study focuses on the British influence in the introduction of railroads into Japan and diplomatic relations between Japan and Britain

INTRODUCTION

during the 1860s.[38] In a similar vein, Yuzawa Takeshi investigates the export of locomotives from Britain to Japan and discusses British responses to the emergence of German locomotive manufacturers.[39] Despite this pioneering research, the international relations perspective faded from subsequent work in this area.[40] As a result, the impact exerted by the changing world environment around the turn of the century on railroads in Japan remains largely ignored. My own previous research, which discusses the multifaceted process of establishing the Japanese railroad industry at the end of the nineteenth century, is limited to a domestic focus with only cursory consideration of how global imperialism in this period influenced these developments.[41] Ericson's comprehensive study of Japanese railroad history also focuses on domestic policies and management rather than the international environment.[42]

On the other hand, noteworthy examples of research on international competition in locomotive manufacturing include Yuzawa's pioneering study of the Japanese market,[43] Sawai Minoru's analysis of trends in Japanese rolling stock importation during the Meiji era,[44] and Peter English's study of the same topic from a British perspective.[45] In this book, I draw on these previous studies while emphasizing and clarifying the importance of international competition in locomotive exports, which the foregoing works do not explicitly examine.

Researchers of railroad history have in recent years begun to reexamine their subject from a global standpoint rather than via the histories of individual countries. Of special note is British historian Christian Wolmar's study of railroads from the start of the nineteenth century to the present day as a "global history" in the truest sense of the term.[46] Although Wolmar's perspective tends toward Eurocentrism,[47] his work nonetheless provides an excellent overview of how railroad systems' diffusion changed the world.[48] It is complemented by Hayashida Haruo's meticulous examination of the introduction of railroads to Japan from the British Empire,[49] and by Steven J. Ericson's studies of Western locomotive manufacturers and technology transfer in the Japanese market.[50] In particular, Ericson's articles are essential references for understanding the process of locomotive importation in Japan and are direct predecessors to this book.

17

INTRODUCTION

Building on these prior findings, I reconsider the formation of Japan's railroad industry during the first global economy by scrutinizing how it procured steam locomotives from all over the world. There is a multidisciplinary body of research on locomotives in Japan, notably Sawai's comprehensive economic history of the formation and development of Japan's rolling stock manufacturing industry.[51] However, Sawai's research is concerned with the establishment of rolling stock manufacturing as a case study of a building-type machine industry,[52] as I explain below. It treats the period that frames this book as a mere prelude to this industry's formation, whereas the analysis here focuses on locomotive supply as an essential part of the railroad industry's propagation. Meanwhile, Aoki Eiichi details the process by which Japan achieved self-reliance in rolling stock manufacturing technology as intertwined with the rollout of railroad policy and discord between civil and mechanical engineers.[53] However, Aoki hardly mentions locomotive supply during the period prior to the nationalization of Japan's railroads. On this topic, rather than scholarship, research by individuals engaged in the railroad business and railroad enthusiasts is highly informative;[54] Usui Shigenobu's exhaustive studies particularly represent a major accomplishment in the field of railroad history in Japan.[55]

Attention has also been paid to the crucial work of trading companies in mediating locomotive imports and exports. A substantial amount of research surrounds the importation activities of Japanese and international trading companies around the turn of the century, notably Ishii Kanji's study of Jardine Matheson, which analyzes the company's account ledgers and clarifies the external economic pressures facing Japan during the end of the Tokugawa era (1603–1867).[56] However, these Jardine Matheson documents were of limited value as historical sources, since locomotive trade records from the 1890s onward are extremely rare and contain few references to transactions involving railroad materials.[57] With regard to Japanese trading companies, research abounds on the business history of Mitsui Bussan (Mitsui & Co.) and its peers.[58] For example, Asajima Shōichi's analysis of Mitsui Bussan's machinery-related transactions includes a detailed examination of transactions involving locomotives and other railroad materials.[59] Concerning machinery trade under the first global economy, Harald Fuess's analysis of the international trade of weapons in Japan

INTRODUCTION

during the Meiji Restoration highlights the crucial intermediary role of Western merchants and consuls in connecting Japan to global arms markets.[60] As I later discuss, a similar situation existed in the locomotive market during the early Meiji era.

Furthermore, Robert Hellyer's study of the Japanese tea trade,[61] mentioned above, sheds new light on the activities of foreign trading companies by vividly depicting their involvement in tea production, distribution, and consumption. I draw on Hellyer's focus on individuals involved in international trade, an approach that facilitates rethinking the actions taken by sales representatives and sales engineers at American manufacturers and businesspersons at Japanese trading companies. The bulk of my study investigates the activities of Japanese and international trading companies responsible for importing and exporting locomotives and delves into the mediations they conducted.

APPROACHES AND SOURCES

This book uses a combination of approaches and sources related to the histories of international relations, business, and technological development, focusing on comparative perspectives in these various fields. In terms of international relations history, I examine the trade in locomotives during the first global economy by analyzing primary sources from four countries—Japan, Britain, the United States, and Germany—related to the production and distribution of locomotives across national borders. Specifically, I have collected as many order ledgers and register books as possible from British, American, and German locomotive manufacturers stored in public archives, university library collections, and company archives, which allow me to investigate locomotive supply to the East Asian market from manufacturers' perspectives. I have also gathered diplomatic, consular, and statistical documents from national archives in Japan, the United States, and Britain to analyze and compare the actions taken by each government. In addition, I examine Japanese records from the Railway Bureau, the Ministry of Communications and Transportation, and railroad companies to clarify the methods and routes of importing locomotives. Furthermore,

INTRODUCTION

I use an array of professional serial publications, including the Japanese journal *Tetsudō jihō* (Japan railway times) and the British journal *The Engineer*, to investigate the state of technology and the market in the period under study. This multi-archival approach opens up multiple perspectives on the global locomotive market and illuminates both the history of railroads and economic history in the context of international relations. In addition, I provide a comparative study of the British, U.S., German, and Japanese approaches to the global market for locomotives in chapters 1, 4, and 6.

With respect to business history, I investigate the companies and individuals who oversaw international transactions related to locomotives around the turn of the century. To this end, I use the files in the Office of Alien Property Records (specifically Record Group 131), which contain documents on Japanese companies in the United States. This collection, stored in the U.S. National Archives at College Park, Maryland, holds records, such as the letter books of the Ōkura Gumi Shōkai (Okura & Co., hereafter Ōkura Gumi), that give detailed accounts of Japanese trading companies' activities concerning the import of railroad supplies. Examining these records in conjunction with Japanese archival collections—chiefly Mitsui Bussan and Ōkura Gumi documents respectively held by the Mitsui Bunko (Mitsui Research Institute for Social and Economic History) and the Tokyo Keizai University library—clarifies not only the mechanisms of transactions related to railroads materials but also the overseas activities of Japanese trading companies during this period.[62]

Lastly, regarding the history of technological development, I consider Japan's social capabilities for industrialization by focusing on its training and organization of engineers capable of working with locomotive technology, particularly in terms of design, manufacture, and institutional changes in resource procurement. At this juncture, we should carefully distinguish between manufacturing and building types when discussing technological formation in machinery industries. According to John Brown, consumer product manufacturers that use the American system, including guns, sewing machines, bicycles, and automobiles, constitute manufacturing-type industries. Building-type industries, on the other hand, consist of

INTRODUCTION

capital equipment builders such as locomotives and steamships.[63] The former is based on bulk or mass production from a basic design that determines a product's general specifications, while the latter's products are at least partially tailored to a customer's detailed requirements.[64]

On the technological formation of building-type mechanical industries, Nakaoka Tetsurō notes the difference between basic design and detailed design in work plans for building large-scale iron steamships. The former process formulates fundamental specifications, functions, and strategies for a product, while the latter ensures stable production by providing numerical figures for individual parts' dimensions, materials, processing, and assembly. Basic design can be taught at universities and other institutions, but detailed design requires accumulating workplace experience.[65]

In Japan, technology transfer in shipbuilding via the import of detailed designs for large steamships from the United Kingdom ended around the turn of the twentieth century.[66] Since locomotive manufacturing is also a building-type machine industry, what path did its development take? Chapters 3 and 6 discuss the characteristics of localization in this industry through a comparative study of steamships and locomotives. Analyzing building-type technology requires a focus on cultivating expertise and human resources in detailed design, which is why this study emphasizes how government and private railroads developed locomotive design skills. Doing so sheds light on the history of railroads in Japan as well as the factors that enabled Japan's rapid industrialization.

CHAPTER OVERVIEW

Chapter 1 explains the process by which locomotive manufacturers in Britain, the United States, and Germany, facing saturated domestic markets after active railroad construction plateaued during the late nineteenth and early twentieth centuries, sought new overseas markets while prioritizing the domestic arena. As a prelude to this, I provide a comparative discussion of the composition of the British, American, and German locomotive manufacturing industries and the histories of major manufacturers to

INTRODUCTION

identify the main locomotive suppliers in this period. Subsequently, I examine the state of competition in the global locomotive market and the international environment that affected Japan's importation of locomotives. Looking at the worldwide state of the industry allows me to explain the structure of the global locomotive market at the turn of the nineteenth and twentieth centuries and provides essential background for subsequent chapters.

Chapter 2 uses railroad technology as a case study to describe the introduction of modern industrial technology as the first step toward nation building taken by the new Meiji government. Here Britain played a significant role in railroads and other fields; as noted at the outset, railroads in Japan started via the introduction of British technology, and Japan looked to the United Kingdom to supply it with personnel, goods, and money. From the late 1870s onward, although Japan advanced steadily toward self-sufficiency in civil engineering technology, for mechanical technology, it remained dependent on hired foreigners, mostly British, until the early 1890s. Britain thus monopolized the supply of locomotives to Japan, especially on the mainland, throughout the 1880s. I then delve into the distribution channels and transactions associated with locomotives in the early stages of Japan's railroad industry, analyzing these issues via the employment system for *oyatoi* hires, the procurement of railway materials through negotiated contracts, and the activities of foreign trading companies.

Chapter 3 takes up the relationship between Japan's Industrial Revolution and the export of American locomotives to Japan. I explain how Japan's economic nation building hinged on the premise of globalization and identify the strategy of the U.S. manufacturing industry, as representative of global capital, toward Japan. For railroads, the second boom in the 1893–1899 period saw the emergence of large numbers of new companies and the expansion of existing ones. This spiked demand for locomotives within Japan, to which Baldwin and other American manufacturers responded promptly and expanded their share of the Japanese market. This chapter discusses the locomotive supply arrangement that supported the swift growth of Japan's railroads at the turn of the century, highlighting the independence of Japanese mechanical engineers and the export of American

22

INTRODUCTION

locomotives to Japan. In addition, I explain how American manufacturers dismantled the British monopoly in Japan's locomotive market while attending to changes in technological and business systems on the demand side (i.e., the railroads). Direct marketing, a key strength of U.S. manufacturers, remains under-researched, which makes it worthwhile to investigate how agents, sales representatives, and sales engineers impacted the marketing activities of American locomotive manufacturers.

Chapter 4 discusses Japan's response to globalization via the overseas expansion of Japanese general trading companies (*sōgō shōsha*). How did these emergent firms accumulate knowledge and expertise in international trade and compete with their established Western rivals? To answer this question, this chapter clarifies how these companies mediated the import of locomotives from the United States to Japan through comparisons with their foreign counterparts. It primarily examines Mitsui Bussan and Ōkura Gumi as case studies of Japanese trading companies that entered and rapidly expanded their role in the locomotive trade at the turn of the century. The growth of such companies crucially enabled the global acquisition of railroad materials, allowing Japanese railroads to procure high-quality locomotives at the lowest prices and shortest delivery times. Investigating the trajectory of their trade in railroad materials thus elucidates an essential aspect of Japan's railroad development.

Chapter 5 describes the impact of Japan's empire building on the East Asian locomotive market in the context of two international wars. Japan began its imperial expansion through the Sino-Japanese and Russo-Japanese Wars while advancing its nation-building efforts. Railroad construction proved a vital tool in this process, and Japan globally imported large numbers of locomotives for war and empire building. This chapter discusses how manufacturers and trading companies enabled this procurement of locomotives. It then studies the impact of establishing a state monopsony through railroad nationalization on the locomotive trade, again focusing on the activities of trading companies and the government. Finally, it examines how Baldwin and the American Locomotive Company grew dominant in Japan and began exporting locomotives to China, a process also related to Japan's imperial ambitions.

INTRODUCTION

Chapter 6 explores the localization of technology through the mass production of domestic locomotives in Japan by reevaluating the role of the government in establishing railroad technology, specifically its critical contributions to localizing locomotives in the face of globalization. Specifically, it considers the impact of the Railway Agency's 1909 policy to manufacture rolling stock domestically, along with the process by which engineers in Japan gained the ability to design and manufacture locomotives. Manufacturers in Britain, the United States, and Germany variously responded to the technological innovation of superheated steam locomotives; meanwhile, the Railway Agency and private locomotive manufacturers in Japan acquired new technology through reverse engineering. Germany, which spearheaded the practical use of superheated locomotives, provided Japan with models for domestic manufacture. In contrast, Britain lagged in this technological revolution and lost its competitive edge in the Japanese market, leading its representative manufacturer, the North British Locomotive Company, to work with Ōkura Gumi and the British government in coercing the Railway Agency to order its model locomotives. This process shows that railroad technology played an important political role as a symbol of national identity even at the beginning of the twentieth century. In closing, this chapter explicates key characteristics in the formation of Japan's domestic locomotive production through a comparison with the shipbuilding industry.

Finally, the conclusion presents an overview of this study's contributions from the standpoint of the international environment related to the locomotive trade in the first global economy, the social capabilities that enabled Japan to utilize this environment in developing its railroad industry, and the structural changes in Asian markets resulting from Japanese government policies and trading company activities in these areas. Overall, Japan's success in industrialization depended on investing in engineering education and effectively introducing technology through global competition. In the conclusion, I consider this point by comparing it with the case of China to discuss the development of Japan's locomotive industry from a comparative perspective and to describe the implications of this story for future research.

1

INTERNATIONAL COMPETITION IN THE GLOBAL LOCOMOTIVE MARKET

The world's first public steam railroad began operating in 1825 between the British towns of Stockton and Darlington. Around the same time, Western nations including the United States, Germany, and France developed prototypes for steam locomotives, leading to the rapid growth of railroads in those metropoles during the early 1830s.[1] Some two decades later, railroads began spreading on a global scale with their construction during the 1850s in the British colonies of Australia and India, as well as in Latin American countries including Argentina and Brazil. In Asia, they began operating in Japan in 1872 and in China in 1876.

Railroads thus ran worldwide in the half-century since their first opening. During this period, the flows of funds, materials, and human resources required for their construction helped build the first global economy. From the end of the nineteenth century to the beginning of the twentieth, following Britain's lead, America and Germany entered the global market for railroad equipment such as locomotives, which sparked intense international competition in this arena.

This chapter links the respective markets that constituted the locomotive manufacturing industry in the era of the first global economy. Critical points of connection emerged between domestic and international locomotive markets and innovation in U.S. production systems: these two elements constituted the premise and driving force of global competition. I begin by explaining how American, British, and German locomotive manufacturers, facing saturated domestic markets after active railroad construction plateaued, sought new destinations overseas. Next, I introduce the major manufacturers in each country, focusing on their markets and relationship to Japan where relevant. I then analyze the impact of the production process known as the American system on international competition in locomotive manufacturing, turning finally to discuss the dynamism of the global locomotive market by comparing British and American locomotives.

LOCOMOTIVE MANUFACTURING
AND ITS INNOVATIONS

THE UNITED KINGDOM

This [Crewe Works] is not the only place in the United Kingdom where locomotives are being manufactured. Locomotives are manufactured in Manchester, Glasgow, Sheffield, and Birmingham, as well as many other locations. If all of the locomotives produced in this small country were used domestically, there would be locomotives everywhere. This leads to the question of where they are being exported. During our subsequent visit to Russia via the Netherlands, on numerous occasions, we came across locomotives that were built in Manchester. Still later, on our tour of Germany and Austria, we learned that several of the railroads we encountered had been constructed by British companies, further deepening our conviction that the British locomotive manufacturing industry is being used widely to Europe's benefit. Even then, the market is too small [for British locomotive manufacturers], and railroads are being constructed in India and Australia, while plans are currently being made to construct a railroad in China.[2]

COMPETITION IN THE GLOBAL LOCOMOTIVE MARKET

The above passage is an excerpt from a record authored by Kume Kunitake, the secretary to Iwakura Tomomi. Iwakura, a prominent statesman of Japan, served as its ambassador extraordinary and plenipotentiary from 1871 to 1873, when he led a large and eponymous mission that traveled to the United States, the United Kingdom, France, Belgium, the Netherlands, Germany, Russia, Denmark, Sweden, Italy, Austria, and Switzerland. The mission's members included Ōkubo Toshimichi, Kido Takayoshi, and Itō Hirobumi, all top leaders in the Japanese government of that era. They had two goals: to negotiate revisions of the so-called unequal treaties that Japan had signed with the United States and European countries toward the end of the Tokugawa period,[3] and to research the contents of Western "civilization."[4] This second part of their mission led them to carefully observe the political institutions, economic systems, industrial technologies, societies, and cultures in their various destinations.

The Iwakura Mission inspected the London and Northwestern Railway at Crewe Works in Cheshire as part of their 1872 tour of the United Kingdom. Astonished by the scale of its operation, they turned their attention to steam locomotives in their subsequent travels. As the quote from Kume's notes shows, they discovered that UK-made locomotives were being exported not only throughout Europe but also as far as India, Australia, and China, supporting railroad construction in multiple places. In the mid-nineteenth century, as Kume astutely observed, British locomotives ruled the world.

Following George Stephenson's 1823 establishment of Robert Stephenson, the world's first locomotive manufacturing firm, the United Kingdom saw a surge in this industry,[5] which had over twenty such companies by 1900[6] and employed 14,853 individuals as a whole in 1903. At the time, Neilson, Reid & Co. in Glasgow employed the greatest number of workers (3,140), followed by its local counterpart, Dübs & Co. (2,423), and the Manchester firm of Beyer, Peacock & Co. (2,165).[7] These companies, sometimes referred to as the "big four," were the largest manufacturers along with a third Glasgow firm, Sharp, Stewart & Co. (1,561). Those next in line employed similar numbers of workers, including the Leeds-based Kitson &

Co. (1,440), indicating the proliferation of small to midsized locomotive manufacturers at the time.[8]

Meanwhile, the United Kingdom's domestic locomotive demand around the turn of the century peaked around seven hundred locomotives.[9] An even smaller number would have been purchased from independent firms, since the major railroads typically built locomotives in their own factories. Given these circumstances, manufacturers naturally looked to overseas markets as the main destinations for their locomotives.

TABLE 1.1 Number of locomotives sold by British major manufacturers

			1860–1889						
	DOMESTIC (# OF CARS)	INDIA (# OF CARS)	COLONIES (EXCL. INDIA) (# OF CARS)	EUROPE (# OF CARS)	LATIN AMERICA (# OF CARS)	JAPAN (# OF CARS)	OTHERS (# OF CARS)	TOTAL (# OF CARS)	EXPORT RATIO (%)
Neilson*	1,291	1,227	170	239	109	0	55	3,091	58.2%
Dübs*	866	817	343	159	156	62	16	2,419	64.2%
Sharp Stewart*	865	380	31	732	164	17	106	2,295	62.3%
Beyer Peacock	918	60	451	870	250	26	52	2,626	65.0%
Kitson	608	439	150	158	136	12	34	1,536	60.4%
Robert Stephenson	595	103	210	200	100	4	127	1,339	55.6%
Vulcan Foundry	419	285	44	33	14	13	15	823	49.1%
Hawthorn Leslie	302	53	19	35	65	0	3	477	36.7%
Nasmyth Wilson	27	54	45	54	43	32	7	262	89.7%
Total	5,891	3,418	1,463	2,480	1,037	166	415	14,868	60.4%
Regional ratio (%)	39.6%	23.0%	9.8%	16.7%	7.0%	1.1%	2.8%	100.0%	
Average per year (# of cars)	196	114	49	83	35	5.5	14	496	

TABLE 1.1 *(continued)*

1890–1913

	DOMESTIC (# OF CARS)	INDIA (# OF CARS)	COLONIES (EXCL. INDIA) (# OF CARS)	EUROPE (# OF CARS)	LATIN AMERICA (# OF CARS)	JAPAN (# OF CARS)	OTHERS (# OF CARS)	TOTAL (# OF CARS)	EXPORT RATIO (%)
Neilson*	814	775	676	52	44	94	37	2,492	67.3%
Dübs*	461	393	556	80	135	226	79	1,930	76.1%
Sharp Stewart*	621	369	87	183	152	28	27	1,467	57.7%
Beyer Peacock	476	98	493	314	816	186	94	2,477	80.8%
Kitson	439	567	252	11	330	15	11	1,625	73.0%
Robert Stephenson	174	216	55	–	139	0	36	620	71.9%
Vulcan Foundry	331	1,179	70	–	115	10	6	1,711	80.7%
Hawthorn Leslie	7	34	103	4	113	15	6	282	97.5%
Nasmyth Wilson	46	256	79	42	33	151	19	626	92.7%
North British Loco.	342	1,655	645	84	1,213	335	96	4,370	92.2%
Total	3,711	5,542	3,016	770	3,090	1,060	411	17,600	78.9%
Regional ratio (%)	21.1%	31.5%	17.1%	4.4%	17.6%	6.0%	2.3%	100.0%	
Average per year (# of cars)	155	231	126	32	129	44	17	733	

Source: Nakamura Naofumi, *Umi wo wataru kikansha* [Locomotives from across the sea] (Tokyo: Yoshikawa kōbunkan, 2016), 48.

Original source: S. B. Soul, "The Engineering Industry," in *The Development of British Industry and Foreign Competition, 1875–1914*, ed., D. H. Aldcroft (Toronto: University of Toronto Press, 1968), 200.

Notes: Unit is number of cars. The total number of overseas sales from 1880 to 1889 differs from the original dates due to a miscalculation on Soul's part. The three companies marked with an asterisk (*) merged in 1903 to form North British Locomotive.

COMPETITION IN THE GLOBAL LOCOMOTIVE MARKET

Exports were a vital part of British locomotive manufacturers' business. For major manufacturers, domestic sales as a share of total sales fell from 40 percent in the 1860–1889 period to 21 percent between 1890 and 1913 (table 1.1). Examining the destinations of these exports in the same table, we see that the share of sales to Europe—the second most common destination after India between 1860 and 1889, accounting for 17 percent of transactions— fell dramatically to 4 percent in the 1890–1913 period. This was likely a consequence of rapid growth in the German locomotive industry, described later in this chapter. Increasingly shut out of Europe, British locomotive manufacturers grew ever more reliant on India and other colonial markets. Sales to these markets, which made up 33 percent of the total for 1860–1889, rose to 49 percent during the 1890–1913 period and made overseas markets the top destination for locomotives. Latin America and Japan also grew in importance, with the share of sales to these two markets increasing from 7 to 17.6 percent and from 1.1 to 6 percent respectively. From the 1890s onward, Japan in particular also became key for American and German manufacturers in the international competition for locomotive exports.[10]

Major British manufacturers emerged as essential locomotive exporters to the global market in this period. Glasgow formed a crucial center of the industry, as it housed the three firms of Neilson, Dübs, and Sharp Stewart, which merged in 1903 to form the North British Locomotive Company (NBL).[11] Below, I examine each of these companies' main characteristics and evolution with reference to figure 1.1.

Neilson, Britain's largest locomotive manufacturer in the latter half of the nineteenth century, originated from Mitchell and Neilson, a firm established by Walter Neilson and James Mitchell in Glasgow around 1836.[12] In 1842, it restructured and changed its name to Neilson, producing its first locomotives in the following year. In 1857, Neilson hired the German engineer Henry Dübs and began full-fledged production of locomotives. From 1860 to 1889, it sold 3,091 locomotives, quickly becoming the top-selling manufacturer in the country (table 1.1). During the same period, exports accounted for 58.2 percent of the firm's sales, with India and other British colonies as the main destinations. In 1898, it reemerged as Neilson, Reid & Co. to reflect a change in partnership.

30

COMPETITION IN THE GLOBAL LOCOMOTIVE MARKET

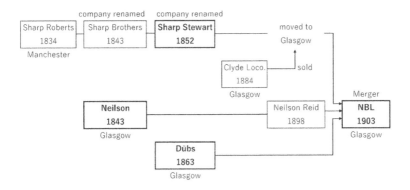

FIGURE 1.1 Origins of North British Locomotive.

Source: Usui Shigenobu. *Kikansha no keifu-zu 1* [Genealogy of locomotives, vol. 1] (Tokyo: Kōyūsha, 1972), 74.

In 1863, Henry Dübs established Dübs & Co. in Glasgow after parting ways with Neilson.[13] His firm produced its first locomotive in 1864 and rapidly expanded its operations thereafter. As of 1900, Dübs had 2,017 employees, making it the second-largest firm in the United Kingdom after Neilson. Although it ranked third in terms of sales, selling 2,419 locomotives between 1864 and 1889, its share of exports (64.2 percent) was high compared to those of Neilson and Sharp Stewart (table 1.1). Dübs's main export destination was India, but it also exported sixty-two locomotives to Japan in this period, accounting for a third of British locomotive exports to Japan at the time. This trend continued into the 1890s and the firm remained the largest British exporter to Japan. After Henry Dübs died in 1876, his partner, William Lorimer, took over the firm's management.

The third manufacturer that would become part of NBL was Sharp Stewart, originally founded as the Manchester-based Sharp Roberts in 1822.[14] In 1834, Sharp Roberts began manufacturing steam locomotives in its "Atlas Works" for the Liverpool and Manchester Railway. Thereafter, the firm was twice renamed to reflect changes in partnership, first to Sharp Brothers in 1843 and then to Sharp Stewart in 1852. In 1888, it purchased the Glasgow-based Clyde Locomotive and moved its factory to Glasgow.

Between 1860 and 1889, Sharp Stewart ranked fourth in terms of sales, selling 2,295 locomotives and shipping 62.3 percent of that total overseas. In the sense that it exported more locomotives to European markets than to British colonies, its character bore resemblance to Beyer Peacock, discussed below, and to other locomotive manufacturers in Manchester. In Japan, Sharp Stewart is best known for providing four of the ten locomotives imported in 1872, when the first Japanese railroad was launched, and for supplying many locomotives to the Imperial Government Railways (IGR) in the early years of the Meiji era.[15]

The 1903 merger of these three major manufacturers marked the birth of a single massive corporation with 7,570 workers and the capacity to produce six to seven hundred locomotives each year.[16] This large-scale merger followed the lead of American companies that were expanding around the turn of the century, whose aggressiveness it intended to combat by leveraging economies of scale. That said, NBL remained small compared to Baldwin Locomotive Works in the United States, which had 12,158 employees in 1902 and continued to have excess capacity for increasing production.

Another industry center emerged in Manchester with the launch of the Liverpool and Manchester Railway in 1830, known as the world's first passenger railroad. Its starting point in Manchester created a cluster of locomotive manufacturers in and around the city's environs. One such firm was Nasmyth Gaskell, founded in 1836 on the outskirts of Manchester by the famous mechanical engineer James Nasmyth with financial backing from Holbrook Gaskell.[17] It produced its first locomotive in 1839, and was subsequently renamed James Nasmyth in 1850 and Nasmyth Wilson in 1860 as it grew into a midsized manufacturer. Nasmyth Wilson sold 262 locomotives between 1860 and 1889 and 626 between 1890 and 1913, with overseas exports accounting for around 90 percent of sales throughout both periods. British colonies, including India, and Japan formed the main destinations for these exports. From 1890 to 1913, Japan accounted for a quarter of all locomotive orders. Although the firm, which had 526 employees as of 1900, was small to medium-sized, its products were praised for their high quality.[18]

Beyer Peacock was established in 1854 by Charles F. Beyer and Richard Peacock in Manchester.[19] After delivering its first locomotive to Great Western Railway in 1855, the firm grew to become one of the United Kingdom's most prominent locomotive manufacturers. Its total sales ranked second only to Neilson in the period 1860–1889 with 2,626 locomotives, and second only to NBL in the period 1890–1913 with 2,477 locomotives (table 1.1). In a noteworthy trend, its exports as a share of total sales soared from 65 percent between 1860 and 1889 to 80.8 percent between 1890 and 1913, and its primary export destination shifted from Europe in the 1880s to South America and surrounding areas from the 1890s onward. This stands in contrast to NBL, which primarily exported to India and other British colonies. Starting in the 1890s, Beyer Peacock's Japan-bound exports also jumped, and it joined Dübs, NBL, and Nasmyth as a key exporter of British locomotives to Japan.

THE UNITED STATES

The first American railroad started operations in 1829 using locomotives imported from Britain. A couple of years later, in 1831–1832, new companies emerged, including Baldwin Locomotive Works, Norris Locomotive Works, and Rogers Locomotive and Machine Works, which enabled the United States to quickly achieve self-sufficiency in locomotive manufacturing.[20] Unlike British railroads, which opted to manufacture locomotives internally, American railroads outsourced production from the outset. For this reason, American locomotive manufacturers' growth depended primarily on domestic demand. The railroad boom in the United States during the 1840s and 1850s caused not only the rapid expansion of existing firms but also the establishment of new ones such as Schenectady Locomotive Works.

Of the main American manufacturers, Norris ranked first in the share of locomotives produced up to the 1850s with 21 percent of the total (table 1.2). It was followed closely by Baldwin and Rogers, each accounting for 20 percent of overall production. These three firms formed the core of the early American locomotive manufacturing industry. However, beginning in the

COMPETITION IN THE GLOBAL LOCOMOTIVE MARKET

TABLE 1.2 Production output of major U.S. locomotive manufacturers

	1830–1859	1860–1869	1870–1879	1880–1889	1890–1899	1900–1909	1910–1919	CUMULATIVE TOTAL
Baldwin	905	1,143	2,861	5,634	6,770	16,834	18,627	52,774
Norris	975	269	–	–	–	–	–	1,244
Rogers+	897	789	867	1,671	1,246	791		6,261
Hinkley	679	260	371	501	–	–	–	1,811
Mason	92	248	276	138	–	–	–	754
Schenectady+	213	393	595	1,805	2,272	916	–	6,194
Portland	103	69	185	244	26	1	–	628
Taunton	270	210	237	265	–	–	–	982
New Jersey–Grant	268	506	623	450	41	–	–	1,888
Cooke+	157	475	464	892	511	256	–	2,755
Manchester+	46	159	587	652	275	74	–	1,793
Dickson+	–	47	196	491	361	235	–	1,330
Pittsburgh+	–	66	329	817	834	364	–	2,410
Rhode Island+	–	162	649	1,505	839	211	–	3,366
Brooks+	–	2	386	1,212	1,802	712	–	4,114
New York (Rome)	–	–	–	564	131	–	–	695
Richmond+	–	–	–	40	641	354	–	1,035
Climax	–	–	–	12	189	446	280	927
ALCO	–	–	–	–	–	15,556	14,709	30,265
Industrial locomotive manufacturers	–	–	361	1,108	1,348	6,038	5,746	14,601
Total	4,605	4,798	8,987	18,001	17,286	42,788	39,362	135,827
Annual average	154	480	899	1,800	1,729	4,279	3,936	1,509

Source: John White, *A Short History of American Locomotive Builders in the Steam Era* (Washington, DC: Bass, 1982), 21.

Notes: Unit is number of cars. "Industrial locomotive manufacturers" included Porter, Lima, Vulcan, Heisler, and Davenport. Plus symbol (+) indicates companies that merged with ALCO.

1860s, Norris and Rogers saw production declines, while Baldwin eventually overtook Norris as the top manufacturer. This trend intensified in the 1870s, with Baldwin accounting for more than 30 percent of all locomotives manufactured. Schenectady's share grew to 13 percent in the 1880s, overtaking Rogers (9 percent) as the second-largest manufacturer. The industry further diversified in the 1870s and 1880s with the rise of many new entrants, including H. K. Porter and the Lima Locomotive Works,

34

which began producing locomotives in 1871 and 1878 respectively. Incidentally, the first American-made locomotive exported to Japan was a small-tank Porter locomotive ordered by the Kaitakushi (Hokkaido Development Commission) in 1880.

In the 1890s, Baldwin's market share increased to 39 percent, which solidified its dominant status. Although other manufacturers continued to grow, the gap between them and Baldwin relentlessly increased. In 1901, aiming to break this deadlock, a group of eight firms—Schenectady Locomotive Works, Cooke Locomotive and Machine Works, Manchester Locomotive Works, Dickson Manufacturing Company, Pittsburgh Locomotive and Car Works, Rhode Island Locomotive Works, Brooks Locomotive Works, and Richmond Locomotive Works—merged to form the American Locomotive Company (ALCO).[21] With this massive merger, ALCO's market share in the 1900s rose to 44 percent; added to Baldwin's 39 percent, the two firms formed an oligopoly accounting for 83 percent of all locomotive production. From that point onward, Baldwin and ALCO competed as America's two main locomotive manufacturers, and they eventually ventured into the international market.

Baldwin played a central role in American locomotive manufacturing since its foundation in 1825 by Matthias Baldwin, whose career started with making various types of machinery before he branched out to small steam engines and eventually locomotives in 1831.[22] After studying a Robert Stephenson locomotive imported from the United Kingdom, he used the design and measurements of its main components as a model for his first commercial locomotive, known as "Old Ironsides." Its initial trials conducted in 1832 garnered rave reviews. Energized by this success, Matthias Baldwin went on to establish the dominance of his enterprise, which churned out locomotives at its factory on North Broad Street in Philadelphia.

The production process that Baldwin innovated was revolutionary in two ways. First, it introduced a uniform system of locomotive types where customers could choose from a number of standardized designs and customize certain components such as the boiler. Second, as chapter 3 details, it pioneered the systematic use of interchangeable parts among different locomotive models.[23] These innovations reduced Baldwin's production costs and delivery times and allowed it to build a wide variety of locomotives based on customer specifications.[24] In the United Kingdom, this production style was referred to as the American system and was considered the source of U.S. manufacturers' competitiveness.

Following Matthias Baldwin's death in 1866, the firm became M. Baird in 1867. Thereafter, it changed its name several times to reflect its evolving partnership and organizational structure: to Burnham, Parry and Williams in 1873, then to Burnham and Williams in 1891, and finally to Baldwin Locomotive Works Inc. in 1909. Despite these frequent changes, "Baldwin Locomotive Works" was consistently used as the brand name for the locomotives produced, and it is this nomenclature that "Baldwin" in the analysis below refers to.

GERMANY

Germany actively developed steam locomotives from the railroad's earliest years. In 1838, Maschinenbauanstalt Übigau in Dresden successfully built the country's first domestic locomotive, known as the Saxonia. Numerous manufacturers emerged in the 1840s, including Borsig Lokomotiv-Werke in Berlin, J. A. Maffei in Munich, Hanomag (Hannoversche Maschinenbau) in Hanover, and Henschel und Sohn in Kassel, transforming Germany overnight into a hub of locomotive manufacturing (see table 1.3).

In 1850, Germany's self-sufficiency rate in this industry—calculated as the proportion of domestically made locomotives within total locomotive production—was 56.6 percent, indicating its achievement of import substitution within just ten years of its inception.[25] This process involved railroads in different national regions ordering locomotives from domestic manufacturers as a rule, thus contributing to the latter's cultivation. Japanese engineer Mori Hikozō, then a factory manager at the IGR's Shinbashi factory, submitted the following report comparing German and British locomotive manufacturers on this point:

The differences between [German railroad factories] and those in the UK include the fact that [in the former] roundhouses are equipped with

TABLE 1.3 Production output of major German locomotive manufacturers

	LOCATION	1880 (CUMULATIVE # OF CARS)	1893 (CUMULATIVE # OF CARS)	INCREASE (CUMULATIVE # OF CARS)	ANNUAL AVERAGE, 1881–1893 (# OF CARS
A. Borsig	Berlin	3,800	4,434	634	49
J. A. Maffei	Munich	1,232	1,720	488	38
E. Kessler	Karlsruhe	1,015	1,400	385	30
G. Egestorff (Hanomag)	Hannover	1,442	2,500	1,058	81
Henschel & Sohn	Kassel	1,147	4,000	2,853	219
Maschinenfabrik Esslingen	Esslingen	1,596	3,000	1,404	108
F. Wöhlert	Berlin	770	–	–	–
R. Hartmann	Chemnitz	1,087	1,720	633	49
Union	Kochsberg	169	753	584	45
M. G. Vulkan	Stettin	800	–	–	–
Schichau	Elving	291	695	404	31
Krauss	Munich	925	2,800	1,875	144
Berliner Maschinenbau (Schwartzkopff)	Berlin	1,094	2,090	996	77
A. L. Hohenzollern	Dusseldorf	148	806	658	51
Total	–	15,516	25,918	11,972	921

Source: Nakamura Naofumi, *Umi wo wataru kikansha* [Locomotives from across the sea] (Tokyo: Yoshikawa kōbunkan, 2016), 50–51.

Original sources: R. Helmholtz and W. Staby, eds., *Die Entwicklung der Lokomotive 1 Band* (Munich: Georg D. W. Callwey, 1981), 441; Eisenbahnjahr Ausstellungsgesellschaft, ed., *Zug der Zeit, Zeit der Zuge: Deutsche Eisenbahn 1835–1985* (Berlin: Siedler, 1985), 135; R. Fremdling, R. Federspiel, and A. Kunz, eds., *Statistik der Eisenbahnen in Deutsceland 1835–1989* (St. Katharinen: Scripta Mercaturae Verlag, 1995), 141–203; Wolfgang Messerschmidt, *Taschenbuch Deutsche Lokomotivfabriken* (Stuttgart: Franckh, 1977); Ogasawara Shigeru, "19 Seiki-zenhan niokeru Doitsu kikai kōgyō no hatten" [The development of German machinery industry in the first half of the nineteenth century], *Shōgaku ronshū* [Journal of commerce, economics and economic history, Fukushima University] 38, no. 2 (1969): 1–55.

Note: The total number of Krauss cars shipped in 1893 is an estimate based on the 1894 figure of three thousand cars.

small manufacturing facilities where repairs are frequently made, and the fact that new models of locomotives, passenger cars, and freight cars are not developed. In other words, in contrast to the common practice of British railroads of centralizing all repair work on locomotives in the railroad's main factory, German railroads are more pragmatic, and repair work is carried out by local branches. Furthermore, whereas new models of locomotives are developed by the railroads themselves in the UK, such development is entirely outsourced to specialized private firms in Germany.[26]

Mori had visited Germany at the start of the 1900s to inspect its domestic railroad industry; his above points show how Germany's locomotive manufacturing industry consequently experienced a rapid growth similar to that observed in the United States. In the railroad boom of the 1860s and 1870s, two new manufacturers further boosted Germany's productive capacity—Locomotivfabrik Krauss & Comp. in Munich, and Eisengießerei und Maschinen-Fabrik von L. Schwartzkopff in Berlin (Berliner Maschinenbau AG from 1870).

This increased productivity explains why, after the domestic railroad boom dissipated, both public and private sectors strove for overseas markets.[27]Germany's major manufacturers produced approximately 12,000 locomotives between 1880 and 1893 (table 1.3). Assuming that around 5,000 of these were intended for the domestic market, it is apparent that a substantially larger number—roughly 7,000—were exported. This indicates an annual export of 540 locomotives, which exceeded the 442 locomotives annually exported by American locomotive manufacturers around the same time (table 0.1).

In terms of innovation, the German locomotive manufacturing industry adopted characteristically aggressive attitudes toward actively reforming firms' production systems and introducing new technologies during the 1890s and 1900s. German firms introduced the American system into machine manufacturing in the late 1890s, which subsequently led to the development of a fitting system in the 1900s and the making of machine-finished interchangeable parts.[28] Borsig Lokomotiv-Werke and its national

COMPETITION IN THE GLOBAL LOCOMOTIVE MARKET

counterparts quickly adopted this system, becoming first in the world to successfully commercialize superheated steam locomotives in the 1900s.

Borsig, which employed over two thousand workers, was also Germany's largest locomotive manufacturer in the latter half of the nineteenth century. However, Henschel und Sohn and Krauss had both eroded its dominance by the turn of the twentieth century. A similar picture emerges from the cumulative number of locomotives produced in between 1880 and 1893. As table 1.3 shows, Henschel und Sohn was the most prolific manufacturer during that period, churning out 2,853 locomotives, followed by Krauss (1,800) and Esslingen in Württemberg (1,404); Borsig ranked sixth (634). The above makes evident that Germany's locomotive manufacturing industry remained strongly regionalized, without massive manufacturers comparable to Baldwin and ALCO in America and NBL in Britain. The following sections examine the histories of Borsig and subsequently Krauss, the latter notable for its proactive efforts to export locomotives to Japan.

Borsig Lokomotiv-Werke, founded in 1837 by the Prussian machine engineer Johann Friedrich August Borsig, produced its first steam locomotive in 1841.[29] It was introduced at the Berlin Industrial Exhibition in 1844 and favorably received, transforming the firm overnight into a prominent manufacturer representative of Prussian strength. Borsig made an estimated 259 of the 392 locomotives manufactured in Germany by 1850, and it continued to grow with the Prussian State Railways as its main customer, producing 583 locomotives by the time of August Borsig's death in 1854. By 1860, its holdings included an ironworks, a hammer-forging plant, and a mine, giving it control over all aspects of production from raw materials to end product. At this point, it counted over two thousand employees, making it the largest firm in Berlin, and its 3,800 locomotives built by 1880 also made it Europe's largest locomotive manufacturer at the time (table 1.3). However, as discussed earlier, the pace of its growth began slowing in the 1890s with stiff competition from Henschel and other firms.

Locomotivfabrik Krauss & Comp. was established in 1866 by Georg von Krauss,[30] a mechanical engineer who had worked for Maffei, an early entrant in the locomotive manufacturing industry, and the Royal Bavarian State Railways. After overcoming substantial opposition from Maffei, he set up a locomotive factory in Munich and grew the firm rapidly, building a second factory near the Munich South station in 1872 and entering the Austrian market in 1880.

Although Krauss was a relative latecomer among German locomotive manufacturers, its swift expansion produced a cumulative total of 4,100 locomotives in the period 1866–1900. Approximately 2,500 of these were sold in Bavaria and other regions of Germany; 1,100 went to the Austro-Hungarian Empire; and the remaining 500 were exported overseas. What distinguished the firm from other manufacturers was the diversity of its product line. Krauss "built locomotives of all types and classes for as many as 105 different gauges."[31] In particular, its small-sized locomotives were known for their high quality. These traits appealed to Japan's private railroads and industrial railroads, which typically used narrow-gauge tank-type locomotives; as I later discuss in detail, this led Japan to import large numbers of Krauss locomotives. In 1931, Krauss merged with Maffei to form Krauss-Maffei, which still exists today.

INTERNATIONAL COMPETITION IN THE LOCOMOTIVE MARKET

THE STRUCTURE OF THE LOCOMOTIVE EXPORT MARKET

International competition in the global market for locomotive manufacturing intensified around the turn of the century, threatening the United Kingdom's once unquestionable dominance in the industry. Starting around 1890, British and American locomotive manufacturers ramped up the battle to improve their performance, cost, and delivery times, resulting in a fierce tussle for market share in South America, Asia, and Britain's colonies.[32] Around 1900, German manufacturers rose to prominence, launching a three-way contest between the United Kingdom, the United States, and Germany. In this process, as the standardization of locomotives enormously increased manufacturers' competitiveness in terms of both cost and delivery time,[33] their willingness to adopt new technologies affected their

COMPETITION IN THE GLOBAL LOCOMOTIVE MARKET

performance. Unlike their German counterparts, who had proactively adopted both standardization and new technologies, British manufacturers lagged in these respects and saw dwindling shares in the first half of the twentieth century, raising concerns at home over the declining world competitiveness of British locomotives.[34] With this in mind, the following section elucidates global competition in locomotives and the international environment that affected their imports to Japan.

The January 1899 issue of *The Engineer*, an influential engineering journal published in London, reported that the Midland Railway, then a major English railroad, had ordered twenty Mogul-type (wheel arrangement 2-6-0)[35] tender locomotives[36] from Baldwin.[37] The Midland went on to order ten additional Baldwin locomotives,[38] and other major railroads followed suit, including the Great Northern Railway and the Great Central Railway, which each ordered twenty locomotives from Baldwin.[39] As earlier mentioned, major UK railroads typically manufactured locomotives in their own factories[40] and purchased the vehicles from domestic manufacturers only if they were unable to manufacture in-house. It had been forty years since a British railroad had ordered foreign-made locomotives.[41] By the end of the nineteenth century, British manufacturers' predominance in the international locomotive market was weakening, and, as discussed in detail below, American locomotive manufacturers had begun expanding overseas in earnest. In this context, news of American-made locomotives landing on British shores was grimly received by the British industrial world, as seen in how discussions about competition between American and British locomotive manufacturers peppered the pages of *The Engineer* from 1899 to the early 1900s. The journal had reporters around the world who meticulously collected and disseminated information on machine technology and the global trade of industrial goods. Its readership included industrialists and dealers in addition to engineers and craftspeople. As such, its articles provided not only technical information but also news on trade, business practices, and business management, while its "Letters to the Editor" column provided a platform for vigorous discussion among readers. Some of these discussions spread to its American counterpart, *The Engineering Magazine*. These journals are valuable sources that explain the circumstances and

TRENDS IN LOCOMOTIVE EXPORTS BY BRITISH AND AMERICAN MANUFACTURERS

First, let us examine trends in British and U.S. locomotive exports in this period.[42] While exports from American manufacturers rose dramatically from the latter half of the 1890s to 1900, the United Kingdom maintained dominance over the entire duration, with British manufacturers exporting over seven times as many locomotives as their American counterparts in 1890 (figure 1.2). During the nineteenth century, observers universally agreed that the United Kingdom stood atop the international locomotive market.[43] However, British exports declined sharply between 1891 and 1893 as a result of growing domestic demand.[44] A sudden spike in UK demand for locomotives around 1896,[45] coupled with a stagnation in British productivity due to an outbreak of large-scale strikes at locomotive plants,[46] fueled the dramatic growth of overseas exports by American manufacturers in the latter half of the 1890s.

It is evident that whereas exports by British manufactures declined sharply in the 1891–1893 period, those by American manufacturers increased steadily through the 1890s (table 0.2). These trends allowed American manufacturers to surpass British manufacturers in exports from 1897 onward, including exports from the United States to the United Kingdom. From 1894 to 1896, although South America was the main export destination for manufacturers in both countries (table 0.2), its markets mattered more to American manufacturers, as they sent over 50 percent of all exports to Asia and Europe. Between 1897 and 1899, the primary export destination for manufacturers in both countries shifted to Asia, including Japan and India. This change proved particularly dramatic for American manufacturers, whose share of Asia-bound exports suddenly climbed to almost half of all exports. For example, Baldwin's exports to Asia jumped from an average of seven locomotives per year between 1890 and 1892 to twenty-five per year between 1894 and 1896 and forty-four per year between 1897 and 1899, or

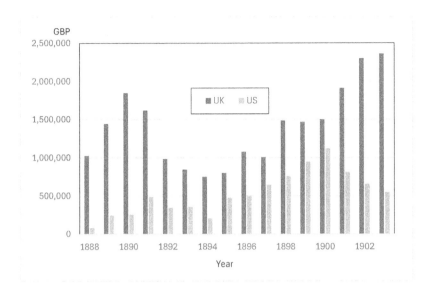

FIGURE 1.2 Comparison between British and U.S. locomotive exports from 1888 to 1903.

Source: W. Pollard Digby, "The British and American Locomotive Export Trade," *The Engineer*, December 16, 1904, 587–588.

from 0.8 percent to 8.4 percent of total exports over this entire period. I discuss this in detail below, but it is already evident from the above that Asian markets played a key role in international locomotive exports during this period.

However, from 1900 to 1902, the primary destination of American locomotive exports shifted to British colonies, which now accounted for 47 percent of total exports (table 0.2) and became the largest market for locomotives in the 1900s. Starting in the 1890s, Britain's manufacturers enjoyed continuous and overwhelming superiority in locomotive exports to its colonies.[47] In many of these territories, including India, Australia, and South Africa, colonial governments drove railroad construction, and most engineers who constructed and operated railroads were British. Accordingly, the British staff responsible for procuring railroad materials tended to purchase from the suzerain state—that is, the United Kingdom.[48]

However, by the latter half of the 1890s, American locomotive manufacturers were making headway in the Indian market, backed by the colonial government's judgment that American locomotives had surpassed British ones. For example, the Indian government signed a contract with Baldwin for the supply of railroad materials in June 1901. In response to British officials who strongly condemned this, Indian officials argued for the necessity of contracting with American manufacturers because of their superior price and delivery time.[49] The arrival of Baldwin locomotives in the United Kingdom thus heralded American locomotive manufacturers' eventual overtaking of their British counterparts.

SOURCES OF INTERNATIONAL COMPETITIVENESS

What enabled American locomotive manufacturers to triumph in an intensely competitive export market and to penetrate British-dominated overseas markets? *The Engineer* published issues around the turn of the century with frequent articles on this transatlantic rivalry as well as numerous essays and letters to the editor comparing the performance and manufacturing methods of British and American locomotives. When organized by year, they show that the points of comparison for each country's products evolved over the first half of the 1890s and the beginning of the 1900s.[50] Whereas discussion in the former period tended to compare the performance of British and American locomotives and market segmentation based on the characteristics of their national terrains, at the end of the 1890s it had come to focus on the pros and cons of adopting the American system of production and standardizing locomotive types. By the beginning of the 1900s, the debate had shifted to the track record of American-made locomotives adopted in the United Kingdom. With this in mind, we can analyze the process of comparing British and American locomotives and consider the source of the latter's competitiveness during this period.

What sparked increased interest in American locomotives in *The Engineer* was the invitation of their manufacturers to the 1890 World's Fair in Edinburgh, Scotland.[51] U.S. manufacturers then prioritized participating in the World's Fair and competing with their British rivals—to promote exports not, as might be expected, to Europe, but rather to South America.[52] Underlying this stance was their pride in how American-made locomotives had surpassed British-made locomotives in all respects.[53]

Baldwin, as the largest American manufacturer at the time, viewed the idea of presenting an exhibit at the World's Fair positively, though it ultimately held back due to the high cost of participating. Still, the lead-up to its decision sparked vigorous debate in the pages of *The Engineer* on the merits of U.S.- and British-made locomotives. Although the discussion initially focused on technical points such as boiler performance and locomotive design, it gradually shifted to reporting and interpreting the results of experiments comparing the performance of each country's locomotives in overseas markets where both were used side by side, including India, Australia, Argentina, and Japan.

In Japan, for example, Francis H. Trevithick,[54] a foreign engineer working for the IGR, conducted experiments comparing British and American 2-6-0 wheel arrangement tender locomotives on the Numazu–Gotenba section of the Tōkaidō line from May 3–6, 1894, and again on September 30, 1895. Although the trials nominally sought to evaluate American (Baldwin-made) locomotives that the IGR had recently entered into service, the fact that Trevithick immediately reported their results to the British journal *Proceedings of the Institution of Civil Engineers*,[55] which circulated internationally, indicates he was well aware of the contemporary discussions surrounding British and American locomotives in the United Kingdom. First, in the pulling comparison conducted on the Numazu–Gotenba section, the American locomotives clearly outperformed in terms of speed, power, and weight pulled.[56] In addition, they consumed less water in both inbound and outbound directions and performed better overall. Next, in terms of coal and oil consumption per mile over a steep stretch of the railroad near Gotenba,[57] the most fuel-efficient contenders were Nasmyth Wilson's 2-6-0, followed by Beyer Peacock's 2-6-0 (figure 1.3), with Baldwin's same type locomotive (figure 1.4) bringing up the rear. In other words, the two British locomotives exhibited better fuel efficiency when climbing steep slopes. Furthermore, given the difference in coal and oil consumption over 200,000 miles,[58] the Nasmyth Wilson locomotive, relative to its Baldwin counterpart, saved an estimated 983 pounds via the 2-6-0 tender model. Based on these results, Trevithick concluded that whereas American locomotives had superior speed and pulling power, British locomotives outperformed them in fuel efficiency and maintenance cost cutting.

The differing characteristics of each country's locomotives stemmed from their respective geographic and socioeconomic environments. The United States' vast area, abundant resources, and low population made it necessary to yield high returns on investment while operating railroads over long distances with high salaries and intense competition. High-speed locomotives capable of pulling heavy loads thus became the American norm, motivating efforts to increase production efficiency through standardized locomotive types and interchangeable production.[59] In contrast, the United Kingdom's small area and short interstation distances made fuel efficiency a priority over speed.

However, on entering the 1890s, demand for heavier and more powerful locomotives grew outside the United States due to the increased volume of rail-transported freight. This change, which led locomotive manufacturers around the world to imitate American designs in terms of weight and type, was especially welcomed in South America, Oceania, and Asia, whose environments resembled that of the United States and where railways consequently faced high costs and long delivery times.[60] However, because American-made locomotives had yet to penetrate the UK market at this point, opinions expressed in *The Engineer* tended to positively view the development of different locomotive types in their respective environments and market segmentation for British and American locomotives.[61]

Discussions in *The Engineer* comparing British and American locomotives briefly declined in 1897–1898.[62] But a January 1899 report on a major British railroad's importation of American locomotives revived a flurry of analyses regarding the comparative advantage of American locomotives, whose superiority in terms of cost and delivery times was already recognized in the United Kingdom by this point. For example, the four American locomotives ordered by the Barry Dock and Railway Company in May 1899 cost 1,800 pounds apiece, whereas a comparable British

FIGURE 1.3 Beyer Peacock's 2-6-0 tender locomotive. It was built for gradient line sections and categorized as a 7700-type locomotive by Japan National Railways.

Source: Iwasaki Collection, © Railway Museum, Ōmiya.

FIGURE 1.4 This photo was taken while driving Baldwin's 2-6-0 type tender locomotive. It was categorized as an 8150 type by Japan National Railways.

Source: Iwasaki Collection, © Railway Museum, Ōmiya.

locomotive would have been 2,800 pounds. Similarly, whereas American manufacturers had an average delivery time of around three months, British manufacturers reportedly could not do faster than twelve months.[63]

By the turn of the century, observers widely accepted that standardized locomotive types and interchangeable production underpinned the comparative advantage of American locomotive manufacturers. As early as 1880, a U.S. census report discussed the process by which interchangeable production had spread within the industry and the advantages of this system.[64] Furthermore, in the 1890s, Indian railroads began shifting to standardized locomotives to increase efficiency in maintenance and operations.[65] The American system, focused on a finite number of types, further proved advantageous in this respect. And, as *The Engineering Magazine* pointed out, the ordering system whereby customers simply had to select their desired locomotive type from a catalog, without the hassle of creating a detailed specification document, suited the needs of colonies under-provisioned in technical expertise.[66]

In the pages of *The Engineer*, witnesses to the ascendance of American manufacturers using this production system increasingly opined that British ones should adopt the same method.[67] However, this could not be immediately achieved. The journal's April 1899 issue, in explaining why the United Kingdom trailed the United States in standardization, observed that efforts to specify a standard type by manufacturers were being hindered by the major railroad companies' in-house manufacture of locomotives.[68] These railroads, also the main consumers of locomotives, only outsourced this work if they could not meet demand internally. As a consequence, manufacturers had to cater to individual demand by producing low volumes of a wide variety of vehicle types, creating an industry structure that hampered standardization.

It is also true that in countries within the British Empire and the sphere of its influence accustomed to using UK locomotives, including Japan, users perceived "the archetypical British locomotive" as "the most suitable for use anywhere in the world as it is in the United Kingdom."[69] One can easily imagine that the strength of Britain's brand gave its locomotive manufacturers little incentive to change their modus operandi. This tremendous confidence in the quality of their own products led some British engineers to arrogantly believe that "they have nothing to learn from Americans or anyone else."[70] *The Engineer* frequently published opinions indicating that "our manufacturers and English engineers will have to look seriously at American competition in Great Britain"[71] in an attempt to draw its readers' attention to the threat posed by American manufacturers.

Starting in March 1900, *The Engineer* published a four-part editorial that reviewed the various comparative evaluations of British and American locomotives as one of the journal's main themes throughout the 1890s. The editors mournfully noted that, "in the discussion of American and English railway practice there seems to be an unfortunate tendency in England to cavil at every point, to deride arguments, to disbelieve statements, to put forward petty objections, and to put aside any suggested measure as impracticable or absurd."[72] They pessimistically concluded that comparing the track records of British and American railroads led them to observe that British railroads performed unfavorably in all respects.

Ironically, as figure 1.2 shows, the following year saw British locomotive exports rapidly expand by a factor of 1.6, going from a total value of 1.5 million pounds in 1900 to 2.36 million pounds in 1903. Exports to British colonies, particularly prolific, showed a 2.4-fold increase from 740,000 pounds in 1900 to 1.79 million pounds in 1903. Meanwhile, the total value of exports by American manufacturers fell by half from 1.12 million pounds in 1900 to 540,000 pounds in 1903. This sudden decline likely resulted from American manufacturers' decreased export capacity due to the explosion in domestic demand. For example, although Baldwin's productivity shot up from 901 locomotives in 1899 to 2,022 locomotives in 1903,[73] the domestic market absorbed all this expanded production.[74] As discussed previously, major American railroads at the time usually placed batch orders for locomotives, which manufacturers were happy to oblige as they could take full advantage of interchangeable production.[75] These circumstances on the U.S. side once again allowed British manufacturers to distance themselves from their American rivals in exports (figure 1.2).

This change in the dynamic of locomotive exports led to remarks in the following vein in *The Engineer*, starting in 1901: "For years before the recent boom railways were running their locomotives to death, and locomotive builders were starving for work. On trade reviving, both British and colonial lines rushed in to renew their stock; British builders were crowded out, American and continental firms stepping in to take the overflows."[76] Furthermore, June 1901 reports regarding the track record of the Baldwin locomotives first imported by Midland Railway indicated that they provided a 20–25 percent increase in fuel costs, a 50 percent increase in oil costs, and a 60 percent increase in maintenance costs compared to British locomotives.[77] These findings set off a convoluted discussion in the journal regarding the cost-effectiveness of British and American locomotives, which sparked a resurgence in national pride: the "British locomotive builder constructs the best machinery of the kind that can be made."[78] This pride also manifested in the criticism leveled by British high officials regarding the Indian government's decision in June 1901 to contract with Baldwin for railroad materials: "it is unacceptable to conclude an agreement with an American manufacturer while disregarding technologically superior British manufacturers."[79]

Such criticisms contained no consideration of customer complaints regarding British manufacturers' "looseness of delivery dates and high costs." Furthermore, discussions that pitted British manufacturers against their American counterparts disappeared from *The Engineer* around 1902. Yet overconfidence in their own superiority delayed British locomotive manufacturers' adoption of technological advances. It slowed their transition from saturated to superheated steam technology, one of the most consequential innovations in twentieth-century locomotive manufacturing, which chapter 6 discusses in detail.

GLOBAL COMPETITION IN LOCOMOTIVE MANUFACTURING

The trends in the foregoing discussion on the global locomotive market around the turn of the century allow us to divide this epoch into three periods based on the changing composition of global competition in locomotive manufacturing: the first half of the 1890s, the end of the 1890s, and the early 1900s. American manufacturers' emergent challenge to British hegemony in South America marked the start of the first period. Here cost and delivery times formed the main points of competition between British and American manufacturers that focused on market segmentation according to the characteristics of each country's locomotives. While the British-made locomotives were superior in fuel efficiency and durability, the American-made locomotives excelled in speed and tractive effort, and these traits shaped their respective shares of the market. Furthermore, comparing the export motivations of both countries, British manufacturers had no incentive to bear additional risk by seeking orders from overseas.[80] In the United States, on the other hand, the decline of domestic demand in the 1890s increased the importance of overseas markets as a safety net.[81] Thus, the domestic market situation in Western locomotive suppliers impacted the shift in the global export market.

The second period is underscored by American manufacturers' aggressive entry into overseas markets, mainly British colonies in Asian and Oceania. In 1899, American locomotives finally landed on UK shores, where their comparative advantage in terms of cost, delivery time, and responsiveness to users' needs led to earnest discussions on adopting the American system perceived as the source of their superiority. However, a domestic market where major railroad companies manufactured in-house and British manufacturers' pride in their own locomotives thwarted the United Kingdom's transition to standardized production.

In the third period, British locomotive exports exhibited a resurgence, especially in their colonial markets, thanks in part to a tumble in American exports following dramatic expansion in the U.S. domestic market. At the same time, American and German manufacturers took up technological innovations epitomized by the development of superheated steam locomotives, with the latter's rise especially striking (and discussed at length in chapter 6). Around 1900, German manufacturers quickly adopted the interchangeable and standardized systems developed in the United States and began manufacturing high-quality locomotives at low cost, taking advantage of cheap labor and state support.[82] In the early 1900s, they developed the world's first superheated steam locomotives and improved their fuel efficiency. In contrast, British manufacturers, blinkered by overconfidence in their own technology, failed to integrate these innovations despite having gained a temporary advantage over their American and German rivals. The loss of their industrial lead to American and German manufacturers was apparent by 1910, a point that marks the sunset of Britain's locomotive industry

* * *

British, American, and German manufacturers were locked in an intense competition in the international market for locomotive exports around the turn of the century. Amid this tussle, two major breakthroughs occurred in succession—the production innovation eventually called the "American system," followed by the technological innovation of superheated steam locomotives in Germany. Competitiveness hinged on the ability to respond to these and other advances, and the British locomotive industry's failure to do so led it off the ramp of its nineteenth-century dominance onto a long path of decline.

Thus, the British monopoly was dismantled through the entry of American and German manufacturers and rapid diversification of the global locomotive market. This competition enabled customers to globally source high-quality, inexpensive locomotives with short delivery times. Such an outcome came to fruition within the first global economy and accelerated the worldwide spread of railroads.[83] Japan's railroads became key global customers of these manufacturers in this era, and the following chapter turns to how they capitalized on this favorable international environment through employing specific mechanisms in locomotive-related transactions.

2

TECHNOLOGICAL TRANSFER AND BRITISH MONOPOLIZATION

This chapter discusses railroad technology as an example of the modern industrial technology that Japan's new government, established in the Meiji Restoration, promoted as the first step toward nation building. Here the United Kingdom had a key role in introducing such innovations during the Meiji period, including for railroads. In particular, I will discuss the critical role of the *oyatoi* system of hired foreigners, technical bureaucracies, and educational system in the formation of Japanese technology.

In 1868, the Tokugawa shogun restored imperial rule, and the Meiji emperor established a new government whose leaders shared a sense of crisis over the threat of colonization, which had grown since the end of the Tokugawa period. They saw catching up with the Western powers in both military and economic terms as pressing issues; hence, they considered the introduction of modern technology from Europe and the United States as the first step toward a solution. The Meiji government aimed to modernize the indigenous silk and cotton industries as well as iron and mining while establishing new industries in shipbuilding, machinery, telegraphs, and railroads. Railroads took high priority not only for their economic role but also because of their anticipated military and symbolic contributions to national prowess, and their building commenced in 1869, just after the Restoration.

As early as 1872, Japan's first government-operated railroad opened between Shinbashi in Tokyo and Yokohama. British technology, materials, and funds aided its operation, and the United Kingdom subsequently monopolized the supply of locomotives to Honshu, Japan's mainland and largest island, from the 1870s to the early 1890s. In contrast, the northern island of Hokkaido introduced its railroad system from the United States, while the southern island of Kyushu procured its own from Germany in the 1880s. Japanese officials in this period lacked the know-how to choose railroad technologies and simply followed the recommendations of the leading industrialized countries. In short, Japan at this point was a late developer subject to the whims of the first global economy.

If we imagine a scenario where a developing country cannot independently build and operate railroads, the logical supposition would be that it relies on developed countries for funds, human resources, materials, outsourcing construction, and operation. To gain the benefits of technology transfer and to procure materials in the early Meiji era, Japan adopted the *oyatoi* system, in which the government hired foreign engineers, managers, and skilled workers to train Japanese staff on the job while building and operating railroads.[1] In parallel, government-established higher education institutions trained engineers and modern industry leaders. Nevertheless, cultivating engineers and managers under this system took time, so Japan continued to rely on hired foreigners, mainly from Britain, for about a decade after establishing its railroads. Consequently, British-made locomotives dominated the Japanese railroad materials market at the end of the nineteenth century.

This chapter examines the distribution routes and transactions related to locomotives in the early development of Japanese railroads from multiple angles, including the employment of foreign engineers and managers, resource procurement based on negotiated contracts, and the activities of foreign trading companies.[2] As a complement to the analysis, I also discuss

Japan's social capabilities in the early stages of its industrialization, focusing on the government's industrial promotion policies and the education of engineers. Finally, I provide a comparative analysis of Japan's railroad formation with that of China, which introduced railroads around the same time.

STARTING THE RAILROADS

From the close of the Tokugawa period to the early Meiji era, in the 1860s and 1870s, Japan received foreign railroad technology by two means: the *oyatoi* system or the use of foreign general contractors.[3] The British preferred the former method, while the Americans encouraged the latter's use. The newly established Meiji government needed railroads to rapidly boost national integration and promote trade and industry. It further sought to establish Western technologies in Japan to grow its industrial capacity.

December 1869 marked the start of railroad construction and the government's official institution of the *oyatoi* system.[4] It ensured Japan would take the lead in railroad construction and management by directly hiring foreign engineers and managers, which also allowed it to require that foreign engineers transfer their expertise to their Japanese colleagues as a condition of employment. Japan's political leaders, hurrying to modernize against Western colonization, particularly emphasized these two points.[5]

A necessary first step in this process was the hiring of a general manager responsible for raising funds, selecting railroad engineers, and procuring materials. An introduction by Harry Smith Parkes, the UK consul general to Japan, led the government to entrust the job of laying rails and securing the necessary funds to one Horatio Nelson Lay (1832–1898).[6] Lay was a former British diplomat who served as the director of customs in Qing China from 1859 to 1864. After leaving his post, he worked as a financial broker and promoted railroad projects in China, but he failed to sell the railroad project to the Qing government. In 1869, he traveled to Japan, and with the help of Parkes's introduction, he lobbied Japanese government leaders to build railroads.[7]

Lay entered into a number of contracts with the government, in which provisions related to the procurement of railroad materials, including locomotives, appeared in an agreement signed on December 22, 1869.[8] This agreement shows that Lay or his proxies had the authority to purchase railroad materials based on specification documents created by foreign engineers and approved by the Ministry of Civil Affairs, for which he received a commission of 2.5 percent. Based on this agreement, Lay hired George P. White as a consulting engineer in London to select and conduct preliminary product inspections in the country of manufacture for the same commission amount.[9] He also hired British engineer Edmund Morel (1841–1871, figure 2.1) as the first chief engineer of Japan's IGR. After studying civil engineering at King's College in London, Morel gained experience as a civil engineer working in colonial territories such as New Zealand (1862–1864) and Australia (1864–1869). In 1869, he signed a contract to become the chief engineer of the IGR and came to the country in April 1870.[10]

Around August 1870, White ordered ten tank locomotives from five British manufacturers, including Sharp Stewart, based on a specification document prepared by Morel.[11] White apparently contracted with five companies to produce a relatively small number of locomotives to speed up delivery time.[12] However, the government rescinded its loan agreement with Lay in December 1870 due to a disagreement over how he had secured funds and designated the Oriental Bank as a new proxy agent. The Oriental Bank and its executives were entrusted with railroad supervision, while the London-based Malcolm Brunker & Co. oversaw materials procurement.[13]

Meanwhile, the Japanese government needed a domestic manager who understood English and had enough familiarity with railroad technology and management to supervise foreign engineers. The best person for the job was Inoue Masaru (1843–1910, figure 2.2), who became the head of the Railway Department (Tetsudō-ryō) in 1871.

Inoue was a member of the Chōshū clan, which had been a driving force of the Restoration. In 1863, he stole passage to England to study at University College London with Itō Hirobumi, Inoue Kaoru, Yamao Yōzō, and Endō Kinsuke, who all served as leaders of the post-Restoration government

FIGURE 2.1 Portrait of Edmund Morel (1841–1871), the first chief engineer of the IGR.

Source: Yokohama shishi hensankakari, ed., *Yokohama Shiryō* [Yokohama historical materials] (Yokohama: Yokohama city, 1928), n.p.

and were popularly known as the Chōshū Five. Inoue Masaru spent four years in London studying civil engineering and mining, and he returned to Japan in December 1868 after gaining practical experience in mining and railroad work. His fluency in English and expertise in railroad technology enabled him to direct and supervise foreign engineers and managers, and he headed the Railway Bureau (Tetsudō Kyoku) for over twenty years, significantly contributing to the development of Japan's railroads.[14]

FIGURE 2.2 Portrait of Inoue Masaru, the first head of the Railway Bureau in Japan.

Source: Murai Masatoshi, *Shishaku Inoue Masaru shōden* [Biography of Viscount Masaru Inoue] (Tokyo: Inoue shishaku dōzō kensetsu dōshikai, 1915), frontispiece.

TECHNOLOGICAL TRANSFER, BRITISH MONOPOLIZATION

After 1874, Inoue's counterparts who had studied railroad technology abroad around the time of the Restoration gradually returned to Japan and gathered at the IGR, becoming the first generation of Japanese engineers to manage railroad construction as it spread nationwide. From the 1880s onward, they replaced foreign engineers as instructors in domestic educational institutions.

THE BRITISH MONOPOLY OF TECHNOLOGICAL TRANSFER

In 1871, the first ten locomotives (figure 2.3) from Britain arrived in Japan one after another, and the IGR line between Shinbashi and Yokohama opened the following year.

At the time, IGR construction and operation relied almost entirely on foreign employees, the vast majority of them British.[15] For all intents and

FIGURE 2.3 Japan's first steam locomotive, built by Vulcan Foundry in the United Kingdom.

Source: Usui Shgenobu, *Kikansha no keifuzu 1* [Genealogy of Locomotives, vol. 1] (Tokyo: Kōyūsha, 1972), 3. © Kōyūsha.

purposes, the director, engineer in chief, locomotive superintendent, secretary, and other managers had the authority to decide the specifications of railroad construction and materials procurement. Furthermore, according to the agreement with Oriental Bank, Malcolm Brunker received the exclusive right to import materials. In this manner, a procurement route was established whereby foreign (British) employees ordered locomotives from British locomotive manufacturers through a British trading company.

This did not mean that foreign employees took unfair advantage of their situation. For example, in 1882, A. S. Aldrich, who lived and worked in Japan for more than twenty-five years as secretary and agent of the Railway Bureau, assisted the IGR by eliminating Oriental Bank as an intermediary and directly contracting with Malcolm Brunker, thereby reducing handling costs from 2.5 percent to 1.5 percent.[16]

Oyatoi engineers played vital roles in transferring railroad technologies to Japan by using Japanese assistants to construct and operate railroads and passing down know-how through on-the-job training. Furthermore, top-level foreign engineers and Japanese engineers educated abroad taught not only skills but theoretical knowledge to their students at the Training School for Railway Engineers (Kōgisei Yōseishō) established by the Railway Bureau.[17] Most students, who served as assistants, understood English and had up to secondary education. They became competent engineers who took over the construction of Japan's railroads from the late 1880s onward.

The *oyatoi* system also exerted considerable influence on industrial policies and the higher education of engineers. In 1870, the Japanese government established the Ministry of Public Works at Morel's suggestion. This office aimed to promote government-owned businesses such as railroads and mines and to train the personnel responsible for these projects. To that end, it directly hired foreigners and introduced the latest technology from Western countries to speed the domestic development of modern industries. Furthermore, it established the Imperial College of Engineering (ICE; Kōbu Daigakkō) in 1873 as an institute of higher education to provide Japanese engineers with advanced training.[18] Yamao Yōzō (1837–1917) crucially enabled the establishment of ICE by drawing on his experience

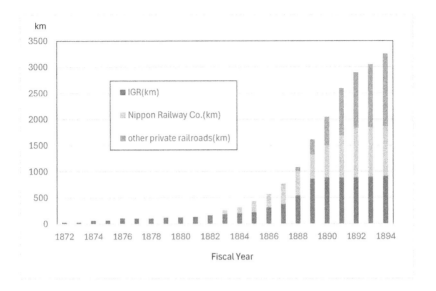

FIGURE 2.4 Railroad operating distances in Japan, 1872–1894.

Source: Tetsudō Kyoku, ed., *Meiji 40 nendo Tetsudō kyoku nenpō* [Annual report of the Railway Bureau in 1907 FY] (Tokyo: Tetsudō In, 1909), appendix, 100–103.

as a student in Britain to implement the concept of a higher educational institute and to select the school's principal.[19] ICE graduates became leading engineers in their respective fields who contributed to Japan's achieving of technological independence after the 1890s, as chapter 3 will discuss. As a whole, technology transfer through the *oyatoi* system boosted the early launch of modern industries in Japan, with the railroads playing central roles in this process.

The length of rail lines operated by private and government railroads (figure 2.4) shows that the IGR played a leading role from the 1870s to the early 1880s. Nippon Railway built Japan's first private railroad in 1881, which began operating between Ueno and Kumagaya in 1883. However, the firm entrusted the construction and operation of its rail lines to the IGR until 1892. The IGR thus monopolized the management of Japanese railroads before the first railroad boom (1886–1889) until the emergence of private railroads such as Sanyo and Kyushu. Consequently, procurement routes for railroad goods remained constant, and Japan continued purchasing locomotives from the United Kingdom in the 1880s, giving UK manufacturers a monopoly on locomotives imported during this period.[20] As late as 1887, 98 percent of locomotives in Japan were British-made (table 0.3). Gerard Lowther, the secretary of the British legation in Tokyo at the time, described these circumstances as follows in his *Report on the Railways of Japan*, sent to the UK government in 1895:

COMPETITION

At the risk of being accused of repeating a warning so frequently addressed by British officials abroad to their countrymen interested in business at home, I would very specially call attention to the vital necessity of manufacturers of railway material in Great Britain, now more than ever taking every possible measure to advance their own interests. Hitherto, as I have pointed out, Great Britain has practically had a monopoly in furnishing rails, locomotives, rolling stock &c. Whether these manufactures may still enjoy this privilege must depend in a great measure on themselves and the exertions they may make. As I have shown, the railways of Japan have been built by foreign advisers. For this term, English advisers might almost be substituted. This being the case, it was evidently convenient that the materials required for the carrying out of designs made by English engineers should be ordered in England.[21]

At a point when British advisers were starting to be let go, Lowther reported that the continued monopolization of railroad materials would depend on British locomotive manufacturers' efforts and awareness of the situation; he particularly emphasized the importance of marketing to them, since changing the purchasing authority would crucially influence the receipt of orders.

BRITISH LOCOMOTIVE EXPORTS TO JAPAN

At this juncture, it is useful to examine British locomotive manufacturers and trends in exports to Japan during this period. Over the forty years stretching from 1871 to 1911, eighteen British manufacturers exported a total of 1,245 locomotives to Japan (table 2.1).

The largest of these was the NBL and its three constituent companies of Dübs, Sharp Stewart, and Neilson, which together accounted for 762 (61.2 percent) of these exports. As Baldwin sent 627 American locomotives

TABLE 2.1 Number of British locomotives exported to Japan

	1871–1889		1890–1911		ACCUMULATED TOTAL # OF CARS	
Vulcan Foundry	13	7.6%	10	0.9%	23	1.8%
Sharp Stewart+	17	9.9%	28	2.6%	45	3.6%
Dübs+	62	36.0%	226	21.1%	288	23.1%
Avonside Engine	2	1.2%	2	0.2%	4	0.3%
Yorkshire Engine	1	0.6%	0	0.0%	1	0.1%
Nasmyth Wilson	32	18.6%	151	14.1%	183	14.7%
Beyer Peacock	26	15.1%	186	17.3%	212	17.0%
Kitson	12	7.0%	15	1.4%	27	2.2%
R. Stephenson	4	2.3%	0	0.0%	4	0.3%
Neilson+	–	–	94	8.8%	94	7.6%
North British Loco.			335	31.2%	335	26.9%
Industrial locomotive manufacturers	3	1.7%	26	2.4%	29	2.3%
Total	172	100.0%	1,073	100.0%	1,245	100.0%

Sources: Peter J. English, *British Made: Industrial Development and Related Archaeology of Japan* (Eindhoven: De Archeologische Pers Nederland ,1982), 13–14; Richard L. Hills, "Some Contributions to Locomotive Development by Beyer Peacock & Co.," *Newcomen Society Transactions* 40 (1968), 99–109; *Nasmyth Papers*, Salford Local Archives; *Vulcan Foundry Records*, National Museums Liverpool; Usui Shigenobu, *Kikansha no keifu-zu 1* [Genealogy of locomotives vol. 1] (Tokyo: Kōyū sha, 1972).

Notes: The three companies marked with the plus symbol (+) merged in 1903 to form North British Locomotive.

TECHNOLOGICAL TRANSFER, BRITISH MONOPOLIZATION

during the same period, this made NBL the top supplier, and the most prolific British manufacturers after it were Beyer Peacock and Nasmyth, with 212 and 183 locomotives respectively. From the numbers of locomotives exported during different periods, Dübs, Nasmyth, and Beyer Peacock were relatively prolific in the period 1871–1889, with exports distributed among several manufacturers. In contrast, for the 1890–1911 period, a large share of the orders for railroad locomotives in public transportation (63.7 percent) concentrated among NBL and its affiliated manufacturers. Starting in the 1900s, Japan began to import smaller locomotives for industrial use, which concomitantly increased the number of manufacturers it used.

THE GLASGOW LOCOMOTIVE MANUFACTURERS

Dübs, Sharp Stewart, and Neilson were all located in Glasgow and exported many locomotives to Japan; Dübs, which sent 288 locomotives over the thirty-one years of 1871–1902, was the largest such exporter.[22] Of these, 202 were tank locomotives, including a large number of locomotives in the B2 (wheel arrangement 0-6-0) and A8 (wheel arrangement 2-4-2, figure 2.5) classes for the IGR.[23] The firm's end customers included the IGR (186 locomotives), as well as private railroads including Nippon Railway (49 locomotives) and Kansei Railway (30 locomotives). Kansei Railway and Osaka Railway imported especially large numbers of A8 locomotives, the same type used by the IGR, reflecting a procurement procedure that relied on the IGR for locomotive selection and testing. Until 1897, British trading companies including Malcolm Brunker, Jardine Matheson, and John Birch served as the IGR's intermediaries; however, Japanese intermediaries emerged in 1898, including Takata Shōkai and Ōkura Gumi.

Similarly, Sharp Stewart exported 45 locomotives to Japan over the twenty-six years for 1871–97. The firm played a critical role in the 1870s, as it supplied 4 of the 10 locomotives used by Japan's first railroad line between Shinbashi and Yokohama.[24] In fact, 15 of the 43 locomotives in operation in 1880 were Sharp Stewart products.[25] Malcolm Brunker, John Birch, and other British trading companies brokered the procurement of Sharp Stewart locomotives for the IGR as their primary end customer. However, from the mid-1890s onward, Sharp Stewart also supplied locomotives to prominent

FIGURE 2.5 Dübs's 2-4-2-type tank locomotive, which was categorized A8 class by the IGR.

Source: Iwasaki Collection, © Railway Museum, Ōmiya.

FIGURE 2.6 A 4-4-0-type tender locomotive made by Neilson, categorized as D9 class by the IGR.

Source: Tetsudō shō, ed., *Nihon tesudō shi chūhen* [A railroad history of Japan, vol. 2] (Tokyo: Tetsudō shō, 1921), n.p.

TECHNOLOGICAL TRANSFER, BRITISH MONOPOLIZATION

private railroads such as Kyushu Railway and Nippon Railway. The latter subsequently tested a large-type tender locomotive, and the IGR purchased 18 tender locomotives in a single order, but Sharp Stewart's exports to Japan ceased in 1897.

Neilson, though the largest and most influential of the three manufacturers that formed NBL, came a far second to Dübs in terms of exports to Japan, sending a total of 94 locomotives over the eleven years for 1889–1900. That said, whereas Dübs and Sharp Stewart mainly manufactured tank locomotives, Neilson primarily manufactured tender locomotives (4-4-0, figure 2.6).[26] Of the 94 locomotives it exported to Japan, 82 were of the tender type, and its customers included trunk line operators such as Sanyo Railway, Nippon Railway, and the IGR.[27] Starting in 1895, the IGR ordered 56 Neilson tender locomotives; as with other British locomotive manufacturers, the intermediaries were all British firms, including Malcolm Brunker, John Birch, and A. R. Brown.

Neilson's *Engine Orders* registry contains entries regarding delivery and ordering conditions for locomotive production.[28] It clearly shows that the company's manufacturing times varied widely in the 1890s, ranging from 90 to 360 days. Using data from table 2.2, Neilson's average manufacturing time in the period 1893–1896 works out to 159.3 days, or approximately double the 75.5 days that Baldwin took during the same period. From the mid-1890s on, Neilson and its fellow British manufacturers came nowhere close to matching American manufacturers in terms of delivery speed. As chapter 5 discusses in detail, this is the reason why British locomotive manufacturers, unable to respond to a spike in demand accompanying the Russo-Japanese War and railroad nationalization, decisively trailed their American counterparts.

THE MANCHESTER LOCOMOTIVE MANUFACTURERS

In Manchester, Beyer Peacock and Nasmyth Wilson both exported locomotives to Japan. Beyer Peacock sent 218 locomotives over the thirty-two years for 1882–1914, making it the second-largest exporter of locomotives behind NBL,[29] and Japan received 20–40 percent of all Beyer Peacock locomotives manufactured during the second railroad boom of 1894–1898.

TABLE 2.2 Comparison of British and American locomotive delivery times

	NEILSON & CO. (BRITISH)				BALDWIN LOCOMOTIVE WORKS (AMERICAN)			
	SHORTEST (DAYS)	LONGEST (DAYS)	AVERAGE (DAYS)	NO. OF SHIPMENTS	SHORTEST (DAYS)	LONGEST (DAYS)	AVERAGE (DAYS)	NO. OF SHIPMENTS
1889	280	335	301	14	100	100	100	3
1890	–	–	–	–	108	316	150	12
1891	–	–	–	–	218	218	218	N/A
1892	–	–	–	–	97	97	97	3
1893	122	214	183	12	64	174	129	25
1894	90	118	105	12	38	158	66	30
1895	109	109	109	6	38	62	53	13
1896	180	302	240	18	30	70	55	31
1897	–	–	–	–	36	102	58	115
1898	–	–	–	–	61	83	68	7
1899	290	390	340	32	105	105	105	9
1900	–	–	–	–	185	302	234	8

Sources: Baldwin Locomotive Works, *Engine Orders*, Smithsonian Institution Archives; Neilson Co. *Engine Orders*, NBL/2/1/1, National Railway Museum.

Notes: Delivery time refers to the number of days from order to shipping, not including transportation days.

TECHNOLOGICAL TRANSFER, BRITISH MONOPOLIZATION

Nippon Railway, by far Beyer Peacock's largest end customer, ordered 142 of their locomotives, or 65 percent of all locomotives the firm exported to Japan; in 1901, 93 of the 286 locomotives the railway owned were made by Beyer Peacock. The firm's prominence was especially evident in the case of tender locomotives, where their products accounted for 44 percent (or 68 of the 154) of those owned by Nippon.[30] The railway preferred Beyer Peacock locomotives due to their fuel efficiency and low maintenance costs, and its records show that the coal consumption per mile of tender locomotives was 1.91 pounds for Beyer Peacock, 1.95 pounds for Sharp Stewart, and 2.22 pounds for Neilson. In terms of repair costs per 40,000 miles traveled, if the costs for Beyer Peacock were 100 yen, those for Sharp Stewart and Neilson were 150 and 108 yen respectively. In other words, Nippon thought that even though Beyer Peacock locomotives were initially slightly more expensive, they promised lower running costs in the long term.[31]

Although Malcolm Brunker handled the purchase of Beyer Peacock locomotives from 1882, Mitsui Bussan took over this role in 1900. In January 1903, Nippon Railway ordered 32 tank locomotives through negotiated contracts.[32] For this trade, Mitsui Bussan purchased 24 Beyer Peacock locomotives as the designated intermediary, and the railroad ordered the remaining 8 from German manufacturers through the German trading company M. Raspe.[33]

The IGR also enthusiastically purchased from Beyer Peacock, ordering 42 of their locomotives between 1889 and 1908. Of these, 8 were rack locomotives for the Usui Pass, located in the mountainous Gunma Prefecture and the steepest section of the IGR's Shin'etsu line.[34] From 1895 onward, the IGR exclusively purchased rack locomotives from Beyer Peacock, which bespeaks the latter's reputation for manufacturing specialized types.[35]

In contrast to the large locomotive manufacturers mentioned up to this point, Nasmyth Wilson was a small to medium-sized company with approximately five hundred employees and an annual production of under 50 locomotives. However, it played a major role in exports to Japan, where it shipped 183 locomotives between 1885 and 1908. This made it the third-largest exporter behind NBL and Beyer Peacock, which sent 762 and 212 locomotives respectively (table 2.1). Accordingly, during the second railroad boom in this period, orders from Japan accounted for more than half of Nasmyth Wilson's total production.

The vast majority of the company's 183 locomotives exported to Japan were tank types, with only six tender types.[36] In marked contrast to Neilson and Beyer Peacock, whose primary customers were trunk line operators, Nasmyth Wilson serviced a wide range of buyers from the IGR to small and medium-sized private railroads. Between 1885 and 1887, the firm developed A8- and B3-class tank locomotive prototypes based on orders from the IGR, entering bulk production after it had selected these production models.[37] From 1893 onward, it delivered large numbers of these same types of tank locomotives, which were used by the IGR as well as small and medium-sized private railroads. The order periods, prices, end customers, and intermediaries for A8-class tank locomotives show that the price varied depending on the order period and end customer. For example, the IGR and Nippon Railway initially purchased serial number 326 through Malcolm Brunker, whose basic design was finalized in 1887, for 1,335 pounds. Then, both railroads purchased eighteen locomotives of the same model at the higher price of 1,620 pounds in 1888–1889.[38] Usui Shigenobu notes the importance of negotiated contracts, carried out under the auspices of Francis H. Trevithick at the IGR, in the relationship between manufacturers and purchasers of Nasmyth Wilson locomotives during the 1880s.[39] Such contracts allowed multiple prototypes to be developed before starting bulk production. Nasmyth Wilson, with advanced technical skill despite its small size, was a vital partner for a country just beginning to construct railroads.

During the second railroad boom, many small and medium-sized railroads purchased A8-class locomotives at a lower price than the IGR. For example, from 1893 to 1896, Sobu Railway purchased ten locomotives of the same type as serial number 326 through John Birch at an average price of 1,378 pounds per locomotive. It was 242 pounds lower than the price during bulk production in 1889. This suggests that, in the late 1890s, small and medium-sized railroads lowered their costs by purchasing the same locomotive types developed by the IGR. These prices, however, shot up dramatically in the 1900s; in 1901, Sobu Railway purchased A8-class locomotives for 1,953 pounds, more than 500 pounds higher than what Narita Railway had paid for the same in 1896.

In addition to differences over time, prices varied among railroads even when the same intermediary was involved. For example, in 1894, three railroads—Sobu, Sangu, and Kobu—bought a total of six A8-class tank locomotives through John Birch. But the purchase price was 1,379 pounds for Sobu, 1,429 and 1,517 pounds for Sangu, and 1,360 pounds for Kobu. The gap between the highest and lowest prices indicates that although these smaller railroads purchased locomotives through John Birch during the same period, they did not share price information. While such variations begat gains for foreign trading companies, they also posed serious problems for Japanese railroads, which attempted to reform their procurement systems and change intermediaries. Chapter 4 explores the process and ramifications of the shift in purchasing intermediaries from British to Japanese firms around 1900.

THE LOCOMOTIVE TRADE AND BRITISH TRADING COMPANIES

THE END OF MALCOLM BRUNKER'S MONOPOLY IN SUPPLYING THE IGR

As outlined at the outset, from the establishment of Japan's first railroad in 1872 up to the 1880s, British trading companies controlled the Japanese locomotive market due to the *oyatoi* system, which strongly favored British engineers, and the primacy of negotiated contracts for purchasing railroad materials. This was especially so in the first decade of Japan's railroads, when the Oriental Bank dispatched agents to oversee the IGR's funding and purchase of materials for railroad construction and the London-based Malcolm Brunker exclusively handled the purchasing of all materials.[40]

In July 1882, A. S. Aldrich, the secretary of the Railway Bureau, proposed that the Japanese government dissolve its contract with the Oriental Bank and enter into a direct agency agreement with Malcolm Brunker. As this would eliminate the 1 percent handling fee paid to the bank, the

TECHNOLOGICAL TRANSFER, BRITISH MONOPOLIZATION

Railway Bureau did so in September of the same year. Although the overall structure of purchasing British railroad materials through a British intermediary remained, the handling charge fell from 2.5 to 1.5 percent.[41]

Let us look at the case of Nasmyth Wilson in the period 1885–1890 to examine the process of purchasing locomotives during the negotiated contract era. First, the superintendent, F. H. Trevithick, would create a locomotive specification document in Japan, which also appears to have designated the workshop. Aldrich would then submit this to Malcolm Brunker in London, which proceeded to send orders to manufacturers. The same information would be delivered to the Japanese government's preliminary product inspector, then Thomas R. Shervinton,[42] a former *oyatoi* back in England. Shervinton would visit the manufacturers to supervise and inspect their progress and check whether products met specifications, after which the finished goods were exported to Japan.[43]

However, the establishment of Railway Bureau regulations on trading goods in 1890 introduced competitive bidding for the purchase of railroad materials and eliminated the ability of *oyatoi* employees to order materials at their discretion through trading companies based in London (as detailed in chapter 3). That said, Aldrich and Trevithick still exercised substantial influence over the purchase of materials and continued to designate British locomotive manufacturers in specification documents up to the mid-1890s.[44] For intermediary companies, the introduction of competitive bidding greatly increased the importance of information gathering within Japan, which advantaged companies with strong personal networks on the ground. Malcolm Brunker's position declined as a result of these developments, paving the way for the emergence of other British intermediaries such as A. R. Brown[45] and John Birch.

For example, John Birch vigorously ordered from the Glasgow-based manufacturers previously handled by Malcolm Brunker. This started with the purchase of 2 Sharp Stewart tank locomotives in 1889,[46] followed by 18 Dübs tank locomotives in 1897,[47] and 20 Neilson tender locomotives in 1899.[48] A. R. Brown also ordered 12 Neilson tender locomotives in 1899 for the IGR.[49] The same type of Neilson locomotives was ordered through John Birch and A. R. Brown because the specification documents designated

Neilson as the manufacturer and because the IGR split its purchase of 32 locomotives across two separate orders. As this case illustrates, the designation of a manufacturer or lack thereof impacted the outcome of competitive bidding. Accordingly, intermediary companies devoted substantial efforts to ensuring that the manufacturers they did business with entered the list of designated manufacturers, as chapter 3 discusses. In this regard, Japanese trading companies enjoyed an edge over their foreign counterparts due to their various government connections, an advantage that underpinned their rise at the turn of the century.

PRIVATE RAILROADS AND LOCOMOTIVE PURCHASES: KANSEI, OSAKA, AND JARDINE MATHESON

In late 1886, plans to establish private railroads began to flourish throughout Japan, setting the groundwork for its first railroad boom, which lasted until 1889. By 1891, the country had approved a string of new railroad companies, eleven of which had launched operations. Four new trunk railroad operators emerged during the same period: Sanyo Railway (the Kobe–Shimonoseki line established in 1888), Kyushu Railway (the Moji-Yatsushiro line established in 1888), Hokkaido Colliery and Railway (the Temiya–Horonai lines established in 1889), and Kansei Railway (the Kusatsu–Nagoya line established in 1888). Along with Nippon Railway, which had begun operating in 1883 on the Ueno–Aomori and Omiya–Takasaki lines, these enterprises would grow into Japan's five main railroads. With the exception of Nippon Railway, which entrusted construction and operation to the IGR, private railroads needed to hire engineers, procure materials, and construct rail lines on their own.[50] For these emergent companies, procuring locomotives and other railroad materials posed major challenges. Almost all private railroads established during this period followed the IGR in procuring materials from the United Kingdom.[51] For example, at the time of its establishment, Sanyo Railway enlisted the IGR's help in purchasing UK railroad materials through Malcolm Brunker.[52]

It was in this context that Osaka Railway (the Osaka–Nara line established in 1888) and Kansei Railway procured railroad materials via a separate route: they did so exclusively through Jardine Matheson, which acted as their sole agent under the auspices of Thomas Blake Glover and his associates. Glover was a British merchant who had famously imported and sold weapons to the rebel factions that overthrew the Tokugawa shogunate and subsequently formed the new Meiji government.[53] After his eponymous trading company went bankrupt in 1870, Glover became a manager at the Takashima coal mine and later an adviser to Mitsubishi.[54] Jardine Matheson, a key British trading company, established itself in Macao in 1832 and succeeded in the Chinese trade after moving its headquarters to Hong Kong in 1841. On entering Japan in 1859, it set up a branch company in the newly opened port of Yokohama and became a central player in trade with the country.[55] For a time, Glover served as one of its agents, but he eventually accrued substantial debt, which contributed to the bankruptcy of his own enterprise.

The list of articles related to Osaka Railway and Kansei Railway[56] excerpted from Jardine Matheson's Yokohama branch office bookkeeping journal for 1888–1889 shows that 700 pounds in expenses and handling fees were paid to a Sasano and a Masudaya on December 27, 1888, for acquiring Osaka Railway as a client. The aforementioned Masudaya is believed to be the famous import merchant Masudaya Kahei, whose Yokohama-based company appears to have mediated contracts between railroad companies and Jardine Matheson. In the case of Osaka Railway, the latter received a handling fee equal to 1 percent of the cost of the ordered goods shipped on March 29, 1889. Notably, Glover received half of this fee on the same day, and in subsequent transactions, the same remuneration was paid to him by Osaka Railway and also to one Yano T. by Kansei Railway. In a letter dated September 13, 1889, written by W. B. Walter of Jardine Matheson's Yokohama branch, this fee is explained as follows:

BALANCE SHEET

Mess. Matheson Co. return 1 percent on all orders they execute on account of the Osaka Railway Company, and this return is divided equally between ourselves and M. T. B. Glover. The business was originally given to us on this understanding (by the ultimate of Railways).[57]

TECHNOLOGICAL TRANSFER, BRITISH MONOPOLIZATION

As the above passage shows, Glover mediated between Jardine Matheson and Osaka Railway, with the former and himself each contracted to receive half of the handling fee. This equaled 1 percent of the invoice price of goods, which was lower than the 1.5 percent handling fee paid to Malcolm Brunker for dealing with the IGR. That said, this was only the fee received from Osaka Railway, and it is highly likely that Jardine Matheson also received another such fee from the manufacturers. As its contract with Kansei Railway included a similar agreement with Yano, this type of settlement was not unique to the company's relationship with Osaka Railway and Glover.[58]

With the above in mind, let us examine the locomotives purchased from the Glasgow-based Dübs by the Osaka and Kansei Railways.[59] Dübs's order records listed the names of its intermediaries, with Jardine Matheson appearing here and there.[60] The first item listed is an 1888 order from Osaka Railway for the purchase of three tank locomotives, described as a "locomotive of the same type as IGR locomotive with serial number 2353." Around this time, the IGR had placed orders with Dübs and other British manufacturers to bulk-produce the A8 tank locomotive originally prototyped by Nasmyth Wilson. By ordering the same locomotive as the IGR, Osaka Railway eliminated the time and effort required to create a detailed specification document. Similarly, Kansei Railway ordered IGR B2 locomotives in 1888 and A8 locomotives in 1889 from Dübs, with all purchases mediated by Jardine Matheson.

Nippon, Sanyo, and other railroads also used this method of ordering the same locomotive models as the IGR from the same manufacturers, with Malcolm Brunker as intermediary. In comparison, using Jardine Matheson enabled the independent railroads of Osaka and Kansei to purchase the same materials at a lower price (minus the 0.5 percent handling fee), and it is likely that these railroads created this arrangement by negotiating with Jardine Matheson through Glover and Yano.

Despite the lower handling fee, this arrangement offered Jardine Matheson merit in the form of reduced risk by ordering customer-specified locomotives from customer-specified manufacturers through negotiated contracts. In fact, the company earned a profit of 1,114 pounds in the four months between December 27, 1888, and April 26, 1889. In short, the trade of railroad goods during this negotiated contract period proved highly profitable for major British trading companies.

Summing up, the structure of the British monopoly in Japan's locomotive market stemmed from the *oyatoi* system of directly hiring foreign staff, which facilitated the rapid accumulation of technology and know-how in railroad construction and operation. *Oyatoi* trained young Japanese engineers and laid the foundation of Japan's technological independence. The domestic talents they cultivated supported the subsequent training of engineers, while government initiatives in industrialization and high educational standards further enhanced Japan's social capability to industrialize.

In contrast to the Japanese government, which directly employed foreign staff and directly managed the construction of railroads, China, which introduced railroads around the same time, adopted a loan system in which railroad construction and operation were entrusted to foreign financiers.[61] This method made sense from the standpoint of reducing the initial cost burden on the recipient and encouraging railroad construction. On the other hand, this method risked losing the railroad concession because the right to build and operate railroads stayed in the hands of foreign capital during the remaining loan period. This lack of control also hamstrung the systematic transfer of technology. Although many railroads were constructed throughout China from the end of the nineteenth century to the beginning of the twentieth, railroad technology transfer did not proceed. After the Xinhai Revolution of 1911, the Guomindang (Nationalist) government began to recover railroad concessions in earnest and shifted to a system of direct management. Despite the *oyatoi* system's initial costs, it enabled Japan to steadily transfer railroad technology and ultimately proved key to the development of the Japanese railroad industry.

On the other hand, regarding locomotives, the Japanese government depended on the British to fund and manage railroads during the 1870s, which resulted in the procurement of locomotives and most railroad materials from the United Kingdom. The then-fledgling state of Japanese engineers made them unable to determine specifications and made them dependent on the *oyatoi* for ordering railroad materials. For instance, the IGR's British engineers wrote specifications in the British way and placed orders with

British manufacturers through British trading companies. From the 1880s, emerging private railroads also followed the IGR in importing British locomotives because they lacked engineers with foreign technical information. British trading companies thus also played a significant role as intermediaries. Jardine Matheson, for example, represented private Japanese railroads and procured all their required materials from the United Kingdom. The global economy made it critical to acquire the latest technical information to optimally procure railroad materials, but emerging countries often faced hurdles in accomplishing this.

As a result, British manufacturers held a near-monopoly in the Japanese locomotive market from its start to the early 1890s. After the mid-1890s, however, the situation shifted. The next chapter investigates structural changes in the global locomotive market by examining the activities of American manufacturers who rapidly expanded their presence at the turn of the century.

3

JAPAN'S INDUSTRIAL REVOLUTION AND AMERICAN LOCOMOTIVES

This chapter examines the relationship between Japan's Industrial Revolution and the export of American locomotives to Japan, a theme that explains how Japan's economic nation building was predicated on globalization and clarifies the strategy of U.S. manufacturers as representatives of global capital toward Japan. The analysis below focuses on the formation of the social capability for industrialization in Japan and the innovations in production and marketing systems that decisively enabled the rise of the American locomotive. It also refers, where appropriate, to the economic situation in the United States that triggered the overseas expansion of American manufacturing.

Japan entered its era of industrialization at the turn of the twentieth century. A study by Fukao Kyōji and Settsu Tokihiko shows its GDP per capita real growth rate at 0.9 percent between 1874 and 1890, during the period of technology transfer, and 1.2 percent between 1890 and 1913, which includes the peak of this era.[1] The primary sector saw a sharp decline in the percentage of workers engaged and in GDP, the latter declining from 60 percent in 1874 to 44 percent in 1890 and 36 percent in

1913. Correspondingly, the secondary sector's share of GDP increased from 9.1 percent to 14.7 percent and 20.6 percent in the same years.[2] Japan's industrial structure underwent rapid changes during this period, led by firms in cotton spinning, silk reeling, mining, and railroads. Private companies established nationwide from the late 1880s to around 1900 became engines of economic growth,[3] even as the government sector declined due to funding straits. Railroads accounted for 26.1 percent of the paid-in capital of private companies in 1894 and 24.3 percent in 1900, far higher than the manufacturing and mining industries combined (16.5 percent in 1894 and 19 percent in 1900); this made up the largest share of total private capital, excluding the financial sector.

Japan had the world's most dynamic locomotive market during the late 1890s. As mentioned in earlier chapters, its railroads experienced two construction booms in in the periods 1886–1889 and 1895–1899, which saw the establishment of over forty companies. After the 1870s, the country excluded foreign investment due to acute wariness of potential financial colonization. In the boom eras, this cautiousness led to railroads being typically constructed by securing funding from Japan's wealthy classes while relying on a joint stock company system and domestic corporate bonds. In effect, landowners and merchants distributed across the country became part of Japan's social capacity for capital accumulation.[4] Furthermore, wealthy locals' active investments in railroads, along with *zaibatsu* such as Mitsubishi and Mitsui, led to the development of a domestic securities market, and the railroads also proved key to the formation of a capital market during Japan's Industrial Revolution.[5]

Railroads revolutionized transportation in Japan, as their passenger traffic increased 4.2 times in ten years, from 726 million passenger kilometers in 1890 to 3 billion in 1900, while freight traffic increased elevenfold from 108 million ton-kilometers in 1890 to 1 billion in 1900. The railroad became an indispensable means of transportation, especially in the development of industries such as coal mining.[6]

The new private railroads needed funds and specialists, especially engineers. From the late 1870s to the early 1880s, the IGR educated Japanese engineers at its in-house vocational school and ultimately achieved independence in civil engineering. And the Imperial College of Engineering, established by the government at Edmund Morel's suggestion, sent graduates to government agencies and industry from 1878 onward. After the late 1880s, these civil engineers moved to the private sector due to the government's financial difficulties and a decline in IGR construction,[7] with their mechanical engineering counterparts following suit in the late 1890s. This process, which widely distributed engineers throughout the government and private sectors, underpinned Japan's technological independence and railroads' nationwide dissemination. From the 1890s, ICE graduates became civil and mechanical engineers with the IGR and private railroads and were central to the formation of railroad technology in Japan.

From the late 1880s to the 1890s, Japan's railroad booms dramatically raised its demand for key components such as locomotives. As mentioned above, Japan at the time had the world's most active locomotive market, and its appetite drew large American manufacturers such as Baldwin and ALCO. Baldwin and its compatriots first responded by expanding their share of Japan's locomotive market and ending Britain's monopoly, and ALCO joined them after 1901. These firms' activities in Japan encapsulate the outward expansion of global capital, characterized by manufacturers' direct approach to the commodity market.[8] But what enabled this rapid increase in imports of American locomotives at the end of the nineteenth century?

Answering this question entails examining the context of technological independence, Japanese railroads' changing procurement system, and American manufacturers' marketing activities. In the following pages, I first explain Japan's social capability for technological development in terms of knowledge accumulation and railroad engineers' skills. Next, I discuss reforms in Japan's railroad procurement system and changes in the locomotive market's competitive environment before shifting to Baldwin and ALCO as examples of global capital's expansion in East Asia. In particular, I unpack American manufacturers' overseas marketing activities through the cases of Samuel M. Vauclain Jr., a sales engineer for Baldwin, and Willard C. Tyler, a sales representative for ALCO.

TECHNOLOGICAL PROGRESS IN JAPAN

RAILROADS' BOOM, DOMINANCE, AND COLLAPSE

The first three-year boom that started in 1886 ended the technological dominance the IGR had enjoyed since the industry's beginnings and diversified the procurement routes for railroad materials. By 1890, the lengths of railroads operated by private companies surpassed those operated by the IGR (figure 3.1), and a similar trend marked the number of privately owned locomotives, which rose to 110 between 1888 and 1890 compared to the IGR's 61 (figure 0.3). This increase occurred despite the opening of the IGR's most busy line, Tōkaidō line, in 1889.[9] Construction by the IGR subsequently stagnated, but private companies continued to expand, ushering the Japanese railroad industry into a new age of market enterprise.

This trend further intensified during the second boom around the time of the first Sino-Japanese War (1894–1895), which launched thirty-four companies in the period 1894–1898 and dramatically increased the length of private lines between 1897 and 1899 (figure 3.1). Many of these newly established companies were small to medium-sized enterprises that operated branch lines connected to trunk lines, but their sheer number spiked the procurement of railroad materials. From 1897 to 1899, private companies added 476 locomotives, while the IGR added several new lines and 160 locomotives (figure 0.3).

The developments that occurred during this boom substantially raised purchases of American locomotives, especially by private companies. This is evident from the following report by the British consulate general in Japan, dated July 16, 1894, which expresses concern regarding the advance of American locomotives into the Japanese market: "For railway locomotives, of which there has also been an increased import, the Japanese private railway companies appear inclined to have recourse rather to the United States than to England; and in one recent instance at least a private company disposed of several of their English built engines to the Government Railways, supplying their place with newly-imported American engines at a cost greatly in excess of the proceeds realised by the sale of the old ones."[10]

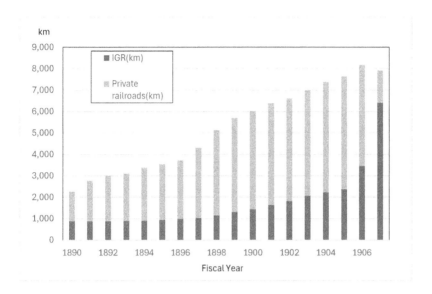

FIGURE 3.1 Operating distance of Japan's railroads, 1890–1907.

Source: Tetsudō Kyoku, ed., *Meiji 40 nendo Tetsudō kyoku nenpō* [Annual report of the Railway Bureau in 1907 FY] (Tokyo: Tetsudō In, 1909), appendix, 101–103.

Twice during the second boom, in 1895 and 1897, the British consul general in Japan, G. Lowther, authored a series of detailed accounts for his government collectively titled *Report on the Railways of Japan*. In the first report, Lowther meticulously described the Japanese railroad boom and advised his leaders not to overlook this opportunity for British locomotive manufacturers.[11] In the second, he optimistically emphasized British locomotives' dominant position in the Japanese market and their superiority over American locomotives in terms of fuel consumption.[12] At the same time, he noted that "we do not have a monopoly in this line," and urged preparations for increased competition in the locomotive export market.[13]

TECHNOLOGICAL INDEPENDENCE AND THE IGR

The erosion of Britain's monopoly in the Japanese locomotive market that Lowther noted was evident not only among the newly established private railroad companies but also in the IGR. Lowther identified the main reason for this as the declining influence of *oyatoi* engineers and managers, which he described in a December 1895 statement: "The influence of the English engineers could not fail to make itself felt in this direction, but, as I have noticed, the tendency of the Japanese government is to dispense with all foreign advice, and the time is possibly not remote when all Japanese lines, government and private, will be built and managed without any assistance from the foreigner in Japan, and the material only will be purchased abroad."[14] The number of *oyatoi* railroad engineers, many of whom were British, continuously declined after peaking in 1874.[15] They numbered less than ten upon completion of the Ōsakayama Tunnel in 1877, which marked a turning point in the independence of Japanese engineers, especially civil engineers,[16] who gradually replaced foreign employees from 1883 onward.

Starting in 1896, hired foreign workers with purchasing authority were successively dismissed. For example, the renowned bridge engineer C. Pownall[17] returned to Britain in February 1896, followed in March 1897 by Aldrich, who had enjoyed absolute purchasing authority as secretary of the Railway Bureau, and F. H. Trevithick, who had served as a superintendent in charge of locomotive procurement. After Japan abolished the train superintendent system in 1898, Japanese engineers began procuring railroad materials themselves.[18] Lowther describes this transfer of purchasing authority from British to Japanese engineers and the resulting change in sourcing of railroad materials in the following passage on bridge materials:

> The English engineer who has been the designer of railway bridges in Japan since 1882 is leaving the country. On his departure, if the Japanese engineers have to design any structure with which they are unable to deal, it will be the easiest plan for them, many of their number having been educated in the United States, to fall back on this American system, obtaining both design and bridge from the manufacturers, and thus transferring the business to Americans, and the leading firms of that country are careful to be represented here.[19]

Here, Lowther predicts that U.S.-educated Japanese engineers would likely procure materials from American manufacturers after becoming independent. As of July 1895, three of the most senior engineers among the IGR's top five officials—Matsumoto Sōichirō (director general of the Railway Bureau), Haraguchi Kaname (head of the Engineering Section), and Hirai Seijirō (head of the Superintending Section)—were graduates of the Rensselaer Polytechnic Institute, and the chief of procurement, Zushi Tamiyoshi (head of the Accounting Section), had also studied in the United States.[20]

Meanwhile, the IGR's train division, which played a central role in procuring rolling stock, underwent substantial transformation. Previously part of the Engineering Section, it became a stand-alone entity called the Train Section (Kisha-ka) in July 1896. In November of the same year, on the retirement of its chief, Sengoku Mitsugu (who also headed the Transportation Section), Miyazaki Kōji, an ICE graduate and director of the Kobe factory, became Sengoku's successor. Miyazaki was a mechanical engineer who had apprenticed under R. F. Trevithick (the older brother of F. H. Trevithick)[21] during his time at the Kobe factory. In 1897, the old Railway Bureau split into the new Railway Bureau and the Railway Operations Bureau,[22] a reorganization that also upgraded the IGR's Train Section into a Train Department (Kisha-bu). Miyazaki was chosen to head this new department as the elder Trevithick's natural successor.

The number of mechanical engineers the IGR employed began to increase around the time of the Train Department's establishment.[23] By 1900, they totaled 78, including 14 engineers and 64 assistant engineers. Of the 14 engineers, 12 were ICE graduates, while 1 came from the Tokyo Technical School (later the Tokyo Higher Technical School and the Tokyo Institute of Technology).[24] Hata Seikichirō, the second head of the Train Department and a mechanical engineer, had graduated from ICE in 1885. Under his leadership, most engineers trained at his alma mater or its domestic higher education counterparts such as Tokyo Imperial University. Unlike civil engineers' achievement of technological independence in the 1880s, Japanese self-reliance in mechanical engineering stemmed largely from the contributions of Imperial University graduates.[25]

In the world of mechanical engineering, where expert techniques reigned, studying at an institute of higher education did not suffice, and successfully training engineers took substantial time. Nakaoka Tetsurō's analysis of how Japan's shipbuilding industry achieved technological independence compares preliminary designs and working plans in the construction of large iron-built ships and points out that while the ICE aimed to produce engineers capable of creating preliminary designs, general layouts, and blueprints, it left their ability to create working plans and all subsequent steps to on-the-job training.[26] The fact that the IGR's Train Section no longer required *oyatoi* engineers around the turn of the century suggests that a cadre of Japanese engineers capable of creating not only designs and specification documents but also working plans had been trained by that time.

The creation of locomotive prototypes at IGR's Kobe factory boosted the nurturing of Japanese engineers. In 1893, the factory produced the first locomotive manufactured in Japan (2-4-2, compound tank, figure 3.2), designed by and built under the direction of R. F. Trevithick.[27]

This was followed by four 4-4-0 tenders in 1895–1896, five 2-6-0 tenders in 1896, ten 0-6-2 tanks between 1899 and 1902, ten 2-8-0 tenders between 1900 and 1908, and four 2-6-2 tanks in 1904. Manufacturing these different classes of locomotives led to the accumulation of skills needed in locomotive production.[28] Notably, they were designed and built by Mori Hikozō and Ōta Yoshimatsu with R. F. Trevithick's supervision;[29] it was these two Japanese engineers who first acquired the skills needed to create working plans and who subsequently took over the duties previously carried out by *oyatoi* engineers.

Based on this accumulation of technical expertise, a Train Department Design Unit was established within the Railway Operations Bureau in 1901 with the following duties: designing for the repair and building of railroad cars and other equipment; supervising construction work and required materials; inspecting designs for factories, railroad yard, and associated buildings; finally, organizing, and storing blueprints held by the IGR headquarters.[30] Unlike the factory, which manufactured locomotives, this unit's primary duty was to create preliminary designs for locomotives and other equipment as well as specification documents needed to procure parts. For this reason, it was staffed by young engineers freshly graduated from the Department of Mechanical Engineering at Tokyo Imperial University,

FIGURE 3.2 The first domestically produced locomotive in Japan, a compound tank engine with a 2-4-2 wheel arrangement, was designed and built under the direction of R.F. Trevithick, a British locomotive superintendent, at IGR's Kobe factory in 1893. It was constructed under the guidance of a foreign engineer in order to train Japanese locomotive engineers.

Source: Iwasaki Collection, © Railway Museum, Ōmiya.

including Aoyama Yoichi, the unit head, Yoshino Matashirō, deputy director of the Shinbashi factory, and Fukushima Nuijirō.[31]

Similarly, a Design Section for rolling stock was established in 1901 within the Railway Operations Bureau that handled all matters related to rolling stock and other railway equipment, such as designs, specifications, leases, and transfers.[32] The IGR's amassing of skills in the above areas shows that it aimed to establish standard rolling stock specifications that applied not only to government but also private railroads. Members of the Design Section thus included key engineers in the Railway Operations Bureau such as Hata Seikichirō and Shiba Gontarō, the Shinbashi factory director, as well as engineers with private-sector experience such as Suzuki Ikuyata and Shima Yasujirō, respectively the former Train Section chiefs of the Hankai and Kansei Railways.

In particular, Shima Yasujirō (1870–1946, figure 3.3) later became a mechanical engineer central to the government railroad, as chapter 6 describes. He joined Kansei Railway immediately after graduating from the Department of Mechanical Engineering at Tokyo Imperial University, and as the head of the firm's Train Section, he gained attention for introducing innovations such as changing the car stripe color based on class, adding lighting to passenger cars, and making improvements to increase locomotive speed. In 1901, he moved to the Ministry of Communications and Transportation and joined the Railway Bureau's newly established Design Section, where he primarily engaged in rolling stock design. In 1908, he was appointed head of the Manufacturing Section of the new Railway Agency and would play a central role in developing a mass-production model for a domestically produced large passenger locomotive.[33]

This domestic cadre of engineers, consisting primarily of ICE graduates, enabled Japan's independence from *oyatoi* experts around the turn of the century. Japanese engineers' acquisition of the technical expertise needed to design rolling stock, build locomotives, and inspect railroad materials resulted in their acquisition of purchasing authority away from their British counterparts. This, in turn, became an important first step in dismantling Britain's monopoly in the railroad materials market.

THE INTRODUCTION OF COMPETITIVE BIDDING

Competitive bidding to procure railroad materials by both state and private railroads further heated Japan's market in the 1890s. The IGR, which had relied on negotiated contracts since its establishment, adopted this new process after the February 1889 promulgation of the Accounting Act. This act, which drew on corresponding legislation in France and Italy, constituted a milestone of modernization in Japan's legal system.[34]

The Accounting Act required all government purchases to be made on the basis of a competitive bidding process, a rule that bound the IGR's activities. Accordingly, in October 1890, the Railway Bureau established

FIGURE 3.3 Shima Yasujirō (1870–1946), a leading locomotive engineer in the late Meiji and Taishō eras. Shima graduated from the Department of Mechanical Engineering at Tokyo Imperial University and joined Kansei Railway in 1894 as the head of the Train Section. In 1901, he moved to the Design Section of the Railway Bureau, and in 1908 he was appointed head of the Manufacturing Section of the Railway Agency. Following this, he played a central role in developing the production capabilities of domestically produced locomotives.

Source: Shima Collection, © Tetsudō Sōgō Gijutsu Kenkyūsho (Railway Technical Research Institute), Tokyo.

regulations that set forth the required procedures for open bidding.[35] From that point onward, the IGR on principle purchased both foreign and domestic materials through such a process. For example, the purchase of thirty locomotives in August 1897 was reported as follows:

> The companies that participated in the competitive tender for thirty locomotives held by the Railway Bureau on the 25th of last month were Mitsui Bussan, Ōkura Gumi, Toa Shōkai, and Takata Shōkai. Among these, a contract for twenty locomotives was awarded to the lowest bidder, which was Takata Shōkai. As for the remaining ten locomotives, based on the Railway Bureau's desire to test Schenectady Locomotive Works products, the only bid tendered was from Mitsui Bussan, which has a strong business relationship with this manufacturer. However, as the bid price of 108,665 USD exceeded the predetermined price, no contract was awarded.[36]

The point here is that the IGR could essentially designate American locomotives in its bidding process based on how the specifications were written. Takata Shōkai won the bid for twenty locomotives at \$8,642 per car and placed orders with Brooks according to plan.[37] For the remaining ten locomotives, the IGR switched from competitive bidding to negotiated contracts and placed orders with Schenectady.[38]

As illustrated by the above example, the bidding process at the time allowed the manufacturer some leeway to make designations. However, this was problematic insofar as the bidder—that is, the intermediary trading company—could not be specified. This made it impossible to exclude bids by inferior vendors, resulting in frequent breaches and cancellations of contracts. Let us consider the problematic aspects of the open bidding process as illustrated by the yearlong case of one Kaminishi Toshimasa, who won a bid for locomotives in 1896 but failed to order them from the manufacturer.

On October 15, 1896, the IGR sought competitive bids to purchase eighteen tank locomotives. The specification documents in this process designated several British manufacturers, and bids were accepted under the condition that the locomotives would be purchased from one of these manufacturers. An individual named Kaminishi Toshimasa won the bid and sent notification on October 20 that he would purchase the locomotives from Beyer Peacock for delivery by a London-based agent, William Duff & Son. On October 21, the Railway Operations Bureau signed a contract with Kaminishi for these eighteen locomotives, and on October 23, it telegraphed this information to Thomas R. Shervinton, the preliminary inspector in Britain. When Shervinton visited William Duff's office to inquire about the contract, he discovered that Kaminishi had not contacted Duff, and, moreover, that Duff had never heard of Kaminishi.

Bidding prices were typically determined by sending specifications to the manufacturer, who then prepared a price quote. A concerned Shervinton subsequently contacted Beyer Peacock and learned that they, too, had had no contact with Kaminishi. On November 6, Shervinton sent a letter explaining these circumstances to A. S. Aldrich, the secretary of the IGR.[39] Upon receiving this letter, the head of the procurement unit submitted the following report to his superior on December 25:

> It is believed that Kaminishi Toshimasa, who entered into a procurement agreement [with the Railway Bureau], has yet to submit orders for the promised products to the manufacturer. As this is highly problematic, one option would be to question Mr. Kaminishi directly about the circumstances. However, taking into consideration Mr. Kaminishi's actions from the time of bidding up to this point, it is extremely dubious whether he can fulfill all terms of the contract. An investigation at this point regarding the existence or non-existence of orders would not only be pointless but might instead stir up unwanted conflict. As such, I would like to leave things as they are and enforce the appropriate punishment when the delivery deadline arrives and the products cannot be delivered.[40]

For corrective action, the head of the procurement unit proposed cancelling the contract without confirming the order. This was based on article 12 of the sales contract to purchase foreign goods, which stated that, "In the case that not all goods are delivered before the delivery deadline, the ordering party has the right to collect a late delivery deposit and to stipulate a contract cancelation deadline before which the products must be delivered, or to seize a portion or the entirety of the contract deposit and immediately cancel the contract."[41] In the end, the IGR sent a notice to cancel the purchase contract and forfeit part of the contract deposit to Kaminishi's agent on March 21, 1897, the date by which nine of the eighteen locomotives should have been delivered.[42]

Without eligibility requirements for bidders, predicaments like the above could not be avoided. Furthermore, the IGR had no choice but to sit idly for more than half a year while it cancelled its contract with a delinquent vendor who had not even contacted the local agent, to say nothing of the manufacturer, prior to bidding. To prevent future such situations, Imperial Edict No. 280, issued in June 1900, introduced a private tender system to be tendered by approved companies.[43] Bidders were limited to designated contractors or their agents who met specific criteria. This shift resulted in competitive bidding for the purchase of locomotives and other imported railroad materials by a small number of designated trading companies recognized for brokering foreign trade.[44]

TECHNOLOGICAL DEVELOPMENT AND PROCUREMENT SYSTEMS IN PRIVATE RAILROADS

As described earlier, Japan's railroad industry saw a wide variety of companies, large and small, emerge between 1890 and 1903. Private companies dominated the industry during this period, operating railroad lines far in excess of the IGR. Accordingly, many railroad engineers at this time worked in both the private and public sectors. As of 1900, Nippon Railway and Kyushu Railway, respectively, employed 10 and 11 of the college-educated engineers at the five top private railroad companies, on par with the 14 employed by the IGR.[45] However, these two companies employed only 7 engineers with bachelor's degrees from Tokyo University, ICE, and Tokyo Imperial University, compared to the IGR's 12 such engineers. Instead, both proactively recruited graduates of the Tokyo Technical School. Compared to the IGR, which had only 1 technical school graduate as of 1900, Nippon and Kyushu employed 4 and 3 such graduates respectively. Nippon Railway was especially proactive about hiring mechanical engineering graduates from the Tokyo Technical School and had 46 such employees by 1900. The company's enthusiasm is evident when compared to the 26 and 24 technical school graduates employed by the IGR and Kyushu respectively.[46]

In the late 1890s, Nippon engineers who had accumulated knowledge on manufacturing rolling stock by reverse engineering[47] locomotives began creating their own specification documents and acquiring the skills to inspect railroad materials and components. With this technical foundation, the railway ordered its first "Mikado" (2-4-2 wheel arrangement) tender locomotive from Baldwin in 1897.[48] Soon thereafter, in 1901, its Omiya factory developed its own 4-4-0 tender locomotive; though an exact copy of the Dübs 4-4-0 tender locomotive, it proves that the company had learned how to manufacture locomotives by the early 1900s.[49]

In comparison, Sanyo Railway, Hokkaido Colliery and Railway, and Kansei Railway, respectively, employed only four, five, and two engineers with bachelor's degrees. Nonetheless, these three railways possessed rolling stock expertise considered cutting-edge for the period. Hokkaido Colliery's Temiya factory built Japan's second locomotive in 1895 (the "Taishō-gō"), while Sanyo and Kansei employed Iwasaki Hikomatsu and Shima Yasujirō, both renowned mechanical engineers. Iwasaki, who graduated from ICE in 1883, served in the navy and the Hokkaido Government Railways before becoming head of Sanyo's Train Section in 1888. As a technical adviser to railways including Kyushu, he was a trailblazer among domestic locomotive engineers in western Japan. In 1896, under his leadership, Sanyo's Hyōgo factory built a tender locomotive modeled after a Vulcan Foundry locomotive, Japan's third such creation.

Thereafter, the Hyōgo factory accumulated manufacturing expertise by copying various European and American locomotives.[50] A comparison of the 4-4-0 tender locomotive manufactured at the Hyōgo factory in 1901 (figure 3.4) and the same type made by Neilson that served as its model (figure 3.5) shows that both had exactly the same physical appearance.

FIGURE 3.4 A 4-4-0 tender locomotive built in-house by Sanyo Railway. Hyogo factory under the supervision of Iwasaki Hikomatsu, who was the head of the Train Section at Sanyo Railway. It was created by replicating a similar engine designed by Neilson (see figure 3.5). Its design closely resembles that of the locomotive it was modeled after.

Source: Iwasaki Collection, © Railway Museum, Ōmiya.

Sanyo Railway's Hyōgo factory built the other tender locomotive based on a Neilson model in 1903, followed by eight more based on a Schenectady model between 1903 and 195. It is likely the repetition of such copying that enabled draftsmen to acquire the skills needed for creating working plans. By 1905, the factory had acquired the ability to build a Vauclain compound tender locomotive with original features distinct from its Baldwin model.[51]

As the above discussion shows, major private railroad companies in the 1890s employed numerous engineers educated in universities and vocational schools who could independently create specification documents and inspect materials and components. By the turn of the century, these engineers had

FIGURE 3.5 Neilson's 4-4-0 tender locomotive. It was built by Neilson, Reid & Co. in Glasgow in 1891 for Sanyo Railway. It was later classified as a JNR 5400 type. Sanyo Railway replicated this design, producing a similarly shaped tender locomotive (see figure 3.4).

Source: Iwasaki Collection, © Railway Museum, Ōmiya.

acquired sufficient expertise to design and build existing locomotive models. Japanese engineers at private railroads thus gained independence earlier than their IGR counterparts, who continued working with *oyatoi* engineers into the early 1900s. Most of these private-sector engineers would join the IGR after the railroad nationalization of 1906–1907.

Unlike the IGR, which was subject to the government's bureaucracy and procurement system, private railroad companies were free to purchase materials through negotiated contracts. Accordingly, each company developed its own unique procurement system. For example, Sanyo, which operated a section of the trunk railroad, was the first to introduce a selective bidding system in 1890. Minami Kiyoshi, then one of its chief engineers, instituted a policy of creating specification documents, drafting contracts in-house, and a system of private tender with designated competitive bidding. This all marked a clean break from IGR-style practices and allowed Sanyo to procure inexpensive goods. Sanyo also gave leading trading companies in Japan opportunities to compete with each other. These companies had established branch offices in Europe and the United States to select and order directly from local manufacturers, which raised their credibility among Japanese railroads.[52] Thus, Minami's initiatives pioneered a departure from the UK-focused procurement method. He subsequently became a technical adviser to Chikuho Railway in 1891 and the chief engineer of Bantan Railway in 1892 while still working for Sanyo, which helped spread his method for procuring railroad components to other railroad companies across western Japan.

Sanyo codified its private tender system in February 1900 under a series of regulations for purchasing goods.[53] Article 2 of these rules defined two procurement methods: designated competitive bidding[54] and negotiated contracts, showing that the company also used the latter system. Specifically, article 1 recommended dealing directly with manufacturers or their agents without an intermediary, and article 5 allowed the purchase of goods without designated competitive bidding in transactions conducted directly with manufacturers. In fact, Sanyo's 1895 proposition for purchasing from Baldwin occurred when the latter was making a full-fledged effort to break into the mainland Japanese market, and it contains a note in the date column indicating that the order was "from K. Minami."[55] In other words, Minami endeavored to optimize his purchases by tactically using designated competitive bidding and negotiated contracts.

Since its establishment as Japan's first private railroad in 1881, Nippon Railway had outsourced the construction and operation of its rail lines to the IGR until 1892 and followed IGR procurement regulations until the 1890s. That said, as explained above, the company had assembled its own team of Japanese engineers capable of independently creating documents and making inspections by the turn of the century. In September 1899, it established a set of provisional regulations for the trade of goods that paved the way for its own materials procurement system.[56] While primarily relying on competitive bidding, these regulations left negotiated contracts as an option and in that sense more closely resembled those of Sanyo than those of the IGR.[57] Moreover, article 15 defined the relationship between competitive bidding and negotiated contracts as follows: "If all bid prices exceed the predetermined price, a second tender shall be held immediately. If all bid prices still exceed the predetermined price, the good shall be procured at or below the predetermined price using a negotiated contract procedure or the purchase shall be abandoned."[58]

One case of actual bidding involved the purchase of thirty-two tank locomotives in 1902–1903.[59] On November 6, 1902, Nippon announced the designated competitive bidding procedure for these locomotives with a specification document that designated as manufacturers the famous British firms of Beyer Peacock, Dübs, Neilson, and Sharp Stewart, as well as their German counterparts of Henschel, Hanomag, and Schwartzkopff. In addition, the document listed Mitsui Bussan, Takata Shōkai, Isono Shōkai, Jardine Matheson, Frazar, and John Birch as bidders. Following a two-month grace period, bidding started on January 10, 1903. The railway explained the specification of locomotive manufacturers as follows: "In this designated competitive bidding procedure, contracts will not necessarily be awarded to the lowest bidder, and it is possible for the highest bidder to be awarded the contract." Moreover, it stated that it would make its selection based on evaluating prices offered by different manufacturers. In other words, Nippon decided that locomotives from manufacturer A could be purchased at a certain price, while those from manufacturer B fetched a different price, and therefore asked bidders to specify the manufacturer in the tender conditions document.[60] However, all bids substantially exceeded the predetermined price, and bidding ended unsuccessfully. At this point, Nippon abandoned the process in favor of negotiated contracts, which it used to purchase twenty-four Beyer Peacock locomotives through Mitsui Bussan. It also acquired eight Henschel and Hanomag locomotives through M. Raspe, which had not been on the original list of bidders.

Essentially, one of the bid's goals was to test German-made locomotives, a subject of great interest at the time, as I explain in detail below. This explains why Nippon, after failing to purchase locomotives by following the official designated competitive bidding procedure, immediately switched to negotiated contracts to order from specific manufacturers. As illustrated above, private railroads such as Nippon and Sanyo could move flexibly. This, however, meant that the authority to make purchases and select models lay with train section directors and chief engineers,[61] which in some cases led to rumors of collusion with suppliers.[62]

THE CHALLENGE FROM AMERICA

THE ENTRY OF AMERICAN LOCOMOTIVES

American locomotives first entered Japan through Hokkaido with the construction of railroads commissioned by the Kaitakushi to develop coal mines.[63] In contrast to Honshu, where railroad construction started with UK-sourced funding, personnel, and materials, railroad construction in Hokkaido—Japan's northernmost island, then under Kaitakushi authority—advanced through technology transfer from the United States. The American engineer Joseph Ury Crawford (1842–1924, figure 3.6) played a central role in this process.[64]

Crawford was born in Philadelphia, graduated from the University of Pennsylvania, and studied civil engineering at a local polytechnic. After serving in the Civil War, he worked as an engineer for several railroads, including the Texas Pacific Railroad from 1871.[65] He arrived in Japan in 1878 at the Kaitakushi's invitation and assumed full responsibility for constructing and operating Horonai Railway as consulting engineer and inspector from late 1878 to early 1881.[66] Despite this short tenure, he accomplished the route selection, design, materials procurement, securing of engineers and technicians, and supervision of construction and testing during this time. Railroad service between Temiya and Sapporo started in November 1880 with materials Crawford had selected and largely procured from the United States.[67] The first American locomotives in Japan, two light locomotives made by H. K. Porter (2-6-0 tender, figure 3.7), arrived in 1880.

Crawford not only brought other American engineers to help build Japan's railroads; he also provided opportunities to Japanese engineers

FIGURE 3.6 Joseph U. Crawford (1842–1924) an American railroad engineer hired by the Kaitakushi (Hokkaido Development Commission). Crawford worked as an engineer for various railroads in the United States before arriving in Japan in 1878. From 1878 to 1881, he assumed full responsibility for constructing and operating Horonai Railway as a consulting engineer.

Source: Nihon Kokuyū Tetsudō ed., *Nihon kokuyū tetsudō hyakunenshi, shashinshi* [One-hundred-year history of Japan National Railways, photo history] (Tokyo: Japan National Railways, 1972), 36.

trained at U.S. universities, such as Matsumoto Sōichirō and Hirai Seijirō, both graduates of the Rensselaer Polytechnic Institute hired as construction supervisors for Horonai Railway. All Hokkaido routes entered operation in 1883, and the region consequently achieved technological independence in its railroads. This contrasted favorably with Honshu's exclusive employment

FIGURE 3.7 Porter's 2-6-0 locomotive for the Kaitakushi in Hokkaido. This locomotive was one of the first to arrive in Hokkaido, built by H. K. Porter and arriving in 1880. It is a typical American locomotive featuring two leading wheels, six driving wheels, and a large cowcatcher. It is currently on display at the Railway Museum.

Source: Iwasaki Collection, © Railway Museum, Ōmiya.

of foreigners and bolstered railroads' presence in Japan. Matsumoto and Hirai grew capable of comprehensively overseeing railroad construction and operation, and they both assumed directorship of the IGR after the 1890s.

Individuals familiar with American-style railroad construction in Hokkaido thus became key players in Japan's railroads from the 1890s onward and decisively influenced the import of American locomotives into Japan. After returning home in 1881, Crawford served as a division chief engineer for the Pennsylvania Railroad before becoming a preliminary inspector for the IGR from the second half of the 1890s. As I discuss in chapter 4, his work in this capacity involved inspecting products and aiding the procurement of railroad materials from the United States.[68]

BALDWIN LOCOMOTIVE WORKS IN JAPAN

The changes to Japan's railroad materials procurement systems in the late 1890s affected its receipt of American locomotive exports. Baldwin Locomotive Works, headquartered in Philadelphia, was the protagonist of American manufacturers' expansion into Japan in the late 1890s.[69] As described in chapter 1, the company underwent rapid growth from the 1860s to the 1870s in America's vast domestic market.

The interchangeable production system and the system of standardized locomotives were essential tools in this process. From the 1850s to the 1860s, Baldwin expanded its system of customizable production based on a large number of standardized components.[70] As part of this process, it redesigned components and strove to achieve interchangeable production through the use of common gauges and tooling. Around 1860, it dramatically increased productivity by shifting to manufacturing with interchangeable components.[71] As a consequence, productivity per worker nearly doubled from 6,064 pounds in 1860 to 12,104 pounds in 1870, boosting the firm's competitiveness in cost and delivery time.[72] Baldwin's installation of a variety of specialized manufacturing machinery in the 1870s further increased its productivity.[73] In short, its innovations established the American system based on efficiently making interchangeable parts using a large number of specialized machines.[74]

For Baldwin, the American system further served as a powerful marketing tool. The large-scale expansion of railroads in the United States at the time meant that companies typically placed batch orders to acquire large numbers of the same type of locomotive at once. For the railroads, interchangeable parts usable on locomotives of the same type were highly desirable as they shortened repair times. Baldwin thus rapidly increased its market share in the 1870s by leveraging the competitive advantage of interchangeable production to win batch orders from major railroads.[75]

Bolstered by domestic success, Baldwin began a full-fledged effort to penetrate international markets. By the end of the 1870s, the company had started expanding abroad, and it began exporting in earnest during the early 1880s. As of 1884, Baldwin sent 39.6 percent of its total production volume overseas, primarily to Brazil, Argentina, and other countries in Latin America (table 3.1). Export ratios briefly dropped in the late 1880s due to a boom in the domestic market, but stagnation in the mid-1890s again produced a rapid increase. At the end of the 1890s, mainline railroad construction in the United States declined significantly, making Baldwin's exports account for an average of 46.6 percent of its production volume in the 1896–1898 period (table 3.1). The railroad industry, which had developed via the domestic market, sought new outlets abroad. For example, during this period, Baldwin developed an international sales network by signing agreements with manufacturer's agents in Havana, Rio de Janeiro, Melbourne, and Yokohama, and it also established a branch office in London.[76] Its agent in Yokohama at the time was Frazar, a relationship later described in detail. By 1897, Japan had become Baldwin's largest overseas market, receiving 23 percent of its total production volume as exports (table 3.1).

Baldwin first entered Japan in 1887 through Hokkaido, which used American technology for its railroad construction. There it received orders for two 0-6-0 tank locomotives for sulfur mines on March 8, 1887.[77] Each locomotive was priced at $6,250, with Frazar receiving an intermediary commission fee of 5 percent. According to the sales contract, Frazar was to pay one-third of the total price up front, another third upon shipment, and the final third upon arrival of the locomotives in Yokohama. In all cases, payment would be made by wire transfer. Baldwin received an 1888 order for two 2-6-0 tender locomotives from Horonai Railway, followed by an 1890 order for two 2-4-2 tank and ten 2-6-0 tender locomotives from Hokkaido Colliery and Railway. In the latter case, the intermediary was Takada Shōkai, paid not with a commission but a shipping discount equivalent to 5 percent of the locomotive price.[78] A onetime payment for the locomotives was required within ten days of shipment in the form of a check guaranteed by the Yokohama Specie Bank. This arrangement differed from IGR and Chikuho Railway orders through Frazar in 1890, which finalized payment after the products arrived.[79] These differences suggest that, by 1890 or thereabouts, Frazar already had Baldwin's trust and effectively acted as its manufacturer's agent in Japan.

TABLE 3.1 Baldwin locomotives produced and exported, 1884–1900

| | PRODUCTS (# OF CARS) | EXPORTS (# OF CARS) | SHIPMENT VOLUME (# OF CARS) BY DESTINATION | | | | | | | | | |
			DOMESTIC	NORTH AMERICA	SOUTH AMERICA	CENTRAL AMERICA	EUROPE	JAPAN	CHINA	SOUTH ASIA	OCEANIA	AFRICA, MIDDLE EAST
1884	429	170	259	6	111	17	3	0	0	0	33	0
1886	550	42	508	–	–	–	–	–	–	–	–	–
1887	653	43	610	1	17	23	0	2	0	0	0	0
1888	737	95	642	3	19	68	0	2	0	0	3	0
1889	898	212	686	9	114	83	1	3	0	0	2	0
1890	946	144	802	3	46	76	3	12	0	0	1	3
1891	899	292	607	13	166	46	1	6	0	0	55	5
1892	731	127	604	1	56	57	8	3	0	0	0	2
1893	772	162	610	1	78	55	1	27	0	0	0	0
1894	313	132	181	4	56	38	2	30	0	0	2	0
1895	401	161	240	1	105	18	22	13	0	0	2	0
1896	547	289	258	5	92	33	126	31	0	0	2	0
1897	501	205	296	10	36	16	8	115	12	0	2	6
1898	755	348	407	63	25	37	164	7	1	0	27	24
1899	901	374	527	41	9	65	134	9	16	45	0	55
1900	1,217	365	852	32	25	70	139	8	33	14	1	43
Accumulated total	11,250	3,161	8,089	193	955	702	612	268	62	59	130	138

Source: Table 1 of Nakamura, "The First Global Economy and the US-Japan Locomotive Trade," *Japanese Research in Business History*, no. 40 (2023): 12.

Original sources: Baldwin Locomotive Works, *Orders for Engines*, 1884–1900; John K. Brown, *The Baldwin Locomotive Works: 1831–1915* (Baltimore: John Hopkins University Press, 1995), 241.

Notes: Japan at this time includes Taiwan (annexed in 1895); China includes the South Manchuria Railway; Europe includes the Chinese Eastern Railway (owned by Russia). Data for 1885 missing.

JAPAN'S INDUSTRIAL REVOLUTION

Baldwin's next entry point was the southwesternmost island of Kyushu, which, like Hokkaido, had a thriving mining industry. On July 18, 1889, Baldwin received an order for one each of its 0-4-2 and 0-4-0 tanks from Chikuho Railway through Frazar. It delivered these locomotives in just over three months and received praise for its rapid turnaround. Thereafter, Chikuho became a valued customer, ordering two more locomotives in October of the same year followed by another three in July 1892 (2-6-0, figure 3.8). In each case, Frazar received an intermediary commission of 5 percent per locomotive, with one-third of the total payment made up front in cash and the remainder paid upon the locomotives' arrival in Japan. This arrangement became the standard practice for transactions involving Baldwin that Frazar brokered.

After its foray into Kyushu, Baldwin finally entered Honshu, Japan's mainland, in 1890. In December 1889, it received an order for two 2-6-0

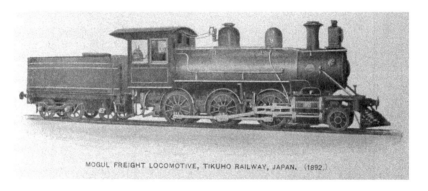

FIGURE 3.8 Baldwin's locomotive for Chikuho Railway in Kyushu. This engine was a 2-6-0 Vauclain compound tender locomotive made by Baldwin Locomotive Works in Philadelphia in 1892. It transported coal from the mines in the Chikuhō coal region to the export port in Wakamatsu. The Kyushu region was the main market for American locomotives along with Hokkaido. Vauclain's compound engine was developed by Samuel M. Vauclain, a president of the Baldwin Locomotive Works and father of Samual M. Vauclain Jr.

Source: Burnham, Williams & Co., ed., *Baldwin Locomotive Works Narrow Gauge Locomotives, Japanese Edition, Frazar & Co. of Japan Agents, Yokohama* (Philadelphia: J. B. Lippincott Co., 1897), 167.

tender locomotives from the IGR through Frazar, which it shipped in March 1890. For the IGR, this was a trial introduction of American locomotives, and after 1893, Sanyo Railway began actively adopting Baldwin's products. Thanks to the enthusiastic endorsement of Sanyo's chief engineer, Minami Kiyoshi, Baldwin received orders for forty-seven locomotives between 1892 and 1894 from Chikuho, Bantan, Hoshu, and other railroads where Minami had influence.[80] In the late 1890s, the IGR, Nippon, and other private railroads previously reliant on British locomotives began to use large numbers of Baldwin locomotives. The changes in Japan's railroad materials procurement system that occurred in the late 1890s influenced the entry of American locomotives into Honshu. By 1897, both the IGR and Nippon Railway had become important customers for Baldwin, ordering thirty-eight and forty-four locomotives respectively in that year.

F. H. Trevithick's experiments in 1894–1895 further facilitated the rise of Baldwin locomotives.[81] As described in chapter 1, these trials compared British 2-6-0 tender locomotives (Beyer Peacock and Nasmyth) to their American counterparts (Baldwin's 2-6-0 tenders), leading to the assessment that, whereas the British locomotives proved superior in terms of fuel efficiency, the American ones had better pulling power and speed. These experiments led Japanese railroads to begin selecting British or American locomotives based on these characteristics and their suitability for specific purposes.

FRAZAR & CO. AS A MANUFACTURER'S AGENT

Frazar & Co., the intermediary for the majority of Baldwin's exports to Japan,[82] was founded in 1834 by George Frazar, the American owner of a clipper ship, in the Chinese city of Guangdong.[83] In 1878, he dispatched a partner, John Lindsley, to establish a branch office in Yokohama, and further began importing American machines into Japan. When he retired, his son Everett Frazar[84] assumed the company's directorship and moved its headquarters to Yokohama, while Lindsley became head of the New York branch office. Frazar's main U.S. customers or agents as of 1898 were the New York and National Board of Marine Underwriters and the

New York–based Atlantic Mutual Insurance, along with Baldwin, Westinghouse Electric and Manufacturing, Newport Engine and Ship Building, and Niles Tool Works.[85]

From this, it is evident that Frazar mainly imported machinery and electrical appliances from American manufacturers. It served as an agent not only for Baldwin but also for major electrical appliance manufacturers such as Westinghouse. In addition to the main office in Yokohama, the company had branch offices in Kobe and New York with a total of seventeen staff members including four partners.[86] The Yokohama main office also had a permanent sales engineer from Baldwin, W. H. Crawford, whose job was to sell rolling stock. As later explained, Crawford played a vital role in the marketing activities of American manufacturers.

In 1900, the existing partnership was dissolved, reestablishing Frazar as an incorporated company with a capital stock of 800,000 yen. Upon Everett Frazar's death in 1901, his son, Everett W. Frazar, took over the management and gained full control of the company in 1902 on acquiring Lindsley's shares. Thereafter, in 1904, Frazar merged with C. V. Sale to form Sale and Frazar, headquartered in Tokyo. By 1919, Sale and Frazar had blossomed into a company with branch offices, sub-branches, and agents in Yokohama, Osaka, Kobe, London, New York, Sydney, Shanghai, Beijing, Tianjin, and Dalian. Mitsui Bussan described its operating structure around 1920 as follows:

> In addition to brokering the import of all types of machinery, metal goods, canned foods, phonographs, typewriters, automobiles, airplane components, and ships, the finance division of Frazar & Co. is currently expanding into the buying and selling of all manner of public debt. Since the recession of March 1920, Frazar & Co. has conducted steady business by carefully selecting clients and collecting deposits for ordered goods. To manage its expanding business, Frazar & Co. has opened a sub-branch in Hakodate and contracted agents in Beijing and Tianjin. The annual value of goods traded by Frazar & Co. is twenty million yen. Among its peers, it is a top-notch, extremely well-trusted company. As of April 1919, it had a paid-in capital stock of one million yen, which increased to two million yen in January 1920.[87]

As the above statement demonstrates, Sale and Frazar maintained its main business of importing and exporting machinery while venturing into financial transactions during the interwar period as "a top-notch, extremely well-trusted company."[88]

Continuous transactions with Baldwin played a crucial role in Sale and Frazar's growth. When we examine the change over time in the composition of intermediaries that brokered exports by Baldwin, we see that Frazar brokered the sale of 234 locomotives over the period 1890–1900.[89] This made Frazar the third-largest intermediary for Baldwin, after Simon J. Gordon, which mainly provided locomotives to the Trans-Siberian Railway, and Norton Megaw, which dealt with business in Latin America.[90] It is further evident that, whereas the value of transactions brokered by the top two trading companies fluctuated dramatically depending on the time of year, Frazar's transactions remained constant. In 1897, during the period when purchases by the IGR and Nippon Railway increased dramatically, Frazar brokered more than 56 percent of Baldwin's exports, though only temporarily.

Such continuous transactions made Frazar a quasi-agent in East Asia for Baldwin, and the manufacturer went so far as to dispatch a sales engineer to the trading company in the latter half of the 1890s. In 1901, Yamada Majirō, who headed Ōkura Gumi's New York branch office, described this special relationship as follows: "because Frazar & Co. has been an agent of Baldwin Locomotive Works for many years, it would be difficult for Baldwin Locomotive Works, as a practical matter, to provide a price quote for any trading company other than Frazar & Co."[91] This shows that, at least during this time, Baldwin considered Frazar indispensable for entering the East Asian market.

AMERICAN MANUFACTURERS' MARKETING ACTIVITIES

American manufacturers commonly used the marketing strategy of dispatching a sales engineer or a sales representative from headquarters to work with local agents and respond to customers' demands.[92] An 1896 report by the British consulate in Japan discusses this point, noting the hundred American locomotives delivered to both the IGR and private railroads over the past five years. It emphasizes that this result stemmed from how American manufacturers had for several years prior worked closely with Tokyo-based trading companies to import locomotives.[93]

The consular report further notes that American manufacturers' aggressive marketing activities, carried out by trading companies acting as quasi-agents, formed a contemporary topic of discussion in Japan. One leading industry magazine described Kansei Railway's competitive bidding process in 1897 as follows: "The trend is for each American locomotive manufacturer to have its own contracted agent in Japan. These agents compete on price with the goal of creating good relations with both public and private railroads."[94] A well-known example of such direct marketing efforts in Japan and East Asia is Willard C. Tyler's promotion of locomotive sales on behalf of ALCO.[95] W. C. Tyler (1856–1936; figure 3.9, left side) was born in Bradford, Massachusetts, and accumulated knowledge of railroads as a journalist for a railroad trade magazine.

Tyler first visited Japan in 1898 as a journalist to observe its burgeoning domestic railroad business. From the winter of 1899 to the fall of 1902, he spent nearly half of each year in the Far East as a sales representative promoting American-made railroad products such as locomotives, brakes, chilled wheels, couplers, and train lights, extending his activities outside Japan to China as well. On trips in 1901 and 1902, he called himself an "engineer" and a "representative of ALCO"; he promoted ALCO's locomotives in the latter capacity and won the manufacturer an order of thirty 4-4-0 tender locomotives (figure 3.10) from the IGR in 1901.[96]

In addition, Tyler simultaneously worked for many other railroad equipment manufacturers whose product mixes did not overlap. In other words, he did not exclusively represent ALCO but served an independent sales representative commissioned by multiple manufacturers. This type of marketing through sales representatives developed in the United States as a system for remote transactions. Railroad equipment manufacturers adapted these marketing techniques of domestic origin to their overseas operations.[97]

My analysis of Tyler's activities as a sales representative in Japan and China using his notebook for 1900–1901 shows that his activities as a sales representative can be summarized in five points:[98] selling products;

FIGURE 3.9 Willard C. Tyler (1856–1936) and Yamamoto Koshirō, his Japanese business partner, in 1901. Tyler (left) was an American journalist and sales representative who promoted American railroad equipment, particularly ALCO's locomotives, to East Asia. Between 1898 and 1902, he visited Japan and China four times to promote new products for American manufacturers. Yamamoto (right) was in charge of railroad materials at Mitsui Bussan at the time.

Source: W. C. Tyler records, © Professor Ellen B. Widmer.

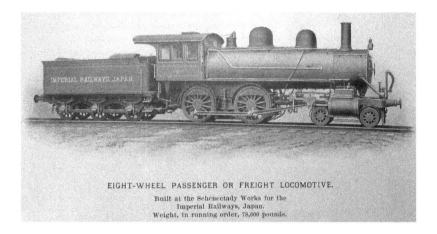

FIGURE 3.10 ALCO's 4-4-0 locomotive for IGR. This tender locomotive had four leading and four driving wheels and was known as an "American-type" engine in the United States. It was one of thirty new ALCO locomotives ordered from the IGR in 1901. W. C. Tyler, a sales representative for ALCO, sold these engines to the IGR with the assistance of a local agent, Mitsui Bussan.

Source: ALCO, *First Annual Report to the Stockholders* (New York: ALCO, 1902), n.p.

researching existing or potential markets; promoting new products and uncovering demand; providing information to and selecting local agents; and seeking new business opportunities.[99] From the contracted manufacturer's point of view, sales representatives provided a variety of information that supplemented the paucity of local data in remote areas. At the turn of the century, East Asia had become the hottest market for the global trade in railroad materials, and manufacturers' primary objective in hiring Tyler as a sales representative was to investigate the demand for railroad materials in the emerging East Asian market.

On the other hand, the relationship between sales representatives and local agents was characterized by both cooperation and tension. Both sides found cooperation essential: local agents gained product information, advice on marketing techniques, and support in product promotion, while sales representatives benefited from perks such as interpretation services and telegraphic communication with their home country. On the other hand, sales representatives' involvement in selecting and monitoring local agents generated tension in the relationship. Tyler, for instance, scrutinized Mitsui as ALCO's local agent and critiqued its poor response to the IGR bidding process. Manufacturers required their sales representatives to monitor local agents so they could maintain a degree of control over marketing in remote areas.

Next, let us use the case of Baldwin to scrutinize American manufacturers' marketing activities using sales engineers in Japan. While independent representatives like Tyler handled different products for various manufacturers, such engineers were exclusive to a specific manufacturer, had in-depth technical knowledge, and specialized in promoting the firm's products. Thus, the sales engineer was a "new type of salesman," even more so than the sales representative.[100] Furthermore, in 1897 Baldwin produced a hardcover catalog of narrow-gauge locomotives for Frazar.[101] In this catalog, Baldwin provided information needed to make sales pitches, such as an explanation of standard gauges as well as careful instructions aimed at sales agents on the ordering method, including the telegram codes to be used. It devoted a large number of pages to explaining the Vauclain compound locomotive, its newest model at the time. Sales engineers with specialized knowledge were dispatched from headquarters to local agents to promote these new products.

W. H. Crawford, the first sales engineer dispatched by Baldwin to Frazar,[102] played a major role in promoting the export of American locomotives to Japan by selling two hundred locomotives to the IGR and private railways in 1897. In addition, he supervised the building of the Mikado-type tender locomotive for Nippon and assisted Sanyo in switching to Baldwin locomotives.[103] His successor, dispatched to Japan in 1904, was Samuel M. Vauclain Jr. (1880–1913, figure 3.11).

Vauclain Jr., born in 1880 in Philadelphia, was the son of Samuel M. Vauclain, the engineer who designed the Vauclain compound locomotive. In 1904, Vauclain was vice president of Baldwin, and his promising young son, at twenty-four years old, was dispatched to Japan as a sales engineer for that country and Australia. However, after falling ill in early 1905, he returned home and passed away in 1913.[104] While overseas, he had traveled

FIGURE 3.11 Samuel M. Vauclain Jr. (1880–1913), a sales engineer for Baldwin Locomotive Works. The company dispatched him to Japan and the Asia-Pacific region in 1904. He spent more than a year promoting Baldwin engines to Japanese customers while also researching market conditions in the region

Source: Samuel M. Vauclain Papers, © DeGolyer Library, Southern Methodist University.

on business and immersed himself in the grueling duties explained below for half a year, which likely contributed to his ill health and untimely demise.

Southern Methodist University holds a trove of documents related to Baldwin, including Vauclain Jr.'s diary and notebook from 1904, which give a clear picture of his marketing activities in Japan and Australia.[105] Vauclain Jr. left Philadelphia on February 3, 1904, arriving in Yokohama via Hawaii on April 20. He began working at Frazar immediately after arriving in Japan and left for his first business trip, an eight-day visit to Hokkaido, on June 1. To get there, he traveled on Nippon Railway by crossing over to Hokkaido from Aomori, where he visited Sapporo, Muroran, Iwamizawa, and Asahikawa. He further met with locomotive superintendents of the Hokkaido Colliery and Railway and the Hokkaido Government Railway Division; on this trip, he aimed to obtain information from the latter regarding bidding on two Mogul-type (2-6-0) tender locomotives and related components. In fact, he participated in a Tokyo bidding on June 20 along with his Frazar colleagues.[106]

Soon thereafter, on June 25, Vauclain Jr. left for another business trip to the Yawata Steel Works in Kyushu. However, on June 27, he suddenly returned to Yokohama after receiving a telegram from Baldwin at Frazar's Kobe branch. It is unclear what drew him back to Yokohama at this point; his subsequent return to Kobe from June 30 to July 2 and travel to Australia thereafter suggests it was related to the Australia trip. At this point, Vauclain Jr. noted in his diary, "Baldwin engines doing all the hard work," hinting at the demanding nature of his activities. On July 12, he left for a three-month business trip to Australia on which he carried out marketing activities around the country and even stopped by Hong Kong, Guangdong, and the Philippines.

After returning to Yokohama on October 2, 1904, Vauclain Jr. quickly began making the rounds to customers in the Kanto area, visiting Hiraoka Hiroshi of Kisha Seizō and the Tokyo Electric Railway Company in Tokyo on October 15 as well as Narashino Horse Tramway in Chiba on October 19. His discussion on October 15 with Hiraoka, Kisha Seizō's vice president, is of particular note regarding the scheme for developing Manchuria and supplying locomotives there. At the time, Japan was embroiled in the Russo-Japanese War and about to place a large order for locomotives to be used on the battlefields of Manchuria. Vauclain Jr. represented Baldwin and attempted to work with Japanese, English, and American locomotive manufacturers to obtain this assignment.[107]

From October 23 to 29, he traveled to Moji, Osaka, and Kyoto to do the same at Kyushu Railway, Sanyo Railway, Kisha Seizō, Osaka Electric Railway, and Kyoto Imperial University. The personages he met included Sengoku Mitsugi (now president of Kyushu Railway), Suzuki Sōjirō (chief engineer and head of Kyushu Railway's Manufacturing Department and Kokura factory), and Iwasaki Hikomatsu (head of Sanyo's Train Section), with whom he reviewed the details of component and locomotive orders. On October 28 at Sanyo, for instance, he discussed a report comparing the performance of Mallet and Vauclain compound locomotives.[108]

Even in the fall, Vauclain Jr. continued enthusiastically calling on customers, visiting the Imperial Japanese Army Nakano Railway Battalion, Kobu Railway, the Railway Bureau, and Tokyo Electric Railway in Tokyo on consecutive days from November 15 to 18. He traveled again to Fukuoka, Kobe, Osaka, and Kyoto from November 23 to 30 to visit three railways: Kyushu, Hakatawan, and Kansei. During this trip, he spoke with Sengoku and Suzuki on November 25 to confirm the production of five hundred freight cars and received blueprints for coal cars from the chief engineer.[109] From December 7 to 12, he again visited Hokkaido via Nippon Railway, where he saw the Hokkaido Colliery and Railway's Temiya factory in Otaru and Iwamizawa factory.

This summary of Vauclain Jr.'s activities in the nine months between April and December 1904 shows that he made a total of 126 days' worth of business trips inside and outside Japan, including Australia. His destinations included major railroad companies, government steel works, the Imperial Japanese Army, electric railroad companies, steam locomotive manufacturing companies, and universities. The purposes of these visits varied widely, from participating in bidding and discussing order details to exchanging information, collecting customer information, and confirming contract details. Of note is that the majority of orders he received were for replacement parts rather than for locomotives. Once a manufacturer had sold a locomotive, they received additional orders for maintenance parts on a continual basis. Accordingly, agents of the trading company or manufacturers periodically made rounds to their customers. Whenever he visited railroad companies, Vauclain Jr. made the acquaintance of the heads and chief engineers of locomotive sections and, in the case of Kyushu Railway, even the company president. From the railroad companies' perspective, the technical information possessed by sales engineers dispatched from the manufacturers was extremely valuable. In Vauclain Jr.'s case, his status as the oldest son of S. M. Vauclain, Baldwin's vice president and a world-renowned engineer, surely made interacting with him worthwhile not just for individuals who had direct business with him but also for top management.

Overall, Japanese railroad engineers cultivated their skills and struggled toward independence from *oyatoi* experts from the 1880s to the early 1890s. During the railroad booms, they moved from the government to the private sector and disseminated their technology nationwide. This enabled the IGR and private railroads to create specifications and order materials from abroad without external support in the late 1890s. In addition, Japanese railroads introduced a competitive bidding system in the early 1890s as a requirement of the modernized national legal system that made it difficult for the *oyatoi* to purchase materials through negotiated contracts. As a result, Japanese engineers grew capable of selecting locomotives worldwide according to need, price, and delivery time. Success in training them and opening up the domestic market enabled the rapid development of the railroad industry during Japan's Industrial Revolution.

American manufacturers such as Baldwin capitalized on this new trend and increased their sales through extensive marketing. They expanded overseas during this period, establishing branches and agents worldwide and marketing on a global scale. As in the cases discussed above, companies' headquarters dispatched sales representatives and sales engineers to extensively and aggressively research global markets. In contrast, British manufacturers failed to react appropriately and lost market share; for them, marketing came under the purview of trading companies, not manufacturers, and they were reluctant to engage in activities such as market research and sales promotion.

This differing perception of global marketing distinguished American and British locomotive manufacturers. In sum, the former's ability to expand their presence in Japan hinged on the rapid expansion of the domestic market, the cultivation of talented domestic mechanical engineers, the introduction of competitive bidding, and extensive marketing activities. Meanwhile, the challenge of American locomotives to British ones at the turn of the nineteenth and twentieth centuries spurred competition for sales in Japan, making it easier for Japanese railroads to procure locomotives at better prices and delivery times. This drove Japanese railroads' growth from the 1890s onward, and in this sense, American locomotives supported Japan's Industrial Revolution.

Another factor enabled Japanese railroads to acquire locomotives on globally favorable terms: the rise of Japanese trading companies. The next chapter examines the entry process and activities of such companies in the railroad materials market through case studies of Mitsui Bussan and Ōkura Gumi.

4

THE RISE OF JAPANESE TRADING COMPANIES

In Japan, a trading company with multinational operations that handles a variety of goods and internally processes diverse functions is called a *sōgō shōsha*, or a general trading company. Mitsui Bussan became the country's first such company in the early years of the twentieth century, initiating a sea change in distribution systems that promoted the country's industrialization.[1] Before the emergence of *sōgō shōsha*, Japan's foreign trade had been controlled by similar companies in its main trading partners, Western countries and Chinese merchants, a trend that lasted from the 1859 opening of ports to the early Meiji era (see chapter 2). The 1870s saw the establishment of Japanese firms that fought for their commercial rights in overseas trade by competing with foreign trading companies. Mitsui Bussan and Ōkura Gumi, its distinguished counterpart, were established in 1876 and 1873, respectively, but such companies handled less than 20 percent of foreign trading transactions until the 1890s.

Japan's handling rate increased gradually from the late 1890s and crossed 50 percent in the late 1900s. During this period, its trading companies accumulated expertise in international commerce and expanded worldwide. For example, Mitsui Bussan set up overseas branches and agencies in the

1880s and 1890s. By around 1900, it imported machinery (including locomotives), steel (including rails), and cotton, while globally exporting raw silk, textiles, and coal; by 1909, in addition to eight branches and twenty sub-branches abroad, it also possessed integrated steamship operations and had invested in manufacturing capacity.

This era further saw the rise of specialized trading companies with expertise in specific areas. These included Takata Shōkai and Ōkura Gumi, which focused on the fields of machinery and railroad materials. Dealing in such specialized fields required staff with the requisite knowledge and know-how, which made it difficult for ordinary trading companies to enter these markets. As a result, only a few Japanese trading companies handled machinery and similarly technical industries. On the other hand, while Western trading companies exclusively handled products from their home countries' manufacturers, their Japanese counterparts traded the wares of manufacturers from all over. As of 1903, Ōkura Gumi had business relationships with Rogers in the United States, North British Locomotive in the United Kingdom, and Borsig in Germany, which enabled it to provide locomotives from those countries that best suited the needs of Japanese railroads. Similar examples existed for locomotives, machine tools, spinning machines, power looms, and mining equipment. In this chapter, I use Mitsui Bussan, Takata Shōkai, and Ōkura Gumi as case studies of the U.S.-Japan locomotive trade to examine how such companies expanded globally and how they acquired the knowledge and know-how to trade machinery and railroad materials. Doing so sheds light on a key aspect of the relationship between Japan's Industrial Revolution and the first global economy.

THE SOCIAL INFRASTRUCTURE FOR TRADING LOCOMOTIVES

When examining the activities of Japanese trading companies, we must consider the underlying social infrastructure in communications, transportation, and finance that supported their work.[2] Transportation and information networks connecting East Asia and North America developed rapidly, especially around 1900. In 1896, Nippon Yusen[3] successfully negotiated an agreement with Great Northern Railroad to connect land and sea services and launched a Japan–Seattle route. In 1898, Toyo Kisen[4] concluded a similar agreement with Southern Pacific Railroad and launched a sea route from Hong Kong to San Francisco. Establishing these transpacific shipping routes and developing international telegraph networks enabled Japanese trading companies in New York to frequently exchange mail and telegram with their head offices in Japan.[5]

With regard to freight transport, numerous new shipping companies connecting New York and East Asia via the Suez Canal entered the market in rapid succession from 1901 to 1902, creating regular shipping routes with newer, faster steamships. As a result, the freight time between New York and Yokohama shrank from four to three months, while the shipping frequency increased to approximately 1.7 ships per month.[6] Meanwhile, with regard to the foreign bills of exchange essential to the trading business, the Yokohama Specie Bank took care of Japanese trading companies, even providing bridge loans when necessary. And the promotion of the Japanese consul in New York to a consul general in 1902 offered complete protection to Japanese expatriates and increased information for Japanese companies doing business in the United States. Japanese trading companies used this external infrastructure to open branch offices with minimal human resources and funds.

THE ENTRY OF JAPANESE TRADING COMPANIES

Around the turn of the century, Japanese trading companies emerged as key intermediaries in the procurement of railroad goods, standing shoulder to shoulder with the British and American firms discussed in previous chapters. One of the first to do so was Takata Shōkai, established in 1881 with a capital stock of 1,500 yen and led by Takata Shinzō (1852–1921), who had experience working for foreign trading companies.[7] In 1870, Takata had commenced employment at H. Ahrens Co. in Germany as an apprentice, where he accumulated experience dealing in machinery. In 1879, he moved to Behr & Co., the firm that succeeded H. Ahrens, and when Behr closed in 1881, he established Takata Shōkai to continue business in the same area. The company, headquartered in the fashionable Ginza district of Tokyo, was a joint investment between Takata, the German H. Ahrens, and the Briton James Scott. On opening, it established a branch office in London and became the agent for firms such as Krupp AG in Germany and the British Iron Works in Sheffield, importing machinery from them for its main clients, the Imperial Japanese Army and Navy.[8] In 1891, it opened a New York office run by Robert Scott, the brother of James Scott, which primarily imported mining equipment. It was right around this time that it started to broker locomotive imports.

Takata Shōkai's first foray into railroads involved importing 12 Baldwin locomotives in 1890–1891 for Hokkaido Colliery and Railway, as discussed in chapter 3.[9] It later imported more locomotives, mostly from Baldwin—3 for the Hokkaido Colliery and Railway in 1893 and 5 for Nara Railway in 1894. Around the same time, the London branch office established itself by importing 3 Vulcan tank locomotives for Osaka Railway in 1894, 18 Dübs tender locomotives for the IGR in 1898,[10] and 1 Nasmyth Wilson tender locomotive for Kobu Railway in 1902.[11]

In this manner, during the competitive bidding era from the 1890s to the early 1900s, Takata Shōkai proactively imported locomotives for both government and private railroads. Around that time, foreign trading companies such as John Birch, Jardine Matheson, and Frazar enjoyed a distinct advantage and higher levels of trust compared to their Japanese counterparts. In this context, Takata Shōkai became the first Japanese company to break into the British and American ranks of locomotive importation thanks to its having the lineage of a foreign trading company as well as German and British partners at the time of its establishment. The firm was thus a pioneer in the Japanese trading of railroad supplies. However, it subsequently entered into an agency agreement with Westinghouse Electric Corporation,[12] and henceforth shifted to importing electrical machines.[13] Thereafter, it gradually stopped brokering all railroad materials except for electric railroad goods.

THE RISE OF JAPANESE TRADING COMPANIES

Mitsui Bussan, the archetype of general trading companies in prewar Japan, entered the locomotive trade after Takata Shōkai.[14] Its opening salvo in the procurement of railroad materials came with its import of Decauville rails from France.[15] However, prior to the First Sino-Japanese War, the company brokered only a small volume of railroad goods and did not import locomotives. In September 1895, it established a position in its head office to oversee railroad goods and machinery, which became the Machinery Section in March 1896; in March 1897, this section was divided into the Machinery and Railway Units, and it began brokering railroad goods in earnest.

In 1895–1896, Mitsui Bussan imported seven Vulcan Foundry's tank locomotives for Osaka Railway.[16] As detailed in chapter 2, Osaka Railway had enjoyed a special relationship with Jardine Matheson that involved the nearly exclusive purchase of British locomotives and materials, but it began using Japanese trading companies in the mid-1890s. Thereafter, Mitsui Bussan worked with manufacturers like Nasmyth Wilson and Beyer Peacock, importing two of the former's locomotives for Kyoto Railway and thirty-six of the latter's for Nippon Railway in 1903–1904.[17]

The critical development that paved the way for Mitsui Bussan's trade in railroad goods during this period was its 1896 establishment of a New York branch office. This started its full-fledged brokering of American locomotives, as described in the following excerpt from a business report the company filed in 1897:

With regard to these railroad goods, in the past, we have mostly demanded British-made materials. However, the American-made goods are cheaper. We have worked to strengthen our relationships with Carnegie Corp., from whom we purchase rails and bridge girders, Pencoyd Iron Works, from whom we purchase bridge girders, and Schenectady Locomotive Works, from whom we purchase locomotives. These manufacturers have become our regular clients, and we are able to derive substantial benefit from these relationships. In addition to increasing the volume of orders from the US, we plan to dispatch an individual with

THE RISE OF JAPANESE TRADING COMPANIES

expertise in the railroad industry to the New York branch office and to further expand our business there.[18]

Japan's second railroad boom, which took place in 1896–1897, dramatically increased its national demand for railroad materials. Recognizing this opportunity, Mitsui Bussan strategically shifted its sourcing focus from the United Kingdom to the United States and aimed to create what it called "regular partners" by concentrating orders from a small number of manufacturers; for instance, Schenectady became one such partner for locomotives.[19] From the first half of 1897 to the first half of 1899, the value of imported railroad goods accounted for an average of 12.8 percent of the value of all goods Mitsui Bussan imported, indicating that this trade had become a key part of its business.[20] This trend was particularly evident for the New York branch office, where profits from the trade of railroad goods accounted for 25 to 53 percent of all profits and represented the greatest share of profits for any category.[21]

That said, with the exception of the second half of 1898, the London office brokered a higher cumulative volume of railroad materials than the New York office.[22] In the latter half of the 1890s, British influence remained strong, especially at the IGR, and in many cases this led to British manufacturers being designated during bids. At that time, however, as British trading companies maintained strong ties with British locomotive manufacturers, Japanese trading companies had to seek other ways of stably procuring locomotives. This explains why Mitsui Bussan in the 1900s began working with American manufacturers such as ALCO, which succeeded Schenectady, and why it expanded its marketing of American railroad goods.

The case of Ōkura Gumi further illuminates the relationship between the emergence of American manufacturers and Japanese trading companies in locomotive exports to Japan around the turn of the century. Like Takata Shōkai and Mitsui Bussan, the company was renowned for its role in the machinery trade during the Meiji era. It was a midsized firm that originated in Ōkura Kihachirō's 1873 founding of the Ōkura Gumi Shōkai. Ōkura Kihachirō (1837–1928), a famous *goyō shōnin* (government purveyor)

120

in the early Meiji period who later founded the Ōkura zaibatsu, was an arms dealer with business interests in guns, munitions trading, and military shoe manufacturing.

Ōkura went on to establish Ōkura Gumi in 1893 with a capital stock of one million yen. His new company mainly engaged in international trade and also sought opportunities in the purveyor business and the mining industry. While Ōkura Gumi had only one overseas branch in London at the time of its founding, it later established agents in San Francisco, New York, Paris, Berlin, Melbourne, Sydney, Colombo, Calcutta, Bombay, Shanghai, Tianjin, and Hong Kong. Within Japan, besides its headquarters in Tokyo, it had six regional branches, a leather manufacturing plant, sixteen sub-branches, and a gun shop.[23] Kadono Chōkurō (1867–1958), a former railroad engineer who managed its European business at the time, supervised agents in Europe and the United States, later becoming a company partner and director. Kadono graduated from the Department of Civil Engineering at the Imperial University in 1891 and got a job in the Pennsylvania Railroad Company in 1892. In 1896, he returned to Japan and became an engineer at Sanyo Railway before joining Ōkura Gumi as the manager of its London branch in 1897. He remained in London until 1907, overseeing branches and agencies in Europe and the United States as a director before returning to Japan as the company's vice president.[24] Kadono's technical knowledge and industry experience were vital to Ōkura Gumi's foray into railroad materials.[25]

Ōkura Gumi began brokering locomotives with a purchase of forty-eight Dübs tank locomotives in 1901–1902 for the IGR.[26] Around the same time, it also purchased six Nasmyth tank locomotives for the Government-General of Taiwan.[27] This makes it evident that the company's railroad trade began in earnest with British goods, but in 1901, it established a branch in New York to broker the sale of American machinery and other railroad components.[28] This office opened on Broadway in 1901 and primarily engaged in the machinery trade together with the London office. Its first director, Yamada Majirō,[29] graduated from the Tokyo Higher Commercial School in 1894 and worked in Ōkura Gumi's London branch until 1900, thereafter making his way alone to New York with the mission of opening

THE RISE OF JAPANESE TRADING COMPANIES

a branch office.[30] Yamada kept a "letter book" from his time in London, and when he first moved to New York, he also left numerous copies of business correspondence with the Tokyo head office overseas department and others in a tracing paper booklet titled *Domestic Letters 1900–1901*. Eight more such booklets, titled *Tokio Letters*, further contain copies of his correspondence with the Tokyo head office from 1901 to 1905. These sources all shed fresh light on the activities of Japanese trading companies in the Meiji era.[31] Hereafter, I use documents from Ōkura Gumi's New York branch to analyze the company's locomotive transactions.

ŌKURA GUMI'S NEW YORK BRANCH AND THE LOCOMOTIVE TRADE[32]

THE HOKKAIDO GOVERNMENT RAILWAY DIVISION TENDER

Yamada arrived in New York to open Ōkura Gumi's new branch office on April 12, 1901.[33] He began enthusiastically collecting information immediately after reaching New York and started full-fledged business activities on June 9 after moving into a space on Broadway.[34] At the time of its launch, the office consisted of one director, one typist, and one messenger boy. For the next ten months, Yamada personally carried out almost every aspect of his work.[35] This included vigorously visiting journalists at American trade magazines such as *The Engineering News* to get technical and industry information related to manufacturing.[36] His office's first major job entailed purchasing six locomotives for the Hokkaido Government Railways.

On June 10, 1901, the Hokkaido Government Railways issued a call for tenders regarding the procurement of six locomotives and other equipment to enhance its facilities in view of route expansions.[37] A quote request for these items arrived at Yamada's office sometime between July 13 and 15, over a month after the initial announcement. Upon receiving the notice, Yamada issued quote requests to major American manufacturers on July 15 and 17.

At this time, as detailed in chapter 1, large-scale consolidation in the U.S. locomotive manufacturing industry had merged eight locomotive

THE RISE OF JAPANESE TRADING COMPANIES

manufacturers centered around Schenectady in July 1901 to establish the American Locomotive Company (ALCO). This narrowed the field to just three companies: ALCO, Baldwin, and Rogers. Yamada informed the London branch office and the Tokyo head office of this change on July 20 and 23 respectively.[38] In these letters, he mentioned that ALCO's vice president and head of sales were both from Schenectady, and that Mitsui,[39] which had many previous transactions and strong connections with Schenectady, would likely serve as the new company's agent in East Asia. Yamada thus speculated that, even if ALCO provided a quote for the six locomotives in this tender to a firm other than Mitsui, it would not be reliable. Indeed, although he visited ALCO repeatedly to conduct negotiations, he ultimately failed to obtain a quote.[40]

Similar to Schenectady and Mitsui, Baldwin had built a strong business relationship with Frazar & Co., as mentioned in chapter 3. Since the Hokkaido tender came after Frazar had already requested a quote, Yamada also failed to obtain a price from Baldwin.[41] The third major manufacturer, Rogers, had temporarily suspended business due to the passing of its former president. Yamada still requested a quote from the company on the basis of having recently heard that a proprietor had been decided and that the factory would soon resume operations. However, given Rogers's situation, he noted that he did not expect it to give Ōkura Gumi a quote.[42]

Consolidation in the American locomotive manufacturing industry increased the advantage of trading companies like Mitsui and Frazar, which had entered the market early and developed long-term relationships with the remaining big firms, leaving little room for latecomers such as Ōkura Gumi. Yamada's initial pessimism is evidenced by the following comment: "Unfortunately, I do not think we [Ōkura Gumi] will be able to participate in this tender for six locomotives."[43]

However, on July 25, 1901, Ōkura Gumi's New York branch received notification that Rogers "would very much like to provide a quote for the tender by the Hokkaido Government Railways for six locomotives." In response, Yamada requested that the company provide a quote by the following Monday, and simultaneously asked the Tokyo head office to consider submitting a bid for the six locomotives based on that price.[44]

Thereafter, on August 4, Yamada visited Rogers in Paterson, New Jersey, where its factory had resumed operations, and he learned from its president that the company planned to produce an average of two hundred locomotives per year.[45] On August 6, quotes from Rogers for six Mogul-type (2-6-0) tender locomotives (figure 4.1) and other railroad goods arrived and were promptly telegraphed to the Tokyo head office.[46] Rogers' per-locomotive price in this quote was $9,833, compared to the usual price of $9,250,[47] indicating that the difference of $583 (6 percent of the price per locomotive) is likely to have been Ōkura Gumi's commission or brokerage fee. Since the average brokerage fee for railroad goods at the time was 5 percent, this quote would have been considered reasonable.[48]

When the Hokkaido Government Railways held its tender on August 10, 1901, it awarded Ōkura Gumi a contract for locomotives, wheels, axles, and springs. Upon receiving news of the successful bid from the Tokyo head office on the same day,[49] Yamada immediately telegraphed Kadono in London and asked him to come to New York as soon as possible.[50] In summoning Kadono, who had approval authority and the know-how of the machinery trade, Yamada, suddenly responsible for the New York branch's first major order—valued at $70,000—hoped to eliminate the time and effort needed to exchange information between New York and London and facilitate the ordering process. Kadono obliged by arriving in New York on August 24, where he remained until the order's settlement on September 17.[51] As transportation and communication systems then remained undeveloped, it was more efficient to have officers with approval authority travel to make decisions on the spot rather than wait for the head office to approve each item. After August 13, Yamada negotiated with the manufacturer on the final price and delivery date, and he further consulted with Kadono as well as Uchiyama Yorikichi, a manager of Ōkura Gumi's gun store in New York for business, and Joseph Crawford, a former *oyatoi*. He then placed the official order with Rogers on August 30.

From January to February 1902, Rogers sequentially shipped six locomotives to Japan via the Suez Canal from New York Harbor on the scheduled service of the New York Oriental Steamship Company. Since the payment for the locomotives was contracted to be made to the manufacturer

THE RISE OF JAPANESE TRADING COMPANIES

FIGURE 4.1 In 1901, Rogers Locomotive Works built and sold this engine for Hokkaido Government Railways, with Ōkura Gumi acting as an intermediary. This tender locomotive had two leading and six driving wheels and was known as a "Mogul-type" engine in the United States.

Source: Iwasaki Collection, © Railway Museum, Ōmiya.

at the time of shipping, Ōkura Gumi procured the necessary funds through a documentary draft with a letter of credit from Yokohama Specie Bank. The bank had a prearranged credit facility for Ōkura Gumi that allowed it to provide bridge financing. In this transaction, the negotiation of the company's documentary draft was delayed for various reasons, but it could still use a bridge loan to pay Rogers promptly.

Yamada Majirō won a massive contract for railroad goods worth over $70,000 in July of the same year and ultimately succeeded in loading these goods onto a ship bound for Japan by February 1902. How did Yamada, who had single-handedly established the company's New York office only a few months earlier, accomplish such a large job with such a short lead time? Besides his own exceptional ability and the support lent to him by colleagues such as Kadono, he received critical aid from Crawford, who served as an American consulting engineer.

As detailed in chapter 3, Crawford had been invited by the Kaitakushi to be a civil engineering consultant in Hokkaido in 1878, where he immersed himself in railroad construction until 1881. From 1880 to 1881, he traveled with the Kaitakushi officer Matsumoto Sōichirō (later the director of the Railway Operation Bureau) to inspect potential routes and estimate construction costs for railroad lines from Tokyo to Aomori and to Takasaki, which lay the foundation of the Nippon Railway Company.[52] While Crawford was honorably discharged from this post during a trip home in 1881, he continued to assist the Japanese railroad industry as an on-site preliminary inspector of railroad goods shipped from the United States to Japan.

Crawford's relationship with the Ōkura Gumi New York branch began on August 12, 1901, when Yamada visited Crawford's home to seek advice on specifications for the locomotives ordered by the Hokkaido Government Railway Division.[53] At the time, Yamada was concerned about discrepancies between the former's specification document and the detailed quote prepared by Rogers, particularly regarding the size of the firebox and the material properties of the track wheel center.[54] Crawford advised that the first was a minor issue that could be resolved simply by recalculating the size using the specified area; on the second, he approved of the cast steel advocated by Rogers, observing that Schenectady had used similar material in its locomotives for Kyushu Railway. Aided by this advice, Yamada submitted an official order to Rogers at the end of August 1901 and asked Crawford to serve as a consulting engineer.[55] To Yamada, freshly arrived in New York, Crawford's intimate knowledge of Japanese railroads, technological expertise, and abundant experience inspecting American locomotives and railroad goods for Japan made him a reliable resource.

Crawford's role as Ōkura Gumi's consulting engineer comprised the following four functions: inspecting and certifying purchased goods, providing price and technical information about railroad goods, technically evaluating discrepancies between specification documents and quotes, and providing product information obtained through his personal connections with Japanese individuals in the railroad industry. Of these, the first function was inspectorial, for which Crawford received a handling fee equal to 1 percent of the product price. The second provided Yamada with information on railroad goods, which was critical to knowing their market price. For example, regarding the previously described price negotiations with Rogers, Crawford told Yamada the actual cost price of the Schenectady locomotives bound for Kyushu Railway, which he himself had inspected.[56]

The third function negotiated technical aspects with clients—namely, the relevant Japanese railroads. If the specifications for a given railroad good had to be changed in the manufacturing stage, Crawford would use his position as consulting engineer to directly contact and negotiate with the source of an order, in this case the Railway Bureau, to obtain acknowledgment that the change was needed. This would have been impossible for Yamada to do given his lack of engineering expertise.

Finally, in regard to the last function, the relationship between Crawford and Matsumoto Sōichiro, his former colleague, is particularly noteworthy.[57] In 1900, Matsumoto, then the director general of the Railway Operation Bureau (i.e., the top official of the IGR), visited Crawford in Philadelphia and discussed his office's evaluation of Rogers locomotives. Yamada learned of this from Crawford himself, which enabled him to confirm the IGR's positive assessment of Rogers's products. Furthermore, the Hokkaido Government Railway Division hired Crawford as a consulting engineer in October 1901.[58] This, too, proved extremely favorable to the Ōkura Gumi New York branch's activities, information gathering, and inspection fees. Yamada's effective use of Crawford as a consulting engineer thus enabled him to successfully purchase railroad materials despite his newcomer status.

SUPPLY MONOPOLIZATION AND AGENT AGREEMENTS

As previously mentioned, the establishment of ALCO in 1901 narrowed the field of American locomotive manufactures to three main companies:

Baldwin, ALCO, and Rogers.[59] During the early 1900s, ALCO and Baldwin's shares were fairly evenly matched and together accounted for more than 80 percent of the American market (table 1.2). The following analysis considers how this supply market oligopolization affected the locomotive trade in tandem with the actions of Mitsui Bussan and Ōkura Gumi.

Iwahara Kenzō, the manager of Mitsui Bussan's New York branch office at the time, described his company's relationship with Schenectady and its business outlook after the establishment of ALCO as follows:

> Because these eight manufacturers each had their own agents, a difficult problem has emerged. . . . ALCO desperately wants to have only one agent in Japan. To this end, the other day, [Willard C.] Tyler, who was in Japan as a traveling agent [of Schenectady], was tasked to investigate and report on the circumstances in Japan. In other words, ALCO believes it needs to create an agent to protect its interests.[60]

In the passage above, after emphasizing Mitsui Bussan's history of marketing Schenectady locomotives in Japan, Iwahara points out a problem arising from the merger: Which of the agents for companies now merged into ALCO would become the new entity's agent? Following this comment, Iwahara, in his capacity as manager of the company's New York office, emphasized that "having or not having an agent agreement substantially impacts our interests, especially when [it] comes to competitive bidding." Moreover, he added that being an agent of the designated manufacturer made it "possible to consult directly with the manufacturer to freely quote a price of their choosing"; conversely, not having this status meant that "one must compete with other trading companies in terms of price, and the ability to win a contract depends on differences in shipping expenses and foreign exchange rates, etc."[61]

Iwahara's statements show how a trading company serving as an agent of the designated manufacturer could negotiate with the manufacturer and set a bid price, enabling contracts that allowed both parties to win reasonable profits without much trouble. If, however, a trading company was not an agent, it had to lower its handling fee to compete with other intermediaries because the manufacturer quoted the same price across the board. As discussed above, Ōkura Gumi also experienced this issue, which was particularly thorny in the railroad goods trade due to its typically low commissions. Similar problems occurred in the competitive bidding to purchase turntables and bridge materials from American Bridge Co. As Iwahara explained, "we have a very close relationship with American Bridge. So even if they receive a request for a price quote from a different trading company, they will work with us." In fact, for IGR's purchase of seven turntables, American Bridge favored Mitsui Bussan by quoting its rival firms a price 7.5 percent higher, and for Nankai Railway's order of bridge materials, it quoted such firms a price 5 percent higher.[62]

On the other hand, Iida Giichi, one of Mitsui's executive directors, raised the inability to broker products from other countries as a shortcoming of being an agent:

> German locomotives are inexpensive. If Japanese railroads start importing these, even if we have agency agreements with American or British manufacturers, we may not be able to compete with the German locomotives. For this reason, leaving aside large companies such as ALCO, we want to be as free from constraints as possible. Even if we don't broker goods from other American manufacturers, I would like us to be able to broker British and German goods.[63]

Here Iida raised the problem that, depending on the details of the agent agreement, a trading company might be prohibited from brokering other manufacturers' goods and thus lose business opportunities. This was a crucial point for Mitsui Bussan, which had branches in the United States, the United Kingdom, and Germany. Japanese general trading companies could take advantage of competitive bidding to beat out specialized foreign trading companies such as Frazar by dealing in products from all countries. In fact, Willard C. Tyler, as an American agent representing ALCO, made this point at an IGR tender in 1902:

> The tender for thirty Imperial Railways locomotives is out. The approved manufacturers are German (Berliner, Hanomag, Henchel), British (Byer Peacock, Dübs, Neilson, Sharp Stewart), & American (ALCO, Rogers).

The Baldwin Co. was not in it. The delivery is February 1904. They are to be side tank six-wheel coupled engines with one pair trailing wheels. . . . Mitsui will probably tender on American, British, & German. An advantage of this is that they know all prices.[64]

For this reason, Mitsui Bussan decided to seek an agent agreement with ALCO that would still allow them to broker British and German locomotives.

JAPANESE TRADING COMPANIES' ATTAINMENT OF AGENT AGREEMENTS

MITSUI BUSSAN AND ALCO

Mitsui Bussan's biggest rival to become ALCO's agent in East Asia was American Trading Co., which served as the agent for Brooks Locomotive Works, one of ALCO's constituent companies.[65] American Trading was a large and influential firm that enjoyed commercial supremacy in South America, an important market for U.S. locomotive manufacturers.[66] ALCO's strategy thus involved making American Trading its agent in South America and Mitsui Bussan its agent in Japan.[67]

Negotiations between ALCO and Mitsui Bussan continued into 1904 and resulted in the signing of an agent agreement in August of that year. In summary, the agreement's main points were as follows: its terms applied to Japan (including Taiwan) and Korea; if ALCO provided a price quote to a different trading company in either of those countries, it would add 5 percent to the price presented to Mitsui Bussan; in the case of a tender, Mitsui Bussan would not contact any American locomotive manufacturers other than ALCO and Porter, which made small locomotives for industrial use.[68]

The agreement's most noteworthy characteristic was the limitation of its scope to Japan and Korea. In 1904, Japan found itself fighting the Russo-Japanese War with northeastern China as the main theater of conflict. This may explain why, despite Mitsui Bussan's predominance in the region, China was excluded from the agreement. However, after said war ended in 1905 and northeastern China came under Japan's sphere of influence—notably through the establishment of the South Manchuria Railway—the agreement expanded to include this region in 1916, making Mitsui Bussan ALCO's sole agent in East Asia.[69]

To alleviate Mitsui Bussan's concerns, the exclusive contract targeted other American manufacturers, which meant that, for all practical purposes, Mitsui Bussan could still deal in British and German locomotives. This agreement enabled the firm to trade the locomotives most relevant to the needs of Japanese railroads from all over, while Japanese railroads could procure high-quality locomotives at the lowest prices and shortest delivery times. Locomotives from ALCO and Baldwin were thus exported to Japan through the agencies of Mitsui Bussan and Frazar during this period.

ŌKURA GUMI AND ROGERS

Yamada Majirō analyzed the outcome of the Hokkaido Government Railway Division's tender based on a detailed table of bidding results that his company's head office sent to its New York branch on August 1901.[70] Based on bid prices, the oligopolization of locomotive manufacturing, and the spread of agent agreements, Yamada concluded that Ōkura Gumi needed to obtain a future agent agreement from Rogers.[71] This goal led him to seek a special relationship with Rogers by attempting to facilitate a mutual understanding with the latter's management and sharing information by providing Rogers with the bidding results.[72]

To put Rogers on the IGR's radar, Yamada met with Utsunomiya Kan'ichi, manager of the Railway Bureau Operations Section, during the latter's visit to New York in February 1902, and took him to see the Rogers factory.[73] Aside from obtaining information from Utsunomiya regarding the reputation of Rogers locomotives and other related affairs, Yamada also urged the Tokyo office to campaign for Rogers to be included on the IGR's list of approved manufacturers. He further requested that it send materials related to past tenders so he could prepare future bids using the

THE RISE OF JAPANESE TRADING COMPANIES

information from Utsunomiya. Furthermore, assessing that Rogers's marketing activities in Japan were insufficient, Yamada called on the Tokyo office to proactively advertise to both private and public railroads in Japan. He had Rogers directly write letters to major Japanese railroads, even enclosing clippings of newspaper and magazine articles demonstrating Rogers's reputation, and requested his head office's help in sending these out.[74] All this aimed to increase the number of trade deals involving Rogers.

Rogers, acknowledging these earnest efforts on its behalf, sought an agent agreement with Ōkura Gumi. At this point, Yamada wrote to Tokyo asking for approval;[75] happily, Ōkura Gumi's head office approved this request on March 24, 1902, and it signed an agent agreement with Rogers on May 2 of the same year.[76] Thereafter, Ōkura Gumi proactively participated in public and private railroad tenders for locomotives and railroad parts while working closely with and receiving information from Rogers. For example, Yamada wrote the following to Tokyo on June 10, 1902: "As can be seen in the attached letter from Rogers Locomotive Works, Rogers received an inquiry from the China Japan Trading Co. about two locomotives. However, I have not heard anything about this from our office."[77] Ōkura Gumi's New York branch sometimes obtained news of tenders in Japan faster through Rogers than its own head office.

In this way, Ōkura Gumi began brokering American locomotives after becoming an agent for Rogers; in 1905, however, Rogers unexpectedly merged with ALCO, which vaporized the trading company's hard-won agent agreement along with its bridgehead in the U.S. locomotive trade. Like American Trading and Jardine Matheson, Ōkura Gumi ended up a victim of ALCO's consolidation. It subsequently stopped brokering American locomotives and worked exclusively with dominant European manufacturers such as North British Locomotive in Glasgow and London as well as Borsig in Berlin.

To sum up the story told in this chapter, Japanese trading companies such as Mitsui Bussan and Ōkura Gumi began establishing branch offices worldwide at the end of the nineteenth century. They accomplished this by utilizing the social infrastructure created in the first global economy, particularly networks of international telecommunications, transportation, and banking, to deepen their business relationships with manufacturers and acquire agency agreements. Ōkura Gumi's New York branch illuminates the significance of Japanese trading companies' offices in the United States and the procedures for importing railroad goods during the Meiji era. As described above, Yamada's actions reveal his ability to identify and exploit business opportunities by collecting relevant and accurate information. He did this through a network of individuals within Ōkura Gumi, which included Kadono Chōkurō, along with an external network of Japanese expatriates employed at the Japanese consulate general and the Yokohama Specie Bank; he also communicated with local experts, including magazine editors as well as Japanese businessmen and technicians who visited New York.

The critical role played by consulting engineers cannot be overemphasized. That Ōkura Gumi's New York office successfully procured such a large account despite its newcomer status hinged on Yamada's hiring of Crawford, whose experience and expertise allowed him not only to conduct parts inspections but also to advise on technical questions, American railroad goods manufacturers, and Japanese railroad companies, which made up for Yamada's inexperience. The timely resumption of manufacturing at Rogers facilitated the locomotive purchases for the Hokkaido Government Railway Division, but Ōkura Gumi's newly opened New York branch undoubtably capitalized on this opportunity thanks to Yamada's multilayered network.

Competitive bidding, as part of the procedures for importing railroad goods, significantly involved quotes from manufacturers. American manufacturers tended to conclude agent agreements with trading companies around the world. Even without a formal agreement, manufacturers often provided preferential price quotes to trading companies with whom they had existing relationships. Thus, trading companies with longer track records of conducting business with specific manufacturers enjoyed a considerable advantage. During the 1900s, Mitsui Bussan and Ōkura Gumi successfully pursued contracts that allowed them to trade goods from countries worldwide according to the requirements of the Japanese railroads who were their customers. In this respect, these companies differed substantially from their foreign counterparts, whose business was predicated on relationships with manufacturers in their home countries. Their expansion and dominance were prerequisites that facilitated Japanese railroads' smooth global procurement of machinery and materials.

These trading companies relied on the contributions of ex-*oyatoi* specialists who served as consulting engineers or inspectors after returning to their home countries. Former *oyatoi* such as Crawford supported the overseas activities of Japanese trading companies in various roles and formed an essential route of knowledge transfer in cross-regional commercial management. Other examples of former *oyatoi* becoming consulting engineers or inspectors for Japanese trading companies after returning home also appeared in the United Kingdom, as in the case of Thomas Shervinton, who served as a civil engineer for the Railway Bureau from 1877 to 1881.[78] The *oyatoi* system, adopted to speed technology transfer to Japan, continued to link Japan with the world even after the country had achieved technological independence.

5

WAR, EMPIRE BUILDING, AND THE LOCOMOTIVE TRADE

This chapter examines the structural changes in the East Asian locomotive market that unfolded as Japan began building its overseas empire in earnest; it also focuses on a new trend in the global locomotive market after the Russo-Japanese War: American manufacturers' and Japanese trading companies' rapid shift toward exporting to China.

I first discuss the relationship between Japan's empire building and railroad development, focusing on the impact of both the First Sino-Japanese War (1894–1895) and the Russo-Japanese War (1904–1905) on the East Asian locomotive market. Japan's imperial expansion, which occurred in tandem with the building of its nation-state, used railroads as a vital tool in this process. During the Russo-Japanese War, railroads emerged as an essential means of military transportation, and they subsequently proved crucial to managing Japan's colonies. The analysis will discuss how it procured locomotives worldwide for war and empire building from the viewpoints of manufacturers and trading companies.

Subsequently, in 1906–1907, the government acquired seventeen major private railroads in Japan to create the new Imperial Government Railways, which owned 90 percent of all railroad tracks and 95 percent of rolling

WAR, EMPIRE BUILDING, AND THE LOCOMOTIVE TRADE

stocks. Nationalization established a demand-side monopsony that eliminated competition to procure materials and gave the IGR crucial sway over the actions of locomotive manufacturers and trading companies. For Japan's developing manufacturers, the government's exclusive determination of locomotive orders provided an opportunity to capture the domestic market from international rivals. On the other hand, Western locomotive manufacturers, locked out of the domestic Japanese market, rapidly shifted to emerging markets in the colonies and spheres of influence that Japan had acquired, particularly those in China. I trace this process to examine how the establishment of a government monopoly through railroad nationalization impacted the trade and local production of locomotives, focusing on the roles of trading companies and the government.

JAPAN'S TWO INTERNATIONAL WARS

Delving into Japan's modern history necessitates attending to the profound impact of two pivotal international conflicts: the Sino-Japanese and Russo-Japanese Wars. Since 1868, the Meiji government's goal of catching up with advanced Western nations had led it to champion industrial development, establish systems of modern governance, and hone its domestic and foreign policies. Railroads contributed to this nation-state building by ushering in industrialization and thereby forging national unity. Amid this transformative process, Japan initiated a war with the Qing Dynasty in July 1894, a move that would transform East Asia's historical trajectory. Although the background to this war is much debated, its direct cause was undoubtedly the conflict between Japan and the Qing over control of Korea. Specifically, while the Qing sought to maintain the traditional *hua-yi* order in which China dominated over what it considered lesser or barbaric polities, Japan aimed to modernize international relations in East Asia while embracing its imperial ambitions.[1] The war ended in a Japanese victory and an April 1895 peace treaty signed in Shimonoseki by which the Qing recognized Korea's complete independence (i.e., the revocation of its vassal status), conceded the Liaodong Peninsula, Taiwan, and the Penghu Islands to Japan, and paid 200 hundred million taels in reparations. Japan ended

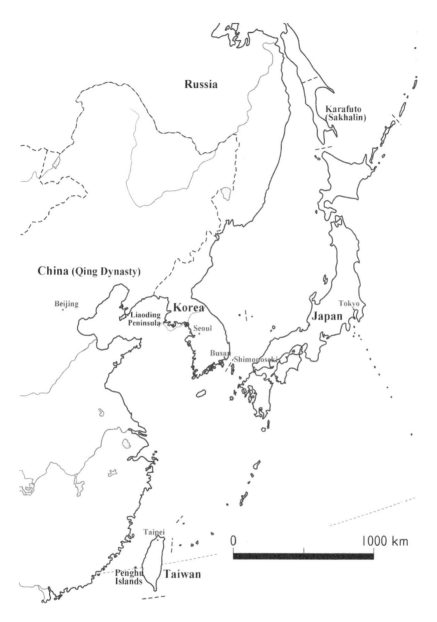

FIGURE 5.1 Map of Northeast Asia after the First Sino-Japanese War. In 1895, following the First Sino-Japanese War, the Qing Dynasty recognized Korea's independence and ceded Taiwan, the Penghu Islands, and the Liaodong Peninsula to Japan. However, Japan eventually relinquished the Liaodong Peninsula due to the intervention of Russia, Germany, and France. In 1898, Russia leased the southern tip of the peninsula and obtained the right to construct the South Manchurian Branch of the Chinese Eastern Railway.

Source: Created by the author.

up ceding the Liaodong Peninsula due to the intervention of Russia, Germany, and France, but it kept Taiwan and the Penghu Islands as its first colonies (figure 5.1).

Japan's triumph in the Sino-Japanese War effectively eradicated China's influence over the Korean Peninsula. However, an ongoing shift in the geopolitical landscape caused its influence to wane while Russia's ascended, partly due to the assassination of Queen Min in October 1895 and the resultant fanning of anti-Japanese sentiment in Korea.[2] In 1898, Russia acquired the right to lease Port Arthur and Dalian on the Liaodong Peninsula, which Japan had returned, and the right to construct the South Manchurian Branch of the Chinese Eastern Railway between Harbin and Dalian (figure 5.2).[3] A series of Russian advances into Korea and Manchuria heightened Japan's sense of crisis, and it concluded the first Anglo-Japanese Alliance with Great Britain in 1902, increasing diplomatic pressure on Russia. At the same time, it sought an agreement with Russia on the scope of its influence in Korea and Manchuria, but these negotiations collapsed in 1904.

In February 1904, the Battle of Chemulpo Bay marked the start of the Russo-Japanese War, which centered on northeastern China. Both sides attempted to use railroads as a tool of aggression in this conflict. Russia tried to mobilize the Trans-Siberian Railway, then still under construction, and the Chinese Eastern Railway, which had been completed, for military transportation; Japan attempted the same using the Keifu and Keigi Railways, both incomplete, and its domestic network of trunk railroads, which was largely finished. However, as Felix Patrikeeff and Harold Shukman observe, Russia lacked sufficient military transportation until the war's end due to logistical difficulties in the unfinished sections around Lake Baikal, poor alignment and track conditions from rapid construction, and inadequate rolling stocks.[4]

Meanwhile, Japan seized control of the Korean Peninsula at the onset by conquering Seoul and forcing Korea to sign the Japan-Korea Protocol, thereby gaining freedom of military action and control over Korea's internal affairs.[5] On February 21, 1904, it also opened the Provisional Military Railway Inspectorate to accelerate railroad building on the peninsula; this hastened the opening of the Keifu network from Seoul to Busan, originally

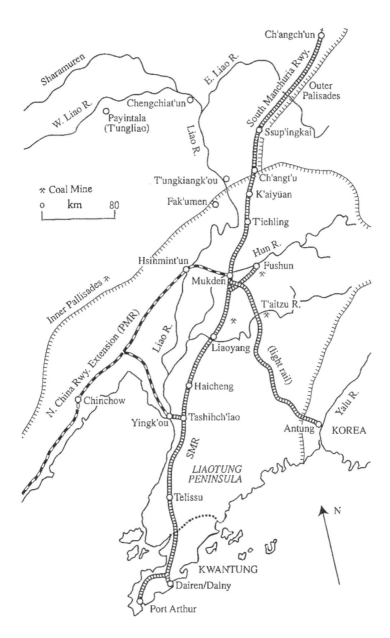

FIGURE 5.2 Railroads in Manchuria after the Russo-Japanese War. After the war, Japan acquired Russian interests in the Liaodong Peninsula and the South Manchurian Branch of the Chinese Eastern Railway between Port Arthur, Dalian, and Changchun. In 1906, the Japanese government merged the branch and the Antung–Mukden Light Railway (Anpō line) constructed by the Japanese army during the war and established the South Manchuria Railway Company.

Source: Reproduced with permission of the Harvard University Asia Center from Yoshihisa T. Matsusaka, *The Making of Japanese Manchuria, 1904–1932* (Cambridge, MA: Harvard University Asia Center, 2001), 67. © The President and Fellows of Harvard College, 2001.

scheduled for 1905, and ramped up the construction of the Keigi line from Seoul to Sinŭiju to a fever pitch.[6] However, as Steven Ericson points out, work on the Keigi Railway encountered difficulties, and military rail transportation on the peninsula did not proceed until April 1905; in addition, Japanese domestic railroads, which consisted of government-owned railroads and over forty private railroads, also faced difficulties in making joint transportation connections through traffic.[7] Furthermore, half of the South Manchurian Branch of the Chinese Eastern Railway, which the Japanese army had taken from Russia during the war, could not be used immediately because the Russians had taken rolling stocks and other materials with them when they retreated. The Japanese Field Railway Headquarters (hereafter the Field Railway HQ), established on June 1, 1904, began converting the broad gauge Chinese Eastern Railway track (five feet) from Dalian to Liaoyang for narrow gauge use (three feet six inches) in July.[8] The Field Railway HQ requisitioned rolling stocks, including locomotives, from the IGR and private railroads, which it sent to northeastern China, and military transportation belatedly began in October 1904.[9] Although the Russo-Japanese War is described as "a war in which railroads played a central role,"[10] neither side could effectively use said railroads.

Nevertheless, the war did significantly determine the market for locomotive imports. The Japanese government ordered large numbers of locomotives from Europe and the United States to fill the hole that requisitioning caused in its domestic market. In 1904–1905, Japan imported 174 locomotives from the NBL and 389 from Baldwin, of which it sent 144 to the Korean Peninsula, and brought in over 230 more from Germany. A surge in imports from the United States and Germany during this period made the share of British locomotives fall to below half for the first time in 1905,[11] and British influence in the Japanese locomotive market declined as Japan increasingly imported locomotives from the United States and Germany during the war.

The war ended in September 1905 with the Treaty of Portsmouth, a settlement whereby Japan acquired Korea as a protectorate along with Russian interests in the Liaodong Peninsula, the South Manchurian Branch of the Chinese Eastern Railway between Dalian and Changchun and its affiliated areas, as well as South Sakhalin (Karafuto). This consequently raised Japan's political interference in Korea, which it finally annexed and turned into a colony in August 1910.

Victory in these two international wars profoundly boosted Japan's efforts at nation-state and empire building. Their immediate impact was evident in the revision of the unequal treaties, a long-standing political and diplomatic issue for Japan since the opening of ports in 1859. In July 1894, just before the Sino-Japanese War, Japan concluded the Anglo-Japanese Treaty of Commerce and Navigation with Great Britain; on the condition that foreigners could reside freely in Japan, it abolished British consular jurisdiction, granted mutual most-favored-nation treatment, and partially restored Japan's tariff autonomy. During the Sino-Japanese War, Japan seized the opportunity to negotiate similar treaties with the other Western powers. And after the Russo-Japanese War, it concluded new treaties in commerce and navigation with the Western powers that fully restored its tariff autonomy. Through a series of treaty revisions, Japanese government leaders dispelled the danger of colonization and completed the formation of a nation-state in terms of politics and diplomacy.

On the economic side, industrial policies using reparations from the Sino-Japanese War and the resumption of foreign capital flows through the shift to the gold standard played a key role in completing Japan's Industrial Revolution. After the war, the Japanese government used part of the reparations to aggressively develop its industrial promotion policy. The IGR, as scheduled under the Railway Construction Act of 1892, began the full-scale building of tracks, which the government also attempted to domestically produce by establishing a state-run ironworks. This industrial policy partly led to a boom in companies in 1895, resulting in many new private railroads and new lines constructed by existing ones. The peak of the expansion induced by the second railroad boom came in 1897, with the largest annual number of new locomotives added by both private and government railroads at 207 and 75 vehicles respectively. While the subsequent collapse caused by the panic after the First Sino-Japanese War slowed the growth of private railroads' locomotive fleets, the IGR steadily increased its own, supported by reparations, adding forty-four locomotives in 1900, forty-six in 1902, and sixty in 1903 (figure 0.3). The Japanese locomotive market thus saw gradual but constant expansion in the first decade of the twentieth century.

Many railroad material manufacturers also emerged during the boom after the Sino-Japanese War. For example, in 1896, Inoue Masaru established Japan's first locomotive manufacturer, Kisha Seizō. As mentioned in chapter 1, Inoue, popularly known as the "father of Japanese railroads," served as the director of the IGR for more than twenty years after Japan founded its first railroad and devoted himself to training Japanese railroad engineers. After retiring from the Railway Bureau in 1893, he took it upon himself to enter locomotive manufacturing, then an incipient industry in Japan. With the odds stacked against them, Kisha Seizō commenced operations in 1899; armed with drawings loaned from the IGR and imported parts, it completed its first tank locomotive in 1901. The company intermittently manufactured locomotives and delivered them to the IGR, private railways, and the Office of the Governor-General in Taipei (Taiwan Sōtokufu), but its production was limited to only fifty-eight locomotives from 1901 to 1908. Notably, nine of these locomotives were for the Taiwan Sōtokufu, and in a move that underscored their commitment to the colony, the company established a Taipei branch factory in 1900. This facility played a crucial role in repairing rolling stocks and bolstered the mechanical operation of the railways in Taiwan. Japan's locomotive manufacturing industry, from its inception, was thus closely connected to the building of the Japanese Empire.

In 1897, Japan adopted the gold standard, using reparations from the Qing as reserves. At that time, since the global economy was led by the United Kingdom and based on gold, this shift significantly impacted Japan's international economic relations by negating foreign exchange risks in financial settlements with advanced Western countries. This was critical for railroads, which required large amounts of capital and imported materials such as locomotives, and around 1900, private Japanese railroads and the IGR, traditionally reliant on domestic financing, began discussing how to facilitate trade through foreign capital. After the Russo-Japanese War, the introduction of foreign capital was key to overcoming the limited

EMPIRE BUILDING AND RAILROADS

funding in the domestic capital market and developing large-scale industries such as railroads and the electric power industry. As a result, during the early 1900s, Japan's Industrial Revolution ended with the completion of the nation-state's economic formation.

EMPIRE BUILDING AND RAILROADS

The Sino-Japanese and Russo-Japanese Wars gave Japan effective control over Korea and Karafuto in addition to Taiwan; the country also wielded influence in the vast sphere of Manchuria, centered on the Liaodong Peninsula and the land appurtenant to the South Manchuria Railway (SMR). During this process of empire building, the railroads served as a tool of domination.

After Japan took possession of Taiwan in 1895 and suppressed fierce resistance from natives and remnants of the Qing, it began constructing trans-Taiwan railways in 1899. At that time, Gotō Shinpei (1857–1929, figure 5.3), the director general of the Civil Affairs Bureau in the Taiwan Sōtokufu and the director of railways, invited Hasegawa Kinsuke (1855–1921) from Japan to serve as the railways' chief engineer.

Gotō initially worked as a doctor in the Health Bureau of the Ministry of Home Affairs. When his old acquaintance Kodama Gentarō became the fourth governor-general of Taiwan in 1898, Gotō was assigned to the Taiwan Sōtokufu as director general of the Civil Affairs Bureau. After thoroughly investigating the situation in Taiwan, he set about building railroads and other infrastructure. He later studied colonial administration and railroad management in Taiwan, was selected as the SMR's first president in 1906, and aided the administration of Manchuria. In 1908, he founded the Railway Agency, which managed the new IGR, and became its first president.[12] He was also involved in localizing locomotives in Japan, as described below.

On the other hand, Hasegawa studied English at the Osaka English School and joined the Railway Bureau as an interpreter for foreign engineers in 1874, learning surveying techniques and other skills through on-the-job training. When the bureau established its Training School for

FIGURE 5.3 Gotō Shinpei (1857–1929), a doctor, bureaucrat, and politician who was the first head of the Taiwan Government Railways, the South Manchuria Railway, and the Railway Agency. In 1899, Gotō began constructing trans-Taiwan railways as a director of railways for the Taiwan Sōtokufu. In 1906, he was selected as the SMR's first president and aided the administration of Manchuria. After studying colonial and railroad management in Taiwan and Manchuria, he founded the Railway Agency in Japan. He was appointed its first president in 1908.

Source: Kinsei Meishi Shashin Hanpukai ed., *Kensei Meishi Shashin sono 1* [Photographs of famous people in recent years, vol. 1] (Osaka: Kinsei Meishi Shashin Hanpukai, 1935), n.p.

Railway Engineers in 1877, Hasegawa became one of the first students who systematically acquired railroad know-how. After that, he worked as an engineer who constructed railroads throughout Japan. In 1892, he transferred to Nippon Railway and became the chief of its construction section.[13] A skilled engineer who represented the second generation of Japanese engineers, he formed a group of engineers around himself during his long career with IGR and Nippon Railway and brought its members to Taiwan. Hasegawa mobilized this cadre of engineers, which included construction contractors, to build the railroad in a colony with little technical capacity in this area.

Japanese engineers designed and managed the construction of the trans-Taiwan railways, and major Japanese contractors handled the work. The Taiwan Sōtokufu selected a narrow gauge of three feet six inches, the same used in Japan. In 1908, when the entire line between Keelung and Kaohsiung commenced operations, this marked a milestone in Taiwan's transportation history.

By that time, Taiwan's railways had amassed a diverse fleet of 54 locomotives, a testament to the global influence on the island's transportation system. Of these, 33 were British, 10 were American, 9 were Japanese, and 2 were German.[14] Many of the British-made locomotives were transfers from the IGR and other companies in Japan,[15] as were 9 locomotives manufactured by Kisha Seizō. During the same period, in the Japanese domestic market, Kisha Seizo was outpaced by imported rivals in terms of delivery time and quality, and the firm could not increase its market share.[16] In the Taiwanese market, on the other hand, the colonial government's support enabled the company to increase deliveries steadily.

On the Korean Peninsula, a significant chapter in railroad history unfolded when the Americans secured the right to build a railroad between Incheon and Seoul in 1896. This marked the beginning of a transformative era, as they embarked on a plan to use standard gauge (4 feet 8.5 inches) and import railroad materials from the United States. However, Japanese capital acquired this pioneering project in 1899 and established the Keinin Railway Company, which continued the original project and completed it in 1900. In 1901, the Keifu Railway, also established with Japanese capital, aimed to construct a line between Seoul and Busan. A variety of plans were drawn up for its gauge: narrow, standard, and wide; in the end, the standard gauge was chosen to connect with railroads in mainland China. Construction of the line began in 1901 but was delayed, and it did not fully open until January 1905.[17] The Seoul–Shinuiju line (Keigi Railway), under the Korean government, was laid as a military railroad under intense pressure from Japan during the Russo-Japanese War and completed at the end of 1905.

The early Korean railroads were built with Japan's full involvement, but because of their standard gauge, they largely used American rolling stock. All ninety-four of Keifu's locomotives at the end of 1906, when the Japanese government acquired the railroad amid its nationalization drive, were manufactured by American companies, mainly Baldwin. Of these, seventy were 2-6-2 tank locomotives imported by Keifu and the Provisional Military Railway Inspectorate during the Russo-Japanese War.[18]

Following the Japanese annexation of Korea in 1910 and the establishment of a Railway Bureau in the Office of the Governor-General in Korea (Chōsen Sōtokufu), the Korean fleet acquired a significant number of American locomotives. By 1914, 151 out of the 165 cars were American-built, a testament to U.S. dominance in the Korean locomotive market. In comparison, while fourteen Borsig tank locomotives (2-6-2) were imported from Germany in 1911 and 1912, American manufacturers had cornered the Korean market before World War I.[19]

Meanwhile, in Manchuria, which became Japan's sphere of influence in the Russo-Japanese War, the Treaty of Portsmouth gave Japan all of the Russian-owned railroad equipment, facilities, and land attached to the Chinese Eastern Railway's South Manchuria line from Changchun to Dalian. Initially, the Field Railway HQ operated this line, but the SMR eventually commandeered it along with the Anpō line from Andung to Mukden. In November 1906, the SMR was established as a joint-stock company with a capital stock of 200 million yen, half of which came from the Japanese government and the other half from private investors. The SMR commenced service in April 1907 and began remaking the converted narrow-gauge tracks into a standard gauge of 4 feet 8.5 inches. The work was overseen by IGR engineers led by Kunizawa Shinbei (1864–1953).[20] Many had been in the Field Railway HQ and were familiar with railroad construction in Manchuria.[21] These engineers played the same role in the SMR as Hasegawa's group in the Taiwan railways.

The conversion from narrow to standard gauge, which was completed on all lines between April 1907 and the end of 1908, led the SMR to hurriedly procure large numbers of standard-gauge locomotives from the United States.[22] While ALCO and Baldwin received orders for 190 and 22 locomotives, respectively, British manufacturers won no contracts and lost their market hegemony in East Asia. Subsequently, from 1910 to 1912, the SMR imported 47 British and 4 German locomotives, comparing their running performance and maintenance costs with those of American locomotives. In 1912, the firm made the groundbreaking decision to construct its locomotives by drawing inspiration from American models. By 1914, its factory had constructed 6 freight locomotives,[23] and it proceeded to independently manufacture various types of locomotives, decreasing its imports of locomotives from Europe and the United States.

In southern Karafuto, ceded to Japan from Russia after the Russo-Japanese War, a military light railway whose construction began in 1906 was transferred to the Karafuto Agency in 1907. In 1910, the agency reconstructed its gauge to the standard three feet six inches used in Japan proper, imported materials from the United States via Japan, and began full-scale railroad construction. However, as of December 1913, the railroad had only six steam locomotives along with two British and four American tank locomotives, making for a tiny locomotive market.[24]

THE COMPETITIVE STRUCTURE OF LOCOMOTIVE EXPORTS TO EAST ASIA

Thus, war and the SMR abruptly expanded the Japanese Empire's locomotive market in its home islands and the territories within its imperial ambit, particularly Korea and Manchuria. However, its newly independent railroad industry, especially in terms of locomotive manufacturing, could not adequately supply materials to these places. American, British, and German manufacturers thus dominated with increased exports to Korea and northeastern China. In light of these points, this section examines the status of European and U.S. locomotive manufacturers' exports to East Asia, starting with the activities of British manufacturers such as North British Locomotive.

Between 1905 and 1911, the number of workers employed in British locomotive manufacturing peaked at 16,821 in 1907 and declined steadily to 13,060 in 1910.[25] As a contemporary journal noted, this indicated a dramatic contraction of the industry.[26] By 1905, NBL employed 52 percent of workers, followed by Beyer Peacock (15 percent), Kitson (10 percent), and Vulcan (9 percent). Although the number of NBL staff fell thereafter, it remained the mainstay of British locomotive manufacturing in this period, employing approximately 50 percent of the industry's employees.

In terms of trends in business operations, NBL's production peaked in 1905 at 573 locomotives,[27] with an average annual production in the 1904–1909 period of 530 locomotives.[28] However, orders shrank from 1909 onward, and its return on assets for 1910–1911 fell below 2 percent. The contraction of the British domestic locomotive market from 1902 contributed to this slump.[29] NBL thus sought overseas markets, and of the 4,370 locomotives it sold between 1903 and 1913, 78.3 percent were exported primarily to India and other British colonies, Latin America, and Japan (table 1.1).

NBL exported 174 tank locomotives in 1905, the majority of which went to the IGR.[30] Of these, 168 were part of the government's massive orders with overseas manufacturers to replace locomotives requisitioned during the Russo-Japanese War. Samuel M. Vauclain Jr. and Ōkura Gumi served as intermediaries in these transactions for 68 and 100 locomotives respectively. As the vehicles needed to be delivered in time for Japan to fight the war, NBL shipped them two to three months after the orders, unusually fast for a British manufacturer.

However, NBL's exports to Japan soon fell dramatically, as it sent only two locomotives to Kansei Railway in 1906–1907 and twelve to the IGR in 1911. The company began exporting to other parts of East Asia through various intermediaries, including Taiwan via Takata Shōkai and China via the Hong Kong offices of Jardine Matheson and J. Whittall.[31] But it could not participate in the SMR's massive orders in 1907 and 1908, which eroded its hegemony in this regional market.

The situation of American manufacturers centered on the top two firms, Baldwin and ALCO. As discussed in chapter 1, the 1901 creation of ALCO led to an oligopoly dominated by this new conglomerate and Baldwin. At this time, American manufacturers as a whole experienced a relative slump, receiving only 2,538 orders in total.[32] Subsequently, when Japanese demand for locomotives soared, orders peaked in 1905 and 1906 but again fell sharply in 1908. For the U.S. locomotive manufacturing industry, this proved a difficult and volatile time. Baldwin continued to maintain a 40 percent share of the American market for the 1901–1906 period, but this plunged from 1907 onward, leaving it in second place after ALCO with a 37 percent average share of orders between 1902 and 1912. ALCO accounted for the greatest share of orders in the same period after 1904, enjoying a market share roughly ten points higher than Baldwin's.

For exports bound for East Asia (table 5.1), the top two American manufacturers peaked at 420 locomotives in 1904–1905. Frazar served as the agent for shipping 381 of these in this period to the main destinations of Japan and Korea; as a result, exports to Japan in 1905 accounted for 11.7 percent of Baldwin's total production.

However, ALCO began to increase its share after the Russo-Japanese War. With Mitsui Bussan as its agent in Japan, it latched on to the last-minute rush of orders before railroad nationalization and exported 99 locomotives to Japan in 1906–1907. Soon thereafter, it sold 190 locomotives to the SMR in 1907–1908 and secured the top spot in the East Asian market almost overnight. ALCO continued to expand its locomotive sales to railroads throughout China from 1907 onward, with exports to East Asia accounting for 17.5 percent of its total production by 1908.

American locomotive manufacturers thus boosted their exports to East Asia by responding adeptly to the opportunities presented by the Russo-Japanese War, the nationalization of railroads in Japan, and the establishment of the SMR, all of which necessitated the speedy procurement of large numbers of locomotives. They successfully did so through the American system, as explained in chapter 1, using interchangeable parts to simplify

TABLE 5.1 Exports of locomotives to East Asia by the top two U.S. manufacturers

| BALDWIN | TOTAL PRODUCTS | EXPORTS BY REGION IN EAST ASIA (SHIPMENT BASIS) | | | | | TOTAL (# OF CARS) | EAST ASIA RATIO (IN TOTAL PRODUCTS) | EXPORTS BY AGENTS | | | FRAZAR RATIO (IN TOTAL PRODUCTS) |
		JAPAN	KOREA	TAIWAN	MANCHURIA	CHINA			FRAZAR & CO.	OTHERS	TOTAL	
1901	1,375	2	2	–	–	2	6	0.4%	2	4	6	0.1%
1902	1,535	1	5	–	–	–	6	0.4%	6	–	6	0.4%
1903	2,022	11	–	–	–	–	11	0.5%	10	1	11	0.5%
1904	1,485	28	97	–	–	–	125	8.4%	117	8	125	7.9%
1905	2,250	217	47	–	–	–	264	11.7%	264	–	264	11.7%
1906	2,666	14	6	–	–	–	20	0.8%	20	–	20	0.8%
1907	2,655	16	15	–	22	–	53	2.0%	53	–	53	2.0%
1908	617	4		1	–	–	5	0.8%	4	1	5	0.6%
1909	1,024	–	–	–	–	–	0	0.0%	–	–	0	0.0%
1910	1,675	–	–	2	–	–	2	0.1%	2	–	2	0.1%
1911	1,606	2	–	–	–	–	2	0.1%	2	–	2	0.1%
1912	1,618	27	12	–	–	1	40	2.5%	21	19	40	1.3%
Cumulative	*20,528*	*322*	*184*	*3*	*22*	*3*	*534*	*2.6%**	*501*	*33*	*534*	*2.4%**

TABLE 5.1 (*continued*)

ALCO		EXPORTS BY REGION IN EAST ASIA (SHIPMENT BASIS)						EAST ASIA RATIO (IN TOTAL PRODUCTS)	EXPORTS BY AGENTS			MITSUI RATIO (IN TOTAL PRODUCTS)
		JAPAN	KOREA	TAIWAN	MANCHURIA	CHINA	TOTAL		MITSUI & CO.	OTHERS	TOTAL	
1901	2,532	5	–	–	–	–	5	0.2%	5	0	5	0.2%
1902	2,091	42	–	–	–	–	42	2.0%	42	0	42	2.0%
1903	1,138	12	–	–	–	–	12	1.1%	12	0	12	1.1%
1904	1,384	10	–	–	–	–	10	0.5%	7	3	10	0.5%
1905	2,698	12	9	–	–	–	21	0.8%	12	9	21	0.4%
1906	3,165	71	–	–	–	–	71	2.2%	71	0	71	2.2%
1907	2,102	28	–	–	110	9	147	7.0%	147	0	147	7.0%
1908	709	24	–	4	80	16	124	17.5%	124	0	124	17.5%
1909	1,935	0	–	–	–	3	3	0.2%	3	0	3	0.2%
1910	1,905	30	9	2	–	2	43	2.3%	43	0	43	2.3%
1911	1,107	16	6	–	5	1	28	2.5%	28	0	28	2.5%
1912	1,989	24	–	3	–	6	33	1.7%	33	0	33	1.7%
Cumulative	22,755	274	24	9	195	37	539	2.4%*	527	12	539	2.3%*
Total cumulative	43,283	596	208	12	217	40	1,073	2.5%*				

Sources: Burnham, William & Co, *Register of Engines*, A-chives Center, National Museum of American History (NMAH.AC.0157); Baldwin Locomotive Works, *Engine Specifications*, Baldwin Locomotive Works Records, Series 2, Specification Books, DeGolyer Library, Southern Methodist University; ALCO, *Register of Contracts*, vols. 1–12 (1900–1912), ALCO Collection, Special Collections Research Center, Syracuse University.

Note: Asterisk (*) indicates average percentages.

WAR, EMPIRE BUILDING, AND THE LOCOMOTIVE TRADE

maintenance and facilitate batch ordering. In contrast, British manufacturers slow to adopt and adapt were forced into decline. Production innovation thus became the main factor in the reversed fortunes of British and American locomotive manufacturers during this period.

Finally, locomotive manufacturers in Germany, the other emerging nation in locomotive manufacturing, commenced exports to Japan in the latter half of 1880. The first two German locomotives exported were A. L. Hohenzollern vehicles delivered to Hankai Railway in 1885. Next, Kyushu Railway, established in 1888, was the first Japanese trunk line operator to use locomotives manufactured by Krauss and Hohenzollern.[33] Yuzawa examines how this occurred,[34] while my previous work shows how Illies & Co., a famous trading company, promoted German products in Japan.[35] These studies suggest that the Japanese government strongly recommended that Kyushu Railway purchase German-made railroad materials to further diplomatic negotiations related to revising Germany's unequal treaties with Japan. Kyushu bowed to pressure on this last point and purchased German technology through Illies, since its receipt of state subsidies meant it had little standing to object; furthermore, it lacked the capacity for railroad construction, which led it to choose a general contract.[36] Moreover, the German government initially introduced its domestically made locomotives to Kyushu through sales promotion, which several German states in the second half of the nineteenth century competitively engaged in to boost industrialization. Heavy industry developed rapidly due to strong protectionism by local governments,[37] and the central government's aggressive marketing to Japan was part of this policy strategy.

In the 1890s, the prices of Krauss's locomotives, one of German locomotives' representatives, were all slightly lower than those of British locomotives in the same class.[38] From this, it is evident that German manufacturers already rivaled British manufacturers in price, with the latter criticizing the former's low prices and blaming the German government for dumping and other protectionist policies.[39] However, German products were already gaining a reputation for quality by the end of the 1890s. Kyushu Railway, apparently satisfied with the quality of Krauss's locomotives, exclusively purchased the same until 1898. As a result, Krauss locomotives

WAR, EMPIRE BUILDING, AND THE LOCOMOTIVE TRADE

accounted for 98 percent of the German locomotives in Japan as of 1897, excepting those used for light railroads.

Germany's sudden emergence marked the most noteworthy change in the locomotive manufacturing industry worldwide at the start of the twentieth century. Japan's interest in Germany around this time is evinced by the inclusion of German firms on the IGR's 1902 list of approved manufacturers.[40] A September 1903 article in the *Tetsudō jihō* pointed out that Germany's locomotive manufacturing industry had "made great strides" and offered "extremely low prices" thanks to heavy subsidization by its government.[41] German manufacturers used this to their advantage in competitive tenders such as the IGR's request for thirty tank locomotives on August 14, 1903. The results reveal that the German trading companies substantially undercut bids by their Japanese, British, and American counterparts.[42] For example, in the first tender for six tank locomotives, whereas the first-, second-, and third-lowest bids (Illies-Schwartzkopff, Ōkura Gumi-Borsig, and M. Raspe-Hanomag) hovered around 12,000 pounds, Mitsui Bussan–ALCO's bid of 12,639 pounds was substantially higher.[43]

Price differentials reflected each country's domestic economic circumstances at the time, as a *Tetsudō jihō* article on competition between German and American manufacturers noted:

> Because the prices of locomotives produced by British manufacturers tend to be high; orders for British locomotives are on a downward trend. Meanwhile, because of sizeable domestic demand, American manufacturers tend to hesitate to accept orders from overseas . . . the bid per locomotive tendered by American manufacturers for a Japanese order was US$1,000 higher than that tendered by German manufacturers. . . . Germany claims that the reason why its manufacturers are able to produce locomotives so cheaply has to do with the extremely low cost of its labor.[44]

A domestic U.S. boom from 1901 to 1903 decreased American manufacturers' overseas exports, of which those to East Asia formed a tiny share of total production (table 5.1). In contrast, as the article notes, the German domestic market experienced a slump that depressed wages and production costs, the latter declining in tandem with the former. Furthermore, led by its machine tool industry, Germany enthusiastically adopted the American system around the turn of the century. In 1897, Ludwig Loewe became the first private machine factory to utilize the limit gauge system; it then developed its own precision fit system in 1903 that enabled interchangeable production with machine finishing, which spread on adoption by Borsig and other domestic manufacturers.[45]

In short, upon entering the 1900s, German manufacturers gained a comparative advantage in terms of pricing, product quality, and time-to-delivery. This led both German government and private railroads to use domestic locomotives on a trial basis, a development the president of Nippon Railway commented on: "German-made locomotives are between JPY 1,500 to 2,000 cheaper per car than British-made locomotives. Compound engines are JPY 3,000 cheaper per car. Although there is no doubt that the German locomotives are less expensive, I have concerns about completely switching to them. For starters, our company has little experience with German locomotives; even if things go smoothly at the start, problems may well arise sometime later. As such, I have decided to first order eight locomotives as a trial."[46] This trial began not with small tank locomotives but with compound engines and other large models. Given Nippon Railway's prominence in Japan, this presented an opportune moment for German manufacturers to demonstrate the superiority of their locomotives to prospective Japanese clients.

Shima Yasujirō, a mechanical engineer for the Railway Bureau, spent a year in Germany in 1903. He did so in part to inspect the production of Nippon's order of compound engines. Shima would later play a key role in Japan's localizing locomotives as head of the Railway Agency's manufacturing section. His series of reports from this period, published in *Tetsudō jihō* throughout 1904 and 1905, described his impressions of the German locomotive manufacturing industry. "I experienced a relatively large number of things new to me," he remarked, "due to my comparatively long stay in Germany and the fact that I had few opportunities to learn about Germany before leaving Japan."[47] He praised the country's enterprising ethos, observing that "the top speed of German trains may be slightly inferior to the top speeds of trains from [the United Kingdom and United States]. However, they have become much faster than before, both trains and rolling stocks are better suited for direct service than their British and American counterparts . . . and they are keen on progress and advancement. They are continuously conducting experiments and research. Germany was quicker to switch to electricity as the motive power for trains in heavy-traffic areas than Britain."[48]

In addition to interchangeable production, Germany's proactive adoption of superheated steam locomotives around this time sharpened its comparative technological edge. At Henschel, Shima observed the development of a train with a top speed of 130 kilometers per hour, and he was impressed by the prospect of high-speed travel based on the newly developed compound engine that used Schmidt-type superheated steam engines. This experience undoubtedly influenced his later decision, as a Railway Agency official, to import superheated steam locomotives from Germany. That said, large German locomotives at the time remained in the testing phase, and Japanese railroads hardly transitioned to new models overnight. The transaction that marked Germany's full-fledged entry into the Japanese market was a batch order, made during the Russo-Japanese War, for over 230 tank locomotives from Henschel, Borsig, Schwartzkopff, and Hanomag.

IMPERIAL EXPANSION AND AMERICAN LOCOMOTIVE EXPORTS

FRAZAR, BALDWIN, AND THE RUSSO-JAPANESE WAR

To learn how locomotive manufacturers and trading companies responded to the substantial changes in the East Asian locomotive market from the Russo-Japanese War up to the start of World War I, let us examine two cases of manufacturers with agent agreements: Frazar-Baldwin and Mitsui Bussan–ALCO. Frazar's unstinting business activities around 1904 drew Japanese interest, as seen from the record of Baldwin locomotive sales it mediated during the Russo-Japanese War.[49] On January 21, 1904, right before the hostilities commenced, Frazar sent Baldwin an order for thirty-six locomotives from the Keifu Railway and another for twenty locomotives from the Keigi Railway.[50] Prior to that point, Frazar had supplied standard-gauge tank locomotives to Keifu, but thirty of the items in this January 1904 order were narrow-gauge tank locomotives for the military's temporary railroads. At the time, the Japanese government was discussing plans for a provisional railroad using the Keifu line to accelerate the construction of a north–south connecting railroad system in the strategically important Korean Peninsula. However, ordering these locomotives directly would expose Japan's preparations for war. Ostensibly for this reason, the orders for this provisional railroad were made under the guise of a private company, in this case Keifu.

Officials ordered fifty-two narrow-gauge locomotives in August 1904 and January 1905, purchasing twenty-five under the name of the government railroad and twenty-seven under that of the Provisional Military Railway Inspectorate. They specified times-to-delivery under one month, scheduling the August order for September and the January order for February of their respective years. These tight temporal margins are even more remarkable considering that the average time-to-delivery in the period 1901–1903 was 7.6 months. Frazar did not only supply locomotives for the military's light railroad; it also received continuous orders for a total of twenty-eight standard-gauge locomotives from Keifu and Keigi between the latter half of 1904 to February 1905, which it supplied with a time-to-delivery around three months. The above illustrates Baldwin's competitive advantage in delivering large numbers of locomotives in a compressed timeframe according to the buyer's needs.

In September 1904, the Railway Operations Bureau allocated one million yen for wartime shipping to speed construction of the provisional railroad.[51] This budget included money for sixty new locomotives and thirteen hundred new freight cars. The locomotives were to be purchased from foreign manufacturers based on negotiated contracts and the freight cars from five domestic manufacturers, including Kisha Seizō.[52] Frazar-Baldwin won contracts to supply fourteen of the locomotives, which were tested before delivery in December of the same year.

In January 1905, the Japanese government simultaneously ordered B6-class (wheel arrangement 0-6-2, figure 5.4) tank locomotives from British, American, and German manufacturers to expand the military railroad fleet—specifically, 174 locomotives from the United Kingdom (NBL), 150 from the United States (Baldwin), and 45 from Germany (Henschel).[53]

For this mass order, Baldwin again had the shortest time-to-delivery, at just two months; it later received another order for fifty F2-class (wheel arrangement 2-8-0) tender locomotives that it sent between August and

FIGURE 5.4 Dübs's 0-6-2 tank locomotive, categorized as a B6 class in the IGR during the Meiji era. The B6 class was a typical tank engine in the IGR. During the Russo-Japanese War, the Japanese government imported many such engines and sent them to the battlefields of Manchuria. After the war, these locomotives returned to Japan, where they were operated by the IGR.

Source: Tetsudō shō, ed., *Nihon tesudō shi chūhen* [A railroad history of Japan, vol. 2] (Tokyo: Tetsudō shō, 1921), n.p.

December 1905. As mentioned above, over 260 locomotives were exported to Japan and the Korean Peninsula in 1905 through mass orders from the government and private railroads to replace locomotives requisitioned for war. As Frazar mediated many of these transactions, it unsurprisingly brokered the sale of 11.7 percent of Baldwin's total production that year.

Frazar-Baldwin's response to the extraordinary demand generated by the war depended on their long-term business relationships with Keifu Railway, the compatibility of American system production with the Japanese military's urgent need for large numbers of locomotives, and sales engineers stationed in Japan. With regard to the last, the role of Vauclain Jr. in Japan, explained in chapter 3, proved particularly important. As mentioned above, in October 1904, deep into the conflict, he met with Hiraoka Hiroshi, the vice president of Kisha Seizō, with whom he exchanged information about locomotive components and agreed to a scheme for supplying locomotives to Manchuria.[54] Because Baldwin had an engineer stationed in Japan, it could negotiate directly with clients and quickly acquire accurate information. The Mitsui Bussan employee responsible for railroad materials at the time praised Frazar-Baldwin's proactive marketing efforts: "Above all else, they work extremely passionately to expand sales. . . . This is carried out by a Westerner . . . who visits railroad companies all around the country to conduct sales activities."[55] These observations by a rival firm dovetail with what we know of Vauclain's active schedule in 1904.

However, it appears that the large numbers of locomotives delivered by Frazar-Baldwin during the war were poorly reputed. Watanabe Hidejirō, an officer of Mitsui Bussan's Machinery and Railway Unit, explained that the locomotives in question used boilers made for temperate climates that could not withstand continental China's freezing weather. This failure, likely the result of a problem with the specification sheet at the time of ordering, affected Baldwin's reputation to the point that its very participation in tenders came into question. On this point, Mitsui Bussan reported in 1906 that Frazar had recently been taking a cautious approach.[56] But on the occasion of the tender conducted by the SMR in 1907, Frazar-Baldwin found itself well behind its rival, Mitsui Bussan–ALCO.

MITSUI BUSSAN–ALCO LOCOMOTIVE EXPORTS TO EAST ASIA

Mitsui Bussan's trade in railroad materials business peaked in the second half of 1900, declined during a recession in Japan, and recovered in 1903 through a materials purchase agreement with the Tokyo Electric Railway. However, the outbreak of the Russo-Japanese War in 1904 produced another contraction.[57] Why did Mitsui Bussan shy away from the locomotive trade right after the start of the war, while Frazar proactively sought and won orders? Some clues to this puzzle appear in its company report issued that year, which offered the following explanation: "Railroad materials . . . yield relatively low profits despite their high prices. They have become even more unprofitable due to difficulties related to financing and shipping caused by the present state of affairs. For this reason, [Mitsui Bussan] avoids taking orders as much as possible."[58] As this document illustrates, Mitsui Bussan adopted a cautious approach immediately after the conflict's inception. This would resemble its later response to World War I and may be considered its basic strategy during emergencies. However, with regard to the business opportunities created by the massive wartime demand in 1904, this stance made it fall behind the rival alliances of Ōkura Gumi–NBL and Frazar-Baldwin.

The East Asian market offered a plethora of business opportunities after the Russo-Japanese War, and following the Railway Nationalization Act of March 1906, Mitsui Bussan received a stream of locomotive orders from companies slated for government takeover.[59] This started with 12 for Nippon Railway and 30 for Kyushu Railway in April, with 3 for Hankaku Railway and 15 for Kansei Railway added in May, and 26 for Hokkaido Colliery and Railway in June 1907. ALCO began production immediately upon receiving these orders at its numerous factories: Rogers took Nippon, Schenectady had Kyushu and Hankaku, and Pittsburgh did Kansei.[60] Kyushu appears to have hurriedly ordered tender locomotives of the same type made by Schenectady in 1904 via negotiated contract. The time-to-delivery for these orders ranged from four to eight months, which was not especially short compared to the two to three months during the Russo-Japanese War. However, because the locomotives had to arrive in Japan by the purchase date (i.e., the start of railroad nationalization), all factories opted for the transpacific shipping route via the Great Northern Railroad, including overland transport, instead of the conventional transatlantic shipping route via the Suez Canal.

The next large order came from the SMR, which as discussed earlier had ordered more than two hundred standard-gauge locomotives from the United States in 1907–1908. Mitsui Bussan–ALCO mediated most of the placements and ordered 143 locomotives in February 1907, of which ALCO's factories manufactured 104 at Richmond, 31 at Cooke, 6 at Rogers, and 2 at Rhode Island. The vast majority of locomotives from this first order went to the Richmond factory, including sixty-nine tanks and thirty-five tenders. The times-to-delivery for these locomotives and for the thirty-one tenders manufactured in the Cooke factory ranged from seven to twelve months, which was considered long for American manufacturers. However, as the Rogers and Rhode Island factories drew on surplus stock from previous orders by the Chicago and Southern Railroad and Minnesota Land and Construction, their locomotives had a time-to-delivery of three weeks. The standard-gauge construction of the SMR locomotives made it possible for manufacturers that usually dealt with custom orders to utilize stock products. Accordingly, the first locomotives reached Dalian at the end of June 1907, just three months after order placement.[61]

The second SMR order occurred from May to July of 1907 and included 40 tender locomotives for delivery between January and February 1908. Of these, ALCO assigned 15 to the Cooke factory and 25 to Richmond. Railroad nationalization and the SMR's establishment resulted in a total of 275 locomotives ordered, a figure that increases to 342 in the 1906–1908 period if locomotives purchased by the IGR and Yokohama Railway are included.[62] Mitsui Bussan's railroad material transactions doubled in value from the second half of 1907 to the first half of 1908 and accounted for 10 percent of all transactions it handled in the second half of the same year.[63] Iwahara Kenzō, who had played a leading role in exporting American locomotives to Japan, triumphantly announced that the company had achieved record-breaking sales for the first half of this year through winning SMR orders.[64] Although Mitsui Bussan–ALCO entered late into the market created by the Russo-Japanese War, their success afterward more than made up for any earlier missed opportunities.

As previously mentioned, the IGR essentially became a monopoly after nationalization, operating 90 percent of railroad tracks and 95 percent of rolling stocks. Shortly thereafter, the head of Mitsui Bussan's Railway Unit, an officer named Yamamoto Koshirō (figure 3.9, right side), expected railroad nationalization to induce the following three changes: increased competition due to the convergence of tenders previously conducted by individual companies into a single tender, the enlarged scale of each tender, and reduced profits from handling fees due to this increased competition. He therefore argued that Mitsui Bussan should do its utmost to win contracts from the IGR and also sell materials to railroads in mainland China.[65]

With regard to Yamamoto's first conclusion, Mitsui Bussan began winning orders from the Railway Agency around 1911. In fact, it garnered a sizeable share of the agency's tenders between 1911 and 1913 compared to its nearest competitors,[66] and it emerged victorious in the fierce competition for orders even amid a domestic market contraction. However, in the first half of 1912, Mitsui Bussan brokered only 3.4 percent of railroad material imports into Japan.[67] Although it enjoyed large slices of the import pie in areas including locomotives and accessories, it had a minute share of rails, bridges, and construction materials, which made up the vast majority of imported railroad goods. Here, trading companies with ties to major British, American, and German manufacturers enjoyed an overwhelming advantage.[68] The intense competition for contracts post-nationalization is likely to have increased the importance of close relationships with manufacturers, especially in developing price quotes and agent agreements or similar arrangements. This explains how Frazar and Illies, both foreign trading companies, maintained shares above 30 percent for railroad goods imports.

On the other hand, Mitsui Bussan had expressed interest in exporting goods to China, and it dispatched Yoshikawa Sanjirō and Ogawa Shigen, both former IGR engineers, to inspect railroads in Fujian, Jiangxi,

WAR, EMPIRE BUILDING, AND THE LOCOMOTIVE TRADE

Zhejiang, Hubei, and Jiangsu around 1900.[69] In particular, Yoshikawa's detailed investigation of the railroad line between Xiamen (Amoy) and Fuzhou from February to June 1900 deserves special attention.[70] After the Russo-Japanese War, Mitsui Bussan–ALCO began full-fledged efforts to sell locomotives in the area south of the Yangtze River known as Nansei, starting with three locomotives to the Yue–Han (Guangdong–Hankow) Railway in February 1907.[71] China at the time was seeing a railroad boom funded by foreign investment. However, as the materials for construction came from merchants with strong ties to their respective governments, Japanese trading companies could not break into this market, which is why Mitsui Bussan concentrated on selling to private Chinese-owned railroads operating south of the Yangtze.[72]

Since the construction of private Chinese-funded railroads was just starting, railroad companies had little expertise in selecting materials and creating specification documents. Mitsui Bussan provided assistance and advice in these areas while trying to sell locomotives, a process Yamamoto described as follows:

> The railroad established in Shanghai, Jiangsu Province, is called the Jiangsu Railway. [Its officials] have not yet decided what kind of locomotives they want to purchase. When I examined the locomotive they said they might want to purchase, it was [a type] suitable for pulling heavy freight cars. After a lengthy discussion, when I explained that it was a locomotive for pulling heavy freight cars and asked if that was okay, they said no, they also needed something to pull passenger cars. I replied that this locomotive was not well suited to that purpose. To which they responded by asking what kind of locomotive would be suitable. When I recommended a certain locomotive, they asked about the price. At the end of extended negotiations, I was finally able to win an order of three locomotives.[73]

As the above description illustrates, building business relationships with private Chinese railroads required diligence and time. Aside from the SMR, selling railroad materials to Chinese firms was far from easy. Mitsui

Bussan's business report from 1909 lamented that "the Chinese railroad industry awards exclusive supply contracts to foreign trading companies in exchange for investing foreign currency into the railroads. As such, we have only received orders for locomotives and freight cars from the handful of private railroads in Nanxun and Zhejiang. Due to the decline in orders from the U.S. according to the SMR's policy and the fact that industries in this country have not yet recovered, our sales remain dull."[74] Nevertheless, the company began full-fledged exports of railroad materials to China from World War I onward.

Overall, the Sino-Japanese and Russo-Japanese Wars sped Japan's empire building and induced structural changes in the East Asian locomotive market by expanding Japan's sphere of influence to Korea and northeastern China. However, the fledgling state of Japanese locomotive manufacturing led American manufacturers, especially Baldwin, to capitalize on this opportunity. For 1904–1905, Japan's imperial sphere was the most significant global market for American locomotives. But after the Russo-Japanese War, the IGR's post-nationalization monopoly reduced profit margins in Japan. Having eliminated competition in procuring railroad materials, the IGR also began promoting domestic locomotives after 1909. This rapidly shrank the Japanese market for imported locomotives, which had temporarily expanded at the time of railroad nationalization.

On the other hand, the Chinese locomotive market grew during this period. In 1906, the imperial Japanese government established the SMR and procured over two hundred locomotives from ALCO and other American manufacturers. In addition, foreign and Chinese capital drove the construction of trunk line railroads in central and southern China. Foreseeing that railroad construction in China's vast terrain would create massive demand, American locomotive manufacturers and Japanese trading companies began expanding into the Chinese market in the late 1900s.

6

LOCALIZING LOCOMOTIVE PRODUCTION IN JAPAN

The last phase of Japan's Industrial Revolution after the Russo-Japanese War saw accelerated progress, especially in the heavy industries. Mitsubishi Nagasaki Shipyard, the oldest shipyard in Japan and one of its largest, designed and built large steamships in the late 1900s and large battleships in the mid-1910s. Around the same time, the government-run Yawata Steel Works began full-scale operations that stabilized the supply of rails and other steel products. Kisha Seizō, the leading domestic locomotive manufacturer, produced lightweight locomotives in the 1900s and began supplying railroads domestically and in Taiwan. The accumulation of skilled workers supported these developments, and large factories began to encourage their long-term employment through paternalism combined with direct hiring and management.[1] Railroads also contributed to this process as providers of traffic services and as customers of heavy industry.[2]

Japan's railroads developed mainly through the private sector since the 1890s. However, after nationalization, the government's role expanded dramatically as the IGR came to operate more than 90 percent of the nation's mainline railroads. The Railway Agency, as the IGR's operating entity, promoted domestic locomotive production, backed by the business community's demand to adopt railroads as a symbol of industrialization. Between 1909 and 1914, the agency cultivated design skills to build powerful locomotives and achieved mass production in collaboration with private manufacturers. And in this final stage of progress, Japan again introduced a cutting-edge mechanism—the superheated steam system—from advanced Western countries.

This chapter examines how railroad nationalization and the establishment of the centralized Railway Agency led to the mass production of domestic locomotives from the viewpoint of localization, focusing on its dynamic interplay with globalization and placing particular emphasis on the role of the state. Crucially, the Japanese government advanced technological localization while strategically leveraging globalization. This nuanced approach provides a comprehensive understanding of government strategies and their impact on Japan's development of technology. The analysis below, which focuses on the role of Shima Yasujirō, the director of the Railway Agency's Manufacturing Section, clarifies the effects of the agency's policy to domestically produce rolling stock in 1909 and the process of how Japanese engineers acquired the ability to design and manufacture locomotives.

Shima and his colleagues absorbed technology by repeatedly imitating advanced locomotives from Europe and the United States to eventually develop original models. Their work typifies a key characteristic of technological development in Japanese manufacturing and shows how Japan localized advanced technology introduced from the West. Building locomotives suited to Japanese terrain and demand and mass-producing them to replace imported models was enabled by the IGR's monopoly of the domestic market, price adjustments through tariff policies, and Japanese railroad engineers' willingness to boost domestic production. The success of this endeavor is the first example of railroads serving as a marker of Japan's national identity.

Railroad technology and the state existed in political relationship. For instance, the superheated steam locomotive, a pivotal innovation of the early twentieth century, originated in Germany and swiftly gained global traction, with the United States among its first adopters. Japan also attempted to import model superheated locomotives for imitation production. But the United Kingdom, which lagged in this advance, saw its manufacturers left off the Railway Agency's designated list for bids on these locomotives. Yet North British Locomotive, a leading manufacturer, asked the British government to force the agency to order its locomotives. Tracing this trajectory demonstrates that railroad technology wielded political meaning not only as technological advances but also as a potent symbol of national identity in the early twentieth century.

Meanwhile, Railway Agency policies impacted the locomotive trade in East Asian markets. After the early 1910s, the IGR stopped importing foreign locomotives and procured original ones from domestic manufacturers. Its withdrawal from locomotive imports slashed the market for imported locomotives in Japan and shifted global trade to Japan's colonies and spheres of influence, including Northeastern China, a process I examine based on the case of Mitsui Bussan.

Finally, this chapter deepens discussion of the characteristics particular to Japan's domestic locomotive production by comparing it to other machinery industries such as shipbuilding. Doing so shows that the success of industrialization in Japan was no mere coincidence but the result of strategic investments in engineering education and the astute utilization of global competition to introduce technology effectively.

PROMOTING DOMESTIC LOCOMOTIVE PRODUCTION

RAILROAD NATIONALIZATION AND MONOPSONY ESTABLISHMENT

In March 1906, the Imperial Diet decided that the government should purchase the tracks of seventeen domestic private railroads and the Keifu Railway in Korea. The purchase prices for the seventeen private railroads were calculated between October 1906 and October 1907 with the formula

$P = C \times R \times 20$, where P was the purchase price, C the construction costs as of the day of purchase, and R the average profit ratio between late 1902 and early 1905.[3] Based on this formula, the purchase price could be maximized only by increasing the construction costs (i.e., capital investment) on the day of purchase. However, since private railroads lacked adequate time to begin new construction of track, they strove to accomplish as much repair work as possible and purchase new locomotives over the remaining period. Accordingly, in 1906 they placed massive bulk orders with American manufacturers that could deliver with short lead times. ALCO received orders for seventy-one cars, as mentioned in chapter 5, while Baldwin received orders for twenty;[4] here, too, British manufacturers found themselves completely shut out.

The Imperial Railway Office, established in April 1907, inaugurated the new Imperial Government Railways that administered the nationalized lines and the former IGR. In December 1908, it merged with the Ministry of Communications and Transportation's Railway Bureau to form a single office, the Railway Agency, which operated and oversaw the national railroad system. The agency managed approximately 4,400 miles of nationalized track, which comprised 90 percent of the total length of Japan's approximately 4,900 miles of track at the time, and it operated 95 percent of locomotives by the end of 1907 (figure 0.3). This established a monopsony that directly reflected the agency's intentions in terms of locomotive demand and created an immediate impact.

The agency did not order significant amounts of materials in 1908, partly due to the purchasing rush during 1906 and 1907 by railroads slated for nationalization. For this reason, locomotive exports to Japan fell dramatically in 1909 (figure 0.2). However, German manufacturers expanded their share after 1909, reflecting the agency's full-fledged trials of their locomotives. Germany emerged as the top exporter to Japan in 1911–1912, when its imported locomotives served as models for domestic manufacturers, and it remained an active exporter of locomotive parts and small-scale locomotives. Meanwhile, American manufacturers began to focus on East Asian markets outside Japan, starting with the SMR's mass purchase of locomotives.

THE RAILWAY AGENCY AND ITS MANUFACTURING SECTION

Gotō Shinpei, the minister of communications and transportation, established the Railway Agency in December 1908 to operate and supervise Japan's railroads, and he assumed the position of its president. The agency set up General Affairs, Transportation, Construction, and Accounting Departments in Tokyo to carry out its primary administrative functions, and it further established five bureaus in Hokkaido, Eastern Japan, Central Japan, Western Japan, and Kyushu to oversee operations in these regions. This organizational structure assigned rolling stock engineers to the Manufacturing Section of the Transportation Department in Tokyo (hereafter the Manufacturing Section) as well as to the manufacturing sections of individual railroad administration bureaus and the factories they operated.

The Manufacturing Section's duties comprised tasks related to the design of rolling stock, tools and equipment, machinery, and traffic signals; the inspection and preparation of materials for manufacture and repair; facilities and factory design; the supervision of manufacturing and repair; finally, the organization and storing of ledgers and charts/blueprints.[5] This list shows that the office was a discrete entity with specific responsibilities in these areas. Notably, the establishment of a section dedicated to designing rolling stock indicating that Japan's technology on this front had fully entered domestic development.

Lower-ranked manufacturing sections within the regional railroad administration bureaus also handled a wide range of tasks, including the design and operation of production factories, the manufacture and repair of rolling stock, the procurement of materials for these purposes, and the settlement of budgets.[6] However, compared to the pre-nationalization period, the supervision of rolling stock design and manufacture concentrated in the Manufacturing Section restricted these lower sections' authority to develop new vehicles.[7]

Here it is worth examining the makeup of engineers in the Manufacturing Section and its counterparts in the five regional railroad bureaus as well as in the main factories of Omiya, Shinbashi, and Takatori.[8] With the exception of the bureau for Central Japan (including the Shinbashi factory), which was strongly influenced by the former Railway Operations Bureau, each of these bureaus retained the influence of the former major railroad companies in their respective regions (i.e., Hokkaido Colliery and Railway in Hokkaido, Nippon Railway in Eastern Japan, Sanyo Railway in Western Japan, and Kyushu Railway in Kyushu). Such residual influence was evident in the case of the Western Japan bureau, where Sanyo's Takatori factory absorbed the functions of the former government factory in Kobe that built Japan's first locomotive.[9] This bureau's inaugural director was Iwasaki Hikomatsu, the former chief of Sanyo's train section, and it was largely staffed by former Sanyo employees.

Moreover, none other than Shima Yasujirō led the Manufacturing Section's rolling stock development efforts. As described in chapter 3, despite Shima's lack of experience with the IGR, Gotō Shinpei chose him to head the locomotive design section over Mori Hikozō and Shiba Gontarō, both older candidates with ample experience at the IGR.[10] At the time, seven of the Manufacturing Section's eight members had graduated from the Tokyo Imperial University's Department of Mechanical Engineering; the exception was Nogami Yaeji, who had worked his way up from being a draftsman. Despite their largely uniform educational history, these engineers had a spectrum of experiences, with two originally employed by the IGR, two by Nippon, one by Sanyo, and two new university graduates. Furthermore, Aoyama Yoichi, previously chief of the IGR Train Department's design section, had studied in the Europe and the United States, while Ikeda Masahiko (ex-IGR) and Akiyama Shōhachi (ex-Nippon) were undergoing their own overseas studies.[11] Takasu Seiji had been the former design leader in Nippon's Omiya factory, and Nogami, the former chief of Sanyo's design section, had worked on the first locomotives manufactured by private railroads. And Ōta Yoshimatsu, a distinguished skilled draftsman, joined as a skilled senior worker who had designed locomotives at the Kobe factory.[12] Gotō and Shima thus sought to improve the Railway Agency's manufacturing capacity by assembling a team of engineers with diverse skills and backgrounds.[13]

LOCALIZING LOCOMOTIVE PRODUCTION IN JAPAN

PROMOTING DOMESTIC LOCOMOTIVE PRODUCTION AND NURTURING PRIVATE MANUFACTURERS

Because the Railway Agency oversaw the seventeen nationalized private railroads and the IGR, it found itself saddled with a wide array of locomotives in varying forms and specifications, which greatly hindered its operations. Furthermore, the Manufacturing Section had to deal with numerous locomotives sent back from Manchuria that had been used during the Russo-Japanese War. On assuming the section's leadership, Shima Yasujirō reported feeling overwhelmed by handling the variegated fleet and returned locomotives.[14] In this context, the section proposed a policy in 1909 to purchase locomotives and passenger cars from domestic manufacturers as much as possible. This policy was also the result of a lobbying effort by major manufacturers including Kisha Seizō, Kawasaki Dockyard, and Nippon Sharyō.[15] These three companies chose the industrialist Shibusawa Eiichi, an auditor for Kisha Seizō and president of the Dai-Ichi Bank, to represent them in an appeal for the government to purchase their products that they made to Katsura Tarō, Gotō Shinpei, and other top bureaucrats at the end of 1908.[16]

As discussed in chapter 5, Kisha Seizō was a rolling stock manufacturer established in 1896 by Inoue Masaru, the former director general of the Railway Bureau. It had the investment and cooperation of notable figures including Shibusawa Eiichi, Inoue Kaoru, and Iwasaki Hisaya, president of the Mitsubishi Gōshi (Mitsubishi Limited Partnership Company). In 1895, after inviting Hasegawa Shōgo, formerly from Nippon Railway, to be its chief engineer, it began constructing a factory in Osaka, but this facility only commenced operation in July 1899 owing to construction delays from the late arrival of imported materials. As a consequence, Kisha Seizō was shut out of the railroad boom after the first Sino-Japanese War and struggled to find its footing. In June 1899, it hired Hiraoka Hiroshi, a former IGR engineer running an independent rolling stock manufacturer in Tokyo. Hiraoka became Kisha Seizō's vice president and merged his firm into the company's Tokyo branch in June 1901,[17] making it Japan's largest locomotive manufacturer by the end of the Russo-Japanese War.

LOCALIZING LOCOMOTIVE PRODUCTION IN JAPAN

Kawasaki Dockyard, a Tokyo-based ship manufacturer established by Kawasaki Shōzō in 1878, provides a study in contrast. In 1886, it purchased the formerly government-operated Hyogo Shipyard, and in 1896 it reorganized as a corporation with a capital stock of two million yen. Matsukata Kōjirō, its president at the time (and the third son of former Prime Minister Matsukata Masayoshi), went on to proactively diversify the firm's business, leading it to open a new factory in 1906 and enter the market for rolling stock. Although this enterprise began with the manufacture of passenger and freight cars as well as electric trains, it gradually accrued the facilities and personnel necessary for locomotive production. After winning its first order for locomotives from the Railway Agency in 1909, it hired Ōta Yoshimatsu of the IGR's Manufacturing Section, earlier introduced, to increase its locomotive manufacturing capacity. Thereafter, it rapidly expanded its facilities and overtook Kisha Seizō as Japan's top locomotive manufacturer in just four years.[18]

Nippon Sharyō, the final company involved, was a rolling stock manufacturer established in 1896 by a group of wealthy individuals and entrepreneurs in Nagoya. For its chief engineer it hired Hattori Tsutomu,[19] an experienced maker of rolling stock at the IGR's Kobe factory. However, it made no locomotives throughout the Meiji era, instead specializing in passenger cars, freight cars, and electric trains. It delivered its first batch of freight cars to the government railroad in 1903 and stood on par with Kisha Seizō in terms of passenger and freight car production.[20]

Around 1909, Kisha Seizō was Japan's only rolling stock manufacturer with the ability to produce locomotives. But the stage for the entry of private locomotive manufacturers was being set as Kawasaki Dockyard and other emergent firms built factories dedicated to rolling stock and hired prominent locomotive engineers. Meanwhile, the Railway Agency, while struggling to organize the diversity of locomotives it had acquired after railroad nationalization, saw domestic production as an opportunity to unify and standardize rolling stock types.[21] It further drafted plans for a special express train to link Tokyo and Shimonoseki, the westernmost city on Japan's mainland, which would facilitate transportation to the Korean Peninsula and South Manchuria as Japan's new imperial territories. The agency's plan for domestic production included a liaison with the SMR, where Gotō Shinpei, its own president, had recently been employed. To succeed, it would require high-speed locomotives and powerful ones designed to climb steep slopes, neither of which existed in Japan.[22] Shima thus imported the latest locomotive models and sought manufacturing expertise through public-private collaboration.[23] In this regard, one of the innovations he emphasized was the superheater technology he had observed in Germany.

THE DEVELOPMENT AND SPREAD OF
SUPERHEATED STEAM LOCOMOTIVES

The difference between superheated and saturated steam locomotives lies in whether the steam generated is sent directly to the cylinder or heated en route to retain its high temperature; in the former, a superheater device performs secondary heating. Although a superheating engine had been formulated in England in the 1850s during the early stages of steam locomotives, it lacked materials suitable for the water pipes, which bore enormous pressure during reheating, and cylinder lubricating oil capable of withstanding high temperatures. But advances in steel manufacturing enabled the practical application of superheaters at the end of the nineteenth century.[24]

In the 1880s, Wilhelm Schmidt developed a type of superheater attached to a fire-tube boiler that he attempted to apply to steam locomotives (figure 6.1).[25] In 1898, this was adopted by the Prussian State Railways, and the Borsig superheated locomotive at the 1900 World's Fair in Paris attracted strong interest, as discussed in *The Engineer*:

> The Paris Exhibition gives evidence of the remarkable activity among continental engineers in the development of the use of superheated steam. The aim of these efforts is, of course, to avoid the immense losses due to cylinder condensation. The seriousness of these losses was probably first fully established in England; but the efficacy of the cure of the evil by

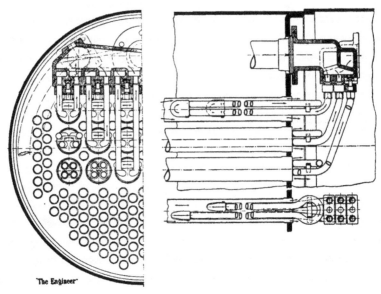

Schmidt Locomotive Superheater

FIGURE 6.1 Internal diagram of the Schmidt superheater. This superheater is attached to the fire-tube boiler and provides secondary heating to improve efficiency by reducing the consumption of coal and water. Wilhelm Schmidt designed and developed this superheater during the 1880s, and it was adopted by the Prussian State Railways in 1898. By the early twentieth century, superheated locomotives had gained popularity worldwide.

Source: Robert Garbe, *The Application of Highly Superheated Steam to Locomotives* (New York: Norman W. Henley Publishing Co., 1908), 32.

means of superheating has been practically proved chiefly through the enterprise and intelligence of Wilhelm Schmidt, of Kassel, whose success in this direction is already well known and recognized in England, and whose patents are now being worked by many different firms in various European countries.[26]

In addition, the journal described the spread of the superheater in Germany as follows:

LOCALIZING LOCOMOTIVE PRODUCTION IN JAPAN

The first locomotive with a superheater seems to have been built [in 1898] at the Vulcan Works in Stettin. It is an express running on the Hanover line, and, considering that it was the first experimental machine built, the results are said to be satisfactory in a high degree. A second improved one followed, and the locomotive we illustrate in this issue is a third, in which the experience gained by the use of the first two on the line was fully utilized in the careful design of all such details as are dependent on, or are influenced by, the superheating. It was built by A. Borsig, of Berlin, for the Prussian State Railways.[27]

In fact, the Prussian State Railways purchased two Schmidt-type superheated locomotives in 1898 and four more in 1899, thereafter expanding its fleet by twenty-four and thirty-nine more such locomotives in 1902 and 1904 respectively.[28] Superheated locomotives thus gained steam in Europe around 1900, and Shima's visit to Germany in 1903 coincided with this expansion.

North America became the next region to adopt superheated locomotives. At the St. Louis World Fair in March 1905, Hanomag's compound locomotive, which boasted a record-setting speed of 82 miles (132 kilometers) per hour, drew much attention.[29] It triggered the growing use of superheated locomotives in the United States in this period,[30] with the Schmidt and Schenectady models used by Baldwin and ALCO, respectively, gaining traction.[31] For example, the Canadian Pacific Railway began the full-fledged introduction of Schenectady-type superheated locomotives in 1906.[32] These reportedly performed well over the first six months, reducing the costs of freight transport by 10–15 percent and those of passenger transport by 15–20 percent relative to conventional locomotives.[33] North American agents thus recognized superheated locomotives' usefulness in the 1900s, soon after their emergence.

Compared to Germany and the United States, which housed emerging locomotive manufacturing companies, Britain, the birthplace of railroads, lagged on adopting superheated systems. Robert Garbe, a German privy councilor and the chief engineer of the Prussian State Railways, published a series of articles in *The Engineer* from October to December 1907 discussing the application of this innovation.[34] In January 1908, the journal followed up with the results of the Canadian Pacific Railway's six-month-long trial of superheated locomotives.[35] This sparked discussion even in the United Kingdom and ultimately led to several British railroads testing superheated locomotives in 1909. Nonetheless, skepticism regarding the efficacy of this technology remained strong until around 1910, for reasons that ranged from the difficulty of adjusting pistons and valves[36] to the theoretical superiority of its fuel efficiency not always being shown in actual results,[37] and even the increased risk of explosions.[38]

The results of trial operations of superheated locomotives conducted in the United Kingdom and its colonies, including Egypt and South Africa, began arriving in early 1910.[39] They demonstrated cost reductions of 20–25 percent and facilitated the spread of superheated locomotives in these areas thereafter.[40] Despite the growing recognition of their advantages,[41] adoption in the United Kingdom progressed slowly due to the persistent view that—in the words of a contributor to *The Engineer*—"there is still no proof that this has any impact on improving horsepower."[42] As a consequence, the United Kingdom soon found itself well behind Germany and the United States.

IMPORTING MODEL LOCOMOTIVES

As previously mentioned, Shima Yasujirō saw German superheated locomotives as a potential method to improve fuel economy in express trains. This, along with the spread of superheated locomotives to the United States, led him to add the use of superheaters on high-speed passenger locomotives to the list of requirements set forth in Japan's 1909 shift to domestic production. Thereafter, mass-produced domestic locomotives developed in three parallel courses: for lightweight passenger trains, high-speed passenger trains, and freight trains, with the last two being superheated types.[43]

Mori Hikozō, chief of the Shinbashi factory, carried out the basic design of locomotives for lightweight passenger trains, with Ōta Yoshimatsu preparing detailed designs. The first model produced in this manner was a saturated steam-type tender locomotive. After completing the design for this model, Ōta, who R. F. Trevithick had described as "conferred with full mastership," took a leave of absence from the Railway Agency in 1910 and moved to Kawasaki Dockyard, where he helped manufacture eighty-eight of these locomotives for lightweight passenger trains between 1914 and 1918.[44]

While lightweight locomotives were thus designed entirely in Japan, no Japanese engineer had experience with large-scale locomotives for high-speed passenger trains intended for the Tokyo–Shimonoseki express service (commenced in 1912) and the Mallet-type compound locomotives for steep grades. Accordingly, models for these had to be imported from Europe and the United States.[45] In 1910, the Railway Agency ordered sixty passenger locomotives and six steep-grade locomotives from the United Kingdom, the United States, and Germany for this purpose. The main specifications for the former group included being of the superheated steam type,[46] while the latter had to be of the saturated steam type.[47]

At the end of March 1910, having decided the locomotives that would serve as models, Shima headed to Europe along with his subordinate Asakura Kiichi[48] for the Eighth International Railway Conference in Bern, Switzerland. After the conference, they planned to move to Germany, where they would study railroad electrification and supervise the production of the Railway Agency's superheated locomotives.[49] Around September 1910, Shima's interim successor as chief of the Manufacturing Section, Shiba Gonzaburō,[50] announced a private tender for the Railway Agency's sixty-six locomotives to the specifications described above.[51] Its designated manufacturers in Germany, the United States, and the United Kingdom included Borsig and Schwartzkopff, ALCO and Baldwin, and the NBL. Through this series of orders, the agency sought to obtain not only the model locomotives but also information regarding their manufacturing process. It thus dispatched Shima to Berlin with the goal of acquiring such knowledge from Borsig and Schwartzkopff.

Locomotive manufacturers greeted this news with excitement partly because it meant that the Railway Agency was once again planning bulk orders, which had not occurred since railroad nationalization. On October 17, Beyer Peacock, which had been excluded from the list of designated manufacturers due to its lack of experience with superheaters, wrote to the British embassy in Japan for support, whose ambassador immediately appealed to the Japanese government for the firm's inclusion in the tender. These efforts paid off, and Beyer Peacock took part through a Japanese trading company with a branch office in London.[52] Its addition raised the number of designated manufacturers to six, with two each from the United Kingdom, the United States, and Germany.

Ōkura Gumi prepared for the tender as NBL's sales agent, with its Tokyo and London offices maintaining close communication. On October 7, the Tokyo office sent a telegram informing its London branch of a slight change in boiler tube dimensions for the six Mallet-type compound locomotives, which the latter immediately conveyed to NBL.[53] However, NBL sent no quote or blueprint, and Ōkura Gumi's London office, concerned that these documents would not arrive in time for the tender deadline on December 1, 1910, issued another letter demanding a response on November 5.[54] Later that month, the London office explained to Tokyo that, although it could relay the price quote on November 28 via telegraph, it had instructed NBL to send the specifications and blueprints directly to Tokyo, as they would otherwise not be delivered in time.[55] In the end, the price quote and required documents from NBL met the deadline, and Ōkura Gumi successfully submitted a bid.[56] But shortly thereafter, the Tokyo office informed London that the announcement of the tender results would be delayed by a few weeks.[57]

In the tender for model locomotives, the sixty passenger locomotives presented the biggest problem. While Borsig and Schwartzkopff submitted blueprints for superheated tender locomotives (figure 6.2) without issue, ALCO's blueprints for a similar locomotive did not meet the specifications issued in the wheel arrangement (figure 6.3),[58] and neither did NBL's blueprints for a saturated steam–type tender locomotive. The Railway Agency thus struggled with handling these latter two manufacturers' deviations from its requirements.[59]

NBL had at that point little experience manufacturing superheated locomotives. According to the firm's order list, it first manufactured such a locomotive for the Buenos Aires and Pacific Railway on July 22, 1909.[60] This

LOCALIZING LOCOMOTIVE PRODUCTION IN JAPAN

inexperience explains why it took so long to prepare a price quote and ended up submitting a proposal for a different kind of locomotive only after Ōkura Gumi's persistent urging. Moreover, because the blueprints were sent at the last minute, neither Ōkura Gumi's London office nor its Tokyo headquarters had time to vet them prior to submission.

Concerned about the risk of NBL's proposal being excluded from consideration, Ōkura Gumi's Tokyo office sent a letter to the London branch office instructing it to ask NBL to appeal to the British embassy in Japan to exert its influence in this matter.[61] The letter arrived on December 23, and the London office telegraphed NBL on the morning of December 24.[62]

FIGURE 6.2 Borsig's 8850-class 4-6-0 tender locomotive. This is a superheated tender locomotive with four leading wheels and three driving wheels. It was one of the model locomotives ordered by the Railway Agency in 1910 and categorized as 8850 class by Japan National Railways. Borsig, a manufacturer of this engine, was one of the leading locomotive manufacturers in Germany. The inspectors of this engine were Shima Yasujirō and Asakura Kiichi.

Source: Tetsudō shō, ed., *Nihon tesudō shi gehen* [A railroad history of Japan, vol. 3] (Tokyo: Tetsudō shō, 1921), n.p.

FIGURE 6.3 ALCO's 8900-class 4-6-2 tender locomotive. This is a superheated tender locomotive built by ALCO with four leading, three driving, and two trailing wheels. It was one of the model locomotives ordered by the Railway Agency in 1910 and categorized 8900 class by Japan National Railways. The original specification did not have the trailing wheels, but ALCO changed the wheel arrangement on its own.

Source: Usui Shgenobu, *Kikansha no keifuzu 4* [Genealogy of Locomotives, vol. 4] (Tokyo: Kōyūsha, 1978), 464. © Kōyūsha.

Upon receiving this request, NBL immediately telegraphed the British Foreign Office and sent a letter addressed to the secretary of state for foreign affairs that made the following case:[63]

> As the international competition for this contract is very keen, we venture to ask the support of your Office in the interests of British industry. The securing of this contract by British locomotive builders would give a much-needed stimulant to the industry, which is at present, and has been for some time past, in a depressed condition. The Entente may count for something in the allocation of the order to this country, and intimation from you that the compliment to their Ally would be appreciated by the British Government would doubtless have great effect.[64]

Of note here is NBL's suggestion that the Anglo-Japanese Alliance of 1902 could impact business affairs; the above exchanges highlight how both a Japanese trading company and a British manufacturer aimed to use this treaty to their advantage.

On December 24, 1910, the British Foreign Office telegraphed its embassy in Japan and asked it to comprehensively support NBL in this matter.[65] Ambassador MacDonald subsequently contacted Gotō Shinpei, in the latter's capacities as Japan's minister of communications and transportation and president of its Railway Agency, to relay the message that NBL would be participating in the tender for model locomotives through Ōkura Gumi and to ask the Railway Agency's consideration therein when awarding contracts.[66] In his response, Gotō hinted that the contract would be split among British, American, and German manufacturers.[67] This was borne out by the tender's results, which were announced soon thereafter. Of the orders for the sixty passenger locomotives, twenty-four went to ALCO-Mitsui and twelve each to Borsig-Ōkura, Schwartzkopff-Illies, and NBL-Ōkura, while ALCO-Mitsui further won the contract for six steep-grade locomotives.

Thereafter, Mitsui Bussan ordered twenty-four superheated tender locomotives and six Mallet-type compound locomotives from ALCO on December 30, 1910, all to be shipped from New York by April 1, 1911. This strict delivery date was due to a pending increase in the ad valorem tax on locomotives from 5 percent to 20 percent, scheduled to take effect on July 15, 1911, which resulted from the ending of fixed tariffs with the full revision of the unequal treaties Japan had been subject to, as mentioned in chapter 5. Therefore, the products had to be in Japanese territory before this date to avoid a 15 percent increase in duties.[68] ALCO manufactured the former group of locomotives in the Brooks factory and the latter in the Schenectady factory, and further managed to ship both batches ahead of the deadline.[69]

Illies appears to have ordered twelve tender locomotives each from Borsig and Schwartzkopff around the same time. As in ALCO's case, the lead times were two to three months,[70] again to avoid the pending tariff increase. Both manufacturers completed production of the locomotives within two months, during Shima and Asakura's sojourn in Berlin as on-site inspectors.[71]

Meanwhile, not until January 28, 1911, about one month after the announcement of the tender results, did Ōkura Gumi send NBL an order for twelve saturated steam 4-6-0 tender locomotives. Although this proposal involving the British government had taken time to negotiate, it was finally approved. However, the late order placement pushed back the delivery date to the end of June 1911, approximately two months later than for the American and German manufacturers. The tariff increase thus proved unavoidable and saddled the Railway Agency with an additional 15 percent in duties.

As described above, the Railway Agency's tender for model locomotives ultimately allowed NBL to maintain its honor as a manufacturer representative of the birthplace of railroads. On February 13, 1911, the company expressed its appreciation to the British Foreign Office in a letter that acknowledged its government's support.[72] Even in the United Kingdom, which purportedly stood for free trade, the Foreign Office began directly and indirectly supporting British businesses operating overseas from the end of the nineteenth century.[73] This example vividly depicts one of the many changes in British policy taking place at the time. That the British brought up the Anglo-Japanese Alliance and urged Japanese government leaders to put the NBL on the designated list further implies that railroads symbolized technological modernization and formed an integral part of British national identity.

In August 1911, ALCO received an order for twelve additional superheated passenger locomotives for the Railway Agency,[74] likely to compensate for NBL's twelve locomotives being of the saturated steam type. In June 1912, the agency ordered additional steep-grade locomotives from ALCO through Mitsui Bussan, Baldwin through Frazar, and Henschel through Takata Shōkai. Unlike the previous order for steep-grade locomotives placed with ALCO, these were for the superheated type; in addition, four more superheated locomotives, ordered from J. A. Maffei through Shin Keita in February 1912, were completed in July of the same year.[75] The fact that all the 1912 orders for steep-grade locomotives were for the superheated type likely reflects input from Shima, who had returned from Germany and resumed his leadership of the Manufacturing Section.[76] Notably, these further rounds of orders marked the Railway Agency's final importation of locomotives for trunk railroads.

LOCALIZING LOCOMOTIVES

As soon as the December 1910 order was placed, Shima and Asakura, in Germany as Railway Agency inspectors, immediately began visiting the Borsig and Schwartzkopff factories on a daily basis and inspecting every drawing for the locomotives' designs.[77] As seen from the statement below, they emphasized the working plans for each part used at the factories:

> Although work is proceeding at a fast pace at each plant, each working plan must be approved by Inspector Shima. As such, although we had to go to the plant as often as possible, because the two factories were quite far apart, we were at best only able to visit each one every other day. A record of the discussions held at each factory was delivered to Mr. Shima the next morning. . . . Looking at the drawings submitted for approval, in both companies, the order [of submission] appears to be random. Although inconvenient for anyone wishing to investigate the design, the drawings for parts requiring the longest time to manufacture must be delivered to the factory floor first. With respect to assembly drawings, we rely on the experience of specialized factories. . . . Although we approved working plans, these require a high level of mastery as a designer and represent highly skilled work.[78]

Shima and Asakura's daily inspections of these leading rolling-stock plants proved crucial not only in preparing for the domestic production of superheated steam engines but also in learning about factory management.[79] The design knowledge and manufacturing know-how they obtained in Germany went on to play crucial roles in Japan's transition to the domestic manufacture of locomotives.[80]

Both engineers' use of their status as inspectors of the ordering company to absorb manufacturing expertise resembles in many respects how the Naval Shipyard developed shipbuilding skills. The shipyard ordered three cruisers from Britain and France in the mid-1880s and sent Japanese engineers to each country as supervisors to inspect the vessels under construction and learn every detail of advanced shipbuilding practices in Europe. On returning to Japan, they used imported naval vessels as models of imitation production, which enabled them to build domestic cruisers in the early 1890s.[81]

The first global economy facilitated technology transfer through Japan's strategy of ordering target machine models from overseas, dispatching domestic engineers as supervisors to absorb the technology, and ultimately acquiring the technology—including the production process—through imitation production. The pivotal role of Japanese engineers in this global technology transfer cannot be overstated. Western manufacturers, in their quest to secure orders amid intense international competition, demonstrated remarkable adaptability. To the maximum extent possible, they strived to meet the demands of orders from Japanese shipyards and railroads. Moreover, the navy was Japan's only consumer of warships, and the IGR monopolized over 90 percent of the country's domestic locomotive market. European and U.S. manufacturers competing for large orders could not ignore the demands of these key customers, while their German peers were obliged to accept Shima and Asakura as inspectors and disclose manufacturing process details at the IGR's request. In this way, the navy and the Railway Agency used global competition to localize technology.

Locomotives from the United States and Germany began arriving in Yokohama one after another between June and July 1911, which the Railway Agency immediately began assembling. Its engineers, along with their counterparts from Kawasaki Dockyard and Kisha Seizō, conducted material hardness tests to evaluate working accuracy,[82] and they also made exact records of each part to manufacture copies of these models.[83] To this end, Kawasaki Dockyard expanded its facilities, increased its workforce, and obtained a patent for a Schmidt-type superheated engine. The Railway Agency subsequently tasked it with making a copy of Borsig's passenger locomotive. Ōta Yoshimatsu developed detailed blueprints alongside the agency's engineers and gained approval from the Manufacturing Section, leading Kawasaki Dockyard to produce twelve copies by 1913.[84] Following the same protocol, Kisha Seizō produced sixteen copies of the NBL saturated steam locomotive that arrived later; though a compromise was forced into the final product, it was sophisticated enough to serve as a model.

This acquisition of expertise by private manufacturers through meticulous imitation led the Railway Agency to announce in 1912 that, starting the following year, it would order new locomotives only from designated domestic manufacturers and cease using imported models.[85] Accordingly, Shima created basic plans for a superheated standard locomotive in 1914 based on Schwartzkopff's passenger locomotive (figure 6.4) and outsourced its production to Kisha Seizō and Kawasaki Dockyard.

This locomotive, known as the JNR class 8620 (figure 6.5), was smaller than its German model; whereas the latter was a large ten-wheeler 17.2 meters long and 50.8 tons, the former was a light Mogul-type 16.8 meters long and 48.8 tons. Yet despite this difference in size, the domestic locomotive's pulling power of 9,300 kilograms almost matched its German counterpart's 9,310 kilograms. Furthermore, it had the same 1,600-millimeter wheel diameter as the German locomotive and could operate at speeds of over 90 kilometers per hour. In transitioning to and standardizing the domestic production of high-speed passenger locomotives, Shima reduced their size and weight and made additional modifications to approximate the performance and pulling power of the model locomotive as closely as possible. A number of factors specific to Japan underlay his design changes, including the country's narrow gauge (3 feet 6 inches) track and its highly curved mountainous areas with soft bedrock. These customizations reflected how meeting domestic conditions had been one of Japan's goals in its longtime cultivation of railroad technology since the early Meiji period.

Other standard locomotives underwent a similar transition to domestic production. For freight types, twelve superheated tender locomotives were produced in 1912. However, after returning from Germany in late December that year, Asakura began working on a brand-new freight locomotive under Shima's supervision. For this, he adopted a design with a higher boiler main line based on Borsig models that aimed to increase power by maximizing the firebox width within the constraints of the narrow gauge.[86] Aided by Ōta's detailed plans, this led to the first domestic mass-produced

LOCALIZING LOCOMOTIVE PRODUCTION IN JAPAN

FIGURE 6.4 Schwartzkopff's 8880-class 4-6-0 tender locomotive. This is a superheated tender locomotive with four leading and three driving wheels, inspected by Shima Yasujirō and Asakura Kiichi. It was one of the model locomotives ordered by the Railway Agency in 1910 and categorized as 8880 class by Japan National Railways. Schwartzkopff, subsequently renamed Berliner Maschinenbau AG, was one of the leading locomotive manufacturers in Germany. This engine was a prototype for Japan's first mass-produced domestic locomotive, known as the 8620 class.

Source: Iwasaki Collection, © Railway Museum, Ōmiya.

freight locomotive in 1913, the JNR class 9600 (figure 6.6). Between 1913 and 1926, 770 of this type were produced, cementing its status as the representative freight locomotive in prewar Japan.

Similarly, in the case of steep-grade superheated steam locomotives, in 1914 Kawasaki Dockyard produced thirty-nine locomotives modeled after Maffei's superheated tank, for which Asakura had served as production supervisor while in Germany. In this instance, Ōta developed detailed blueprints using documents that Asakura had obtained during this time.[87] This type did not exactly mimic its model and should be considered a

LOCALIZING LOCOMOTIVE PRODUCTION IN JAPAN

FIGURE 6.5 Kisha Seizō's 8620-class 2-6-0 tender locomotive. This is a superheated passenger locomotive with two leading wheels and three driving wheels, categorized as 8620 class by Japan National Railways. Shima Yasujirō designed this engine with Schwartzkopff's 8880 class as a reference. The unique aspect is the reduction of the leading wheels, which shortens the overall length and lightens the weight.

Source: Tetsudō shō, *Nihon tesudō shi gehen*, n.p.

domestically manufactured locomotive that drew on the original German design.[88]

Together with private manufacturers, the Railway Agency thus developed a domestic fleet of locomotives and began mass-producing them just prior to World War I. Shima's accommodation of local circumstances while matching the performance of European and American locomotives proved vital to this effort and shaped the subsequent development of railroad technology in Japan.[89] Critical roles were played not only by elite engineers such as Shima and Asakura, both Imperial University graduates, but also by their colleagues with less distinguished backgrounds; these included technicians such as Ōta who realized engineering plans through their

FIGURE 6.6 Kawasaki's 9600-class 2-8-0 tender locomotive. This is a superheated freight locomotive featuring two leading wheels and eight driving wheels. Japan National Railways classified it as 9600 class. This engine was initially designed by Asakura Kiichi. Known for its excellent traction and user-friendly design, this locomotive was manufactured in large quantities and became a representative freight locomotive in Japan.

Source: Tetsudō shō, *Nihon tesudō shi gehen*, n.p.

expertise in design and production. Highly skilled workers with practical experience were just as crucial to Japan's self-reliance in locomotive manufacturing as college graduates with theoretical knowledge.[90]

Japan successfully produced domestic locomotives over forty years after the foundation of railroads. This achievement undoubtedly stemmed from the government-led process of technology transfer since the early Meiji period and the training of engineers through the development of national educational institutions. It is highly commendable that engineers such as Shima Yasujirō accumulated technology through repeatedly imitating locomotives from Europe and the United States and developed locomotives compatible with their own country's environment.

However, developing domestic locomotives was not always a rational choice from an economic standpoint. At the time, American and German manufacturers were supplying inexpensive, high-quality locomotives with short delivery times amid fierce global competition, and daring to purchase expensive domestic locomotives had little economic merit. In fact, in the early 1910s, large domestic locomotives cost much more than those imported from the United States and Germany: a Japanese-German comparison of the price of the 8850-class superheated steam locomotive shows that the Borsig product cost 27,387 yen, while Kawasaki Dockyard's version cost 35,072 yen, or 28 percent more than the former.[91] The Japanese government revised tariffs in 1911 to compress this difference, raising the tax rate on locomotives and their parts from 5 to 20 percent. It insisted on domestic production even by raising tariffs and wielding the monopoly it enjoyed in its home market through railroad nationalization because nationally made large locomotives symbolized the development of modern technology in Japan.[92] This also held true in the United Kingdom, and as mentioned earlier, it was why the British government used its diplomatic power to maneuver the NBL onto the Railway Agency's designated list. Domestic locomotive production thus formed the origins of how, as Jessamyn Abel demonstrates, the Shinkansen became a national identity in postwar Japan.[93]

FROM JAPAN TO CHINA: MITSUI BUSSAN'S RESPONSE TO DOMESTIC PRODUCTION

The shift to domestic production substantially impacted trading companies that had agent agreements with foreign manufacturers to import locomotives. As Mitsui Bussan's Machine Division explained:

> The tariff revision enacted in 1912 (Meiji 45) has led to the protection of domestic manufacturers. The Railway Agency has since adopted a policy whereby all supplementary locomotives are to be manufactured in domestic factories and that absolutely none may be imported. . . . Up to now, our division . . . has acted under an agent agreement with the American

Locomotive Co. and imported locomotives needed by the Railway Agency. The order for 24 Mallet-type compound locomotives (approximate value JPY 5 million) will be the last. After that, we will shift our focus to supplying necessary railroad materials to Kawasaki Dockyard and Kisha Seizō. Presently, the lost orders from the Railway Agency are offset by orders from these two manufacturers.[94]

As this document indicates, although the official policy called for domestic locomotive production, trading companies maintained a certain level of overseas business by supplying railroad materials for passenger and freight cars to domestic manufacturers. Mitsui Bussan's revenue from the sale of wheels, axles, tires, spring couplers, and other components to the Railway Agency, Kawasaki Dockyard, Nippon Sharyō, and Kisha Seizō amounted to about one million yen annually, implying the continuation of imports.[95] Imports of rails (track) and bridge materials also remained vigorous, with values hovering around three to four million yen in the period just before World War I.[96]

However, having been excluded from the Railway Agency's monopsonistic procurement of locomotives, Mitsui was well aware of the domestic market's limitations, which explains its heightened expectations regarding exports to China in the 1910s. Its sales of railroad goods in China had stagnated at the start of that decade; orders from the SMR slumped from the latter half of 1913 to the latter half of 1914.[97] In contrast, World War I led to Mitsui's full-fledged exports to China via SMR's heavy investment in facilities and its winning of a contract to supply materials to the Shandong Railway, which the Japanese army had confiscated from Germany. In 1919, the Machine Division sold 81 locomotives valued at 12.3 million yen to China, of which 51 went to the SMR, 12 to the Shandong Railway, 10 to the Jinpu (Tianjin–Pukou) Railway, and 8 to the Beijing–Zhangjiakou Railway.[98]

The Chinese market continued accruing importance up to the early 1920s, with exports to it peaking in 1921 at 58 locomotives (table 6.1). ALCO sold 180 locomotives to Chinese railroads and 30 to the SMR between 1913 and 1929; during this period, these sales made up 70.7 percent of all its

TABLE 6.1 ALCO's locomotive exports to East Asia, 1913–1929 (number of cars)

| | INTERMEDIARY | | | DELIVERY | | | | | |
	SHIPPING TOTAL	MITSUI TOTAL	OTHER	JAPAN	KOREA	TAIWAN	KARAFUTO	MANCHURIA	CHINA (EXC. MANCHURIA)
1913	5	5	–	–	–	1	–	–	4
1914	27	27	–	–	9	–	–	–	18
1915	7	7	–	–	–	–	–	–	7
1916	11	1	10	1	–	–	–	–	10
1917	7	3	4	3	–	–	–	–	4
1918	45	45	–	3	12	–	–	25	5
1919	44	44	–	1	12	–	7	–	24
1920	51	51	–	1	–	11	–	–	39
1921	70	70	–	–	–	7	5	–	58
1922	8	8	–	–	6	–	–	–	2
1923	2	2	–	2	–	–	–	–	–
1924	5	5	–	–	–	–	–	5	–
1925	6	6	–	6	–	–	–	–	–
1927	2	2	–	–	–	–	–	–	2
1928	1	1	–	–	–	–	–	–	1
1929	6	–	6	–	–	–	–	–	6
1913–1929 total	297	277	20	17	39	19	12	30	180

Sources: ALCO, *Register of Contracts*, vols. 13–21 (1913–1929), ALCO Collection, Special Collections Research Center, Syracuse University; *John White, A Short History of American Locomotive Builders in the Steam Era (Washington, DC: B*ass, 1982), 21.

exports to East Asia compared to the 5.7 percent it sent to Japan's domestic market. By this point, China had become the largest locomotive export market in East Asia.

THE REORGANIZATION OF
THE DOMESTIC MARKET

Japan's railroad nationalization plan called for the Railway Agency to centrally manage trunk lines and granted private railroads subsidies to construct and operate branch lines according to the Light Railway Act and the Light Railway Subsidy Act (1910–1911). This led to a first nationwide boom in light railroads from 1913 to 1915.[99] Railroad operators more than doubled from 116 in 1912 to 249 in 1915, and 4,211 kilometers of lines were operating by the end of this period.[100] This rapid expansion is even more striking considering that the Railway Agency then operated 9,268 kilometers of lines. These light railroads and tramlines relied on small steam, electric, and oil-burning locomotives for motive power. The number of steam locomotives began to increase after the Light Railway Subsidy Act took effect in 1911; in 1914, private railroads added 115 locomotives and the Railway Agency added 129, illustrating that public and private railroads were on par in this area.[101]

The small steam locomotives used by light railroads and tramlines fell into one of three cases: newly manufactured by domestic rolling stock manufacturers, disposed of by the Railway Agency and other governmental entities, or imported from overseas. Small to medium-sized rolling stock manufacturers played an important role in the first case, as exemplified by the Amenomiya Ironworks; an accurate estimate is elusive, but the company is believed to have manufactured approximately 100 locomotives by 1915.[102] That would mean that this single manufacturer produced slightly under a quarter of the 411 locomotives newly added to light railroads and tramlines in the 1909–1915 period.[103] Without a doubt, medium-sized rolling stock manufacturers were key suppliers of locomotives that supported the light railroad boom.[104] The second case occurred when the Railway Agency was dealing with the great variety of locomotives it had inherited during railroad nationalization. It disposed of 53 such locomotives in 1914–15, which went to private railroads and provided a critical supply route for light railroad and tram operators during this period.

In the third case, the volume of imported locomotives rose sharply after the Light Railway Subsidy Act took force in 1911. The main sources of exports to Japan around this time appear to have been H. K. Porter in the United States and Orenstein & Koppel in Germany. It is hard to obtain a comprehensive picture of small steam locomotive imports before the start of World War I as they had a wide range of destinations, including coal mines, mineral mines, ironworks, and railroad companies, making it difficult to calculate the total number imported. Furthermore, although a portion of small locomotives were made to order, others were ready-made products, which complicates the picture on the manufacturers' side. For example, Usui Shgenobu observes that H. K. Porter offered low-cost locomotives for light railroads and industry entirely through catalog sales of standardized locomotives and cut its production costs through using interchangeable parts in multiple models.[105]

Adhering even more strictly to this approach, Orenstein & Koppel exported large numbers of small steam locomotives to Japan from the 1910s to the 1920s.[106] It began full-fledged exports to Japan in 1909 and exported more than 450 locomotives by 1928, even with a temporary suspension during the chaos of World War I.[107] Their greatest appeal was their low cost; in 1922, the price of an Orenstein & Koppel 0-6-0 wheel arrangement tank locomotive was reportedly 20 percent less than that of a comparable Japanese model.[108] Imports of such inexpensive small steam locomotives continued even after their domestic production began in 1914. This created one market for Japanese-made large locomotives and another for small locomotives of domestic and overseas manufacture, a dual structure that survived into the 1920s.

COMPARATIVE PERSPECTIVES

The development of Japanese locomotive technology and its characteristics is usefully compared to shipbuilding as another representative example of a building-type machinery industry. Japan's modern shipbuilding industry started in the late 1850s and relied on *oyatoi* engineers until after the Meiji Restoration. Production of small iron steamships began at the end of the 1880s, when Japanese engineers from the Imperial University and other domestic institutions acquired expertise from their foreign counterparts. At the close of the 1890s, the Mitsubishi Nagasaki Shipyard successfully manufactured the Hitachi Maru, a large iron-build steamship that incorporated UK technology. Japanese engineers also designed a large steamship in the late 1900s, the Tenyō Maru, and built large battleships in the mid-1910s.[109] These all indicate this national industry's achievement of technological independence.

In contrast, as this book shows, locomotive manufacturing remained reliant on foreign engineers until the 1890s. From the late 1890s to the early 1900s, the IGR and private railways repeatedly produced imitations of various imported locomotives. In the process, Japanese engineers' design skills improved enough to domestically produce lightweight locomotives in the late 1900s and large locomotives in the early 1910s. Thus, Japan's shipbuilding and locomotive manufacturing industries both achieved technological independence from developed Western countries prior to World War I. But the former, faced with global competition and few environmental limitations in its operation, created one of the world's largest passenger vessels by pursuing larger and faster steamships.[110] In contrast, the latter aimed for smaller, lighter, and more efficient locomotives rather than larger and faster ones, constrained by Japan's environmental factors of its railways' narrow gauge, soft soil, and mountainous terrain.

Even in the same type of machinery industry in the same country, technological development took divergent courses depending on the environment in each case. In particular, it is apparent that locomotive manufacturing, like other building-type machinery industries based on custom or batch production, drew strong influence from international and social environments and consequently took diverse paths in technological development. In fact, within Japan's imperial sphere, Taiwan was a similarly mountainous terrain whose railroads had adopted Japanese locomotives with the same narrow gauge early on (see chapter 5). In contrast, the SMR, which ran on Manchurian plains in standard gauge, continued to import locomotives from the United States instead of Japan. It then developed original locomotives based on American models and collaborated with Japanese manufacturers to mass-produce them.[111] Following SMR's lead, Korea's railways also began to use Japanese locomotives for their standard gauge. The localization of locomotives in imperial Japan's territories thus advanced significantly in the late 1920s.[112]

* * *

On the whole, Japanese railroads effectively utilized their country's social capability to industrialize and developed rapidly through fierce international competition in the locomotive trade. After the Russo-Japanese War, railroad nationalization integrated the domestic market, and the Railway Agency began replacing imported locomotives with domestic products. In 1911, a dramatic rise in import tariffs on locomotives made it difficult to import very large models, but the Railway Agency and private manufacturers cooperated to mass-produce domestic locomotives. Japanese engineers initially imitated German models and then created original designs tailored for domestic use. Their ability to innovate depended on training colleagues skilled in design and the growth of manufacturers who could produce in-house, both social capabilities formed from the 1880s to the early 1900s.

Prior to World War I, Japan's railroad industry achieved self-sufficiency with respect to locomotives and could reproduce without relying on foreign suppliers. Notably, Japan's withdrawal from the global locomotive market coincided with the beginning of the first global economy's decline.[113] As Japan changed from customer to supplier, the primary locomotive market in East Asia shifted to its colonies and spheres of influence, including China. For example, Mitsui Bussan shifted its main business away from the Japanese homeland to these overseas markets, which made selling to the SMR and Chinese railroads critical for its operations after World War I. Conflicts in the decades between the two great wars undermined the cohesiveness of international relationships, which led individual countries to form trading blocs. During the 1920s, the Ministry of Railways (established in 1920 as the successor to the Railway Agency) and major Japanese locomotive manufacturers formed a quasi-monopolistic bilateral market and began transferring railroad systems to territories under Japanese control, including Taiwan, Korea, and Manchuria.[114] And in the 1930s, Japan's imperialistic ambitions created a full-fledged Japanese imperial market bloc in East Asia.[115]

CONCLUSION

This book opened by asking how Japanese railroads successfully procured locomotives and other necessary components to rapidly develop amid the intense market competition that characterized the era of the first global economy. The preceding chapters answered this question by analyzing historical trends in the global locomotive market, the social capabilities of industrialization that supported railroads' progress in Japan, and the role of trading companies in linking the global economy and the Japanese market. In this conclusion, I summarize and compare two perspectives that are threaded through the key findings of this study: the rivalry between globalization and localization as well as the interrelationship between empire building and nation-state building. I then compare these perspectives and consider their implications for the present day.

GLOBALIZATION AND JAPANESE LOCOMOTIVE MARKETS

Starting from Britain in the first half of the nineteenth century, locomotives and railroads soon spread to regions including the United States and

CONCLUSION

Germany. In the 1850s, Britain began exporting steam locomotives to territories in its formal and informal empire in Asia, Africa, Oceania, and Latin America, driving a worldwide boom in railroad construction in the latter half of that century. This dominance explains the new Japanese government's decision in 1869, just after it had taken power in the Meiji Restoration, to source locomotives and a complete railroad system from Britain.

However, around the end of the nineteenth century, American and German locomotive manufacturers entered this British-founded market, causing significant fluidity. The former, buoyed by large batch orders by domestic railroad companies, developed the American system as a production method that standardized model types and interchangeable parts to enable shorter times and lower costs. From the 1880s, American manufacturers carried out global marketing activities by dispatching sales representatives and engineers to agencies and business offices in locations worldwide. Meanwhile, their German counterparts, whose main customers were state-owned railroads, adopted the same system and other emergent technologies to export aggressively with government support. During this period, American and German locomotive manufacturers rapidly reorganized the industry, while their laggard British counterparts began to decline. As a consequence, Britain's global monopoly crumbled and was replaced by a competitive market structure. Then, at the turn of the twentieth century, American manufacturers rushed into the Japanese locomotive market, which was one of the significant objects of global capital.

The export of locomotives in this period entailed international competition not only in cost and lead times but also in quality and the incorporation of technological innovation. This is evident from the comparative performance evaluations of British and American locomotives as well as the superheated locomotive tests carried out around the world and widely reported in industry publications, which enabled railroad operators as end users to acquire high-quality, low-cost locomotives with short lead times. These factors should be emphasized as crucial background to railroads' rapid spread worldwide in the late nineteenth century and their contribution to deepening the first global economy. The market environment from

CONCLUSION

the 1880s up to around 1910 favored the development of railroad industries in late-starter countries. However, these countries' ability to utilize market conditions depended on their social capabilities for industrialization.

JAPAN'S SOCIAL CAPABILITIES AND LOCALIZATION

Three elements are vital to a consideration of how Japan's railroads developed: international transportation infrastructure, which enabled the smooth import of railroad materials; a nominated competitive bidding system, which created a competitive procurement system; and financing for the purchase of materials. These social capabilities promoted the formation of Japan's railroad industry, leading to two boom periods between the 1880s and 1900 and the speedy growth of private companies.

First, the social infrastructure that facilitated imports of materials included the establishment of transportation and communications systems in the form of a steamship network with regularly scheduled trips and the laying of submarine telegraph cables. All these constituted the foundation of the world economy, which centered on the United Kingdom. The branch offices established by Takata Shōkai, Mitsui Bussan, and Ōkura Gumi in major Western cities exported locomotives to Japan by forming relationships with major overseas manufacturers using *oyatoi* connections and this transport infrastructure. The dominance of Japanese trading companies and their international matrix of offices thus enabled optimal procurement within Japan's railroad industry.

Second, as an institutional innovation to spur competition in procurement, governmental and private railroads introduced competitive bidding systems in the 1890s that made designated bidding (private tenders) the norm in the 1900s. The ability to select both manufacturers and intermediaries let railroad operators efficiently and stably procure locomotives of specific quality and price in a given period. Meanwhile, as competition among the limited number of bidders also reduced administrative costs, special relationships between trading companies and manufacturers often

CONCLUSION

determined bidding outcomes. Trading companies such as Mitsui Bussan, Ōkura Gumi, and Frazar thus devoted substantial efforts to conclude agency contracts with major American, British, and German locomotive manufacturers.

Lastly, the circumstances of securing capital for the purchase of materials differed substantially before and after the First Sino-Japanese War. Japan constructed its first railroads using British capital in the early 1870s, but afterward it excluded foreign investment due to the risk of financial colonization. From the 1880s to 1890s, railroad construction relied on funding from wealthy domestic elites coupled with a public corporation system and internal loans.[1] Japan's determination to avoid subjugation to the Western powers underlay its choice to shut out foreign investment at a time when the creation of a gold standard and multilateral settlements system had stimulated international financial transactions. After its victory in the Sino-Japanese War alleviated the threat of colonization, its 1897 participation in the gold standard led to discussions of foreign investment in both government and private railroads, which began in the 1900s via corporate and public bonds.[2] Since then, global capitalism has directly influenced Japan's railroads. In the era of imperialism, these railroads' ability to choose their funding methods independently became a national social capability in terms of finance.

At the same time, Japan's ability to develop original railroads in this international environment depended on its capability to receive and localize new technology. The first step of the formation of Japanese railroad technology required cultivating engineers and technicians able to create specification documents, select materials, and inspect products. The successive dismissals in the latter half of the 1890s of A. S. Aldrich and F. H. Trevithick, the last *oyatoi* administrators, prove that Japan's railroads had achieved technological independence. In their place, engineering graduates of the Imperial University and other Japanese institutions of higher education assumed the authority to select and order materials as steam locomotive section chiefs and factory directors at state-owned and private railroads. These new administrators abandoned the practice of purchasing materials from a single country in favor of optimal procurement globally.

CONCLUSION

The second stage of technology formation saw the emergence of engineers capable of designing and manufacturing locomotives themselves. Locomotive manufacturing by imitation production began around 1900, when Japanese engineers' creation of working plans in addition to basic designs and specification documents evinced the maturing of domestic production technology.[3] These engineers accurately copied advanced technology as a prerequisite to attain the end result of developing original locomotives to suit Japan's topography. Japanese railroads, therefore, attempted to accumulate design and manufacturing skills by imitating a wide variety of locomotives from the United Kingdom, the United States, and Germany. In the 1910s, they had accumulated technology and know-how and were able to develop large locomotives compatible with Japan's soft ground and mountainous terrain, while Japanese engineers succeeded in converging technologies learned from a diversity of locomotives into their original models.[4] The key players in this development were Imperial University engineers clustered in the Railway Agency, whose monopoly on demand due to railroad nationalization and the protectionist spike in tariffs also facilitated this technological progress.

There is no doubt that the Japanese state was the most important player in the localization of railroad technology through human resource training and institutional development. Its leaders emphasized domestically produced large locomotives as a symbol of national identity and boosted their development. In this way, the government's will to localize industry also formed a social capability of Japanese industrialization.

EMPIRE BUILDING AND THE REORGANIZATION OF THE EAST ASIAN MARKET

Since the Meiji Restoration, Japan has worked to build a nation-state while resisting the waves of globalization, and its Industrial Revolution between the late 1880s to the early 1900s was an economic milestone in this process. Railroads were a leading sector of this revolution, and the market for their materials in Japan expanded amid two boom periods. In East Asia, Japan's relatively advanced progress in railroads saw the locomotive trade in the latter half of the nineteenth century and the start of the twentieth primarily occurring within its borders. After the First Sino-Japanese War, Japan began to build its empire alongside its nation-state, its capital began to construct railroads in Korea and Taiwan, and it also imported locomotives, albeit on a small scale.[5] For this reason, Baldwin, ALCO, and other American manufacturers sent sales engineers or sales representatives from their headquarters to work with local agents in Japan, where they sought to expand sales in its home islands, its colonies, and its sphere of influence. The Japanese imperial sphere consequently became the most significant export destination for American locomotive manufacturers in the early twentieth century and formed one of the world's most active locomotive markets. Here a key characteristic of U.S. manufacturers was that they developed their own overseas marketing, in contrast to British manufacturers who left sales to the trading companies.

The United States had developed two main methods of industrial product marketing at the end of the nineteenth century: marketing through local agents or sales representatives and marketing through branch offices. American manufacturers mainly used the former during the market exploration phase and shifted to establishing the latter as the volume of transactions increased, which constituted an effective strategy for marketing new industrial products in remote areas.[6] The activities of Tyler and Vauclain Jr. in Japan, as mentioned in chapter 3, mainly concerned the former method, which ALCO and Baldwin used to expand their business internationally.

Meanwhile, the Russo-Japanese War accelerated Japan's empire building and expansion of railroads in Korea, southern Karafuto, and Manchuria as its sphere of influence. In 1906–1907, domestic railroad nationalization led the government to acquire seventeen major private railroads in Japan and the Keifu Railway in Korea. This, along with the SMR's establishment in 1906, generated a substantial reorganization of the East Asian locomotive market. Nationalization created a monopsony of the IGR/Railway Agency and dramatically increased government control over the domestic locomotive market. Japanese manufacturers such as Kisha Seizō, Nippon Sharyō, and Kawasaki Dockyard seized this opportunity to lobby for public orders

CONCLUSION

of Japan-made rolling stocks. In 1912, this created a shift toward domestic manufacturing and imposed high import duties on locomotives as part of the 1911 tariff reform, which induced a precipitous drop in imports of large locomotives for trunk lines.

Railroad construction and improvements proceeded at breakneck pace in Korea and Manchuria, where the Russo-Japanese War had created substantial demand for locomotives. Japanese locomotive manufacturers, then in their infancy, could not sustain overseas exports, which opened the market for imports. Seizing this opportunity, American manufacturers shifted their attention from Japan to China and Korea, marketing locomotives to the SMR and other railroads in both territories.[7] Japanese and foreign trading companies were deeply involved in this shift as manufacturers' agents. The former, such as Mitsui Bussan, used its extensive branch office network in East Asia to probe new markets, conducting detailed analyses based on local information and connecting local customers and global suppliers. And as Japanese trading companies also promoted sales of American locomotives in China, Western manufacturers found them indispensable for developing emerging markets in East Asia.[8]

The railroad, introduced and developed as an essential tool for Japan's nation-state building, was transformed into a tool for empire building. In civil engineering, Japan completed its domestic transfer of Western technology at the end of the 1880s, after which it immediately began exporting designs and construction technology to the overseas territories it controlled. In this aspect, the *oyatoi* system of government-led technology transfer promoted domestically educated engineers and rapidly grew Japan's empire.

In comparison, for the field of mechanical technology, as represented by locomotive manufacturing, it took Japan too long to acquire the technology required to build railroads in its empire. Thus, in the short term, Japan's empire building provided an expanded market for Western locomotive manufacturers. However, Japan succeeded in localizing and mass-producing large locomotives just before World War I and began transferring and exporting them to its colonies and spheres of influence after the 1920s. Japanese locomotive manufacturers did not simply send their locomotives developed for the domestic market to Japanese colonies and spheres of

CONCLUSION

influence; instead, they worked with local railroads like the SMR to create locomotives better suited to each region's specific conditions.[9] This gradually drove Western locomotives out of the Japanese imperial market and shifted then to the Chinese market from the late 1920s onward.

COMPARISON BETWEEN CHINA AND JAPAN

Finally, I compare the characteristics of railroad and locomotive manufacturing development in Japan and China through considering the differences in technological advancements across developing countries. For the locomotive industry, both Japan and China introduced technologies from countries including the United Kingdom, the United States, and Germany. However, while Japan consolidated its original technology in the 1910s, China was slow to do the same,[10] and it continued to import locomotives from Western countries until World War II. This contrast stems from how both countries established their railroads and trained engineers with locomotive design and production skills. On the first point, the Japanese government ended its dependence on foreign capital to build and operate its railroads, which allowed it to make its own technological choices. In addition, it rapidly established domestic institutions of higher education and systematically cultivated engineers who accumulated expertise and experience through repeated repair and imitation to create locomotives adapted to Japan's specific environment. Moreover, graduates of domestic institutions became chief engineers in government and private railroads and contributed to the domestic production of locomotives in the 1910s.

In China, on the contrary, the cultivation of Chinese engineers was delayed because many railroads were built with foreign loans and foreign engineers continued to make technological decisions. Graduates of domestic institutions of higher education established in the 1910s also had difficulty finding employment in loaned railroads controlled by foreign engineers.[11] In 1921, the Republic of China merged three technical colleges and established Jiaotong University, whose graduates increasingly replaced foreign engineers in decision-making positions at the Ministry of Railways and

CONCLUSION

railroad companies in the late 1920s and early 1930s.[12] However, the outbreak of the Second Sino-Japanese War in 1937 halted domestic locomotive production until the 1950s, after World War II and the Chinese Civil War.

Even if locomotive manufacturing industries introduced technologies in the same way, the process and degree of development differed with the availability of technological choices, the cultivation of human resources, and employment opportunities in their respective countries. Compared with China, Japan's success in railroad development is attributable to the government's direct involvement in railroads and the early education of engineers.

EPILOGUE: IMPLICATIONS FOR THE SECOND GLOBAL ECONOMY

A century after the story described in the preceding chapters, the world has entered the peak era of the second global economy.[13] The focus of competition in railroads has shifted from steam locomotives to high-speed trains such as the Shinkansen, and Japan is leading in technological development along with Germany, France, and China. However, in terms of market share, Hitachi and Kawasaki are lagging behind the "new big three" in rolling stock: CRRC (China), Alstom (France), and Siemens (Germany).[14] In particular, China's rolling stock manufacturing industry has made remarkable progress in recent years.

In 2004, China signed a contract with German and Japanese rolling stock manufacturers to introduce high-speed railroads, whose rapid construction opened the Beijing–Tianjin line in 2008 and the Beijing–Shanghai line in 2011. And in 2010, the high-speed CRH-380 train developed by CSR (part of CRRC from 2015 onward) achieved a maximum speed of 486 kilometers in a test run. In July of the same year, a high-speed rail collision occurred in Wenzhou, Zhejiang Province. However, this slowed neither the network's expansion nor the subsequent inauguration of the Beijing–Guangzhou line in 2012. China thus constructed 16,000 kilometers of high-speed rail in less than a decade, surpassing Japanese rolling stock

CONCLUSION

manufacturers at least in terms of speed. Although critics in Japan and Germany have labeled the swift advance of Chinese rolling stock technology as "stealing" or "imitation," Chinese manufacturers have not simply copied foreign technology wholesale; instead, their rapid catch-up comes from developing their own systems through the integration of existing technologies from abroad.

A century ago, as examined in this book, Japan accumulated technology in the exact same way. They introduced technologies from advanced countries and developed their own through convergent imitation, which led them to dominate the global market. On the other hand, the United Kingdom, which flaunted its technological advances at the end of the nineteenth century, fell behind these emerging countries in terms of price and delivery. Globalization does not permit resting on one's laurels nor the naive notion that "if it is good, it will sell even if it is expensive," a commonly held belief among Japanese manufacturers prior to the 2000s. British manufacturers' overweening concern with craftsmanship hamstrung their response to rapid changes in production technology. Their experience of success prevented them from making subsequent advances, a failure clearly shown in how the United Kingdom used its political power to market its products despite being a supposed advocate of free trade.[15]

There is no shortage of examples where the development of a unique technology or system becomes a success that prevents successive innovation. In order for Japanese railroads to avoid following their British counterparts' missteps of the previous century, manufacturers must shun excessive adherence to proprietary technologies and over-specification and learn from a diversity of technologies and systems with humility. Since the comparative advantage of Japanese companies lies in their technological capabilities, they must overcome their own histories of success and continue to innovate if they wish to open new frontiers in the export of railroad systems and rolling stock.

NOTES

INTRODUCTION

1. The category of rolling stock includes, among other vehicles, locomotives, tenders, passenger cars, freight cars, and electric cars. Tenders are coupled to locomotives and carry coal and water.
2. The first export of Japanese high-speed trains went to Taiwan in 2004.
3. Kawasaki Takeshi, Mochida Toshihiko, and Yamaguchi Takashi, "Ōshū tetsudō muke sharyō gijutsu [Rolling stock technology for European railways]," *Hitachi hyōron* 89, no. 11 (2007): 66–69.
4. In 1986, Kawasaki built a factory in Lincoln, Nebraska, and began local production in earnest.
5. See part 1 of Geoffrey Jones, *Multinationals and Global Capitalism: From the Nineteenth to the Twenty-First Century* (Oxford: Oxford University Press, 2005). The term "global economy" refers to the worldwide system of finance, industry, and trade that developed due to globalization. In chapter 2, Jones suggests that the first global economy peaked before World War I, declined during the interwar period, and ended in the Great Depression, a persuasive historical hypothesis on international economic relations that also recalls Harold James, *The End of Globalization: Lessons from the Great Depression* (Cambridge, MA: Harvard University Press, 2002).
6. This book draws on source material from my Japanese monograph, *Umi wo wataru kikansha* [Locomotives from across the sea] (Tokyo: Yoshikawa Kōbunkan, 2016), with extensive revisions and new additions for anglophone audiences.
7. Defined by Nakaoka Tetsurō and developed by Suehiro Akira, this concept explains the essential factors for late-adopter countries to achieve industrialization, including

INTRODUCTION

government policies, education, human resources, entrepreneurship, and capital accumulation. See Nakaoka Tetsurō, ed., *Gijutsu keisei no kokusai hikaku: Kōgyōka no shakaiteki nōryoku* [International comparisons of technological formation: Societies' abilities to industrialize] (Tokyo: Chikuma Shobō, 1990), and chapter 3 of Suehiro Akira, *Catch-Up Industrialization: The Trajectory and Prospects of East Asian Economies* (Singapore: NUS Press, 2008).

8. Naofumi Nakamura, "Diversification and Convergence," in *The Development of Railway Technology in East Asia in Comparative Perspective*, ed. Sawai Minoru (Singapore: Springer, 2017), 41–65.

9. See Elisabeth Köll, *Railroads and the Transformation of China* (Cambridge, MA: Harvard University Press, 2019).

10. See Sawai Minoru, *Nihon tetsudō sharyō kōgyō shi* [A history of Japan's rolling stock industry] (Tokyo: Nihon Keizai Hyōronsha, 1998).

11. As I mention later, previous studies also argue for the role of trading companies during Japanese industrialization. For a conceptual framework and historical overview of such companies' multinational activities, see Geoffrey Jones, *Merchants to Multinationals: British Trading Companies in the Nineteenth and Twentieth Centuries* (Oxford: Oxford University Press, 2000).

12. Glenn Porter and Harold C. Livesay, *Merchants and Manufacturers: Studies in the Changing Structure of Nineteenth-Century Marketing* (Baltimore: Johns Hopkins University Press, 1971).

13. Jones, *Merchants to Multinationals.*

14. Andrew Gordon, *Fabricating Consumers: The Sewing Machine in Modern Japan* (Berkeley: University of California Press, 2011); Robert Hellyer, *Green with Milk and Sugar: When Japan Filled America's Tea Cups* (New York: Columbia University Press, 2021).

15. On the historical methodology related to commodity chains, see Terence K. Hopkins and Immanuel M. Wallerstein, "Commodity Chains in the World-Economy Prior to 1800," *Review* (Fernand Braudel Center) 10, no. 1 (1986): 157–170.

16. While both Gordon and Hellyer discuss consumption and culture in depth, this book does not cover the cultural history of railroads and locomotives. Jessamyn R. Abel provides an interesting discussion of the cultural-historical aspects of bullet trains in *Dream Super-Express: A Cultural History of the World's First Bullet Train* (Stanford, CA: Stanford University Press, 2022).

17. See the conclusion to Steven J. Ericson, *The Sound of the Whistle: Railroads and the State in Meiji Japan* (Cambridge, MA: Harvard University Asia Center, 1995).

18. Ryōshin Minami, *The Economic Development of Japan*, 2nd ed. (London: Macmillan, 1994), 103–110.

19. A recent study that focuses on the role of imitation in this vein is Eugenia Lean, *Vernacular Industrialism in China: Local Innovation and Translated Technologies in the Making of a Cosmetics Empire, 1900–1940* (New York: Columbia University Press, 2020).

20. Abel, *Dream Super-Express*, chap. 5.

21. League of Nations, Economic and Financial Section, ed., *International Statistical Year-Book 1926* (Geneva: League of Nations, 1927), 121–127; John Westwood, *The Historical Atlas of World Railroads* (London: Cartographica Press, 2008).

22. League of Nations, *International Statistical Year-Book 1926*; Westwood, *Historical Atlas*. The order of passengers per kilometer of rail was as follows: United Kingdom, 4,757; Germany, 2,704; Japan, 1,967; France, 1,335; India, 821.

INTRODUCTION

23. League of Nations, *International Statistical Year-Book 1926*; Westwood, *Historical Atlas*. The order of freight per kilometer of rail was as follows: United Kingdom, 1,118; Germany, 886; United States, 501; France, 492; Japan, 387.

24. Alexander Gerschenkron, *Economic Backwardness in Historical Perspective* (Cambridge, MA: Belknap Press of Harvard University, 1962), chap. 1.

25. Gerschenkron, *Economic Backwardness in Historical Perspective*.

26. In contrast, Japan saw delayed domestic production of complex machines for industries such as cotton textiles; while weaving machinery manufacture began in the Meiji period, spinning machinery was not domestically produced until the 1920s by companies like Toyoda Automatic Loom Works, the parent firm of Toyota Motor, which began making spinning machines in 1929.

27. Sawai, *Nihon tetsudō sharyō kōgyō shi*. In contrast, large steamships for oceangoing vessels could be built domestically at the end of the 1890s due to the government's industrial encouragement of that sector. However, imports of more technically complex large battleships continued until 1915. See Inoue Yōichirō, "Nihon kindai gijutsushi no ichi kenkyū [A historical study of Japan's modern technology]," *Keizai ronsō* 99, no. 1 (1967): 87–89.

28. Akita Shigeru, "Ajia kokusai chitsujō to Igirisu teikoku, hegemonī [International order in Asia, the British Empire, and hegemony]," in *Gurōbaru histori no chōsen* [Challenges of global history], ed. Mizushima Tsukasa (Tokyo: Yamakawa Shuppansha, 2008), 102–113; Angus Maddison, *Contours of the World Economy, 1–2030 AD* (Oxford: Oxford University Press, 2007), 81. On debates related to global history in Japan, see also the introduction to Robert Hellyer and Harald Fuess, eds., *The Meiji Restoration: Japan as a Global Nation* (Cambridge: Cambridge University Press, 2020).

29. Figures for the United Kingdom are probable underestimates given that the period started in the 1860s and many locomotives were manufactured in-house by major railroad companies' workshops. However, as only locomotive manufacturers (contract builders) exported locomotives, export figures likely reflect the actual situation on this front. In contrast, railroad shops in the United States and Germany generally did not build locomotives and only performed repair work, while their railroads purchased locomotives from contract builders.

30. Daniel R. Headrick, *The Tools of Empire: Technology and European Imperialism in the Nineteenth Century* (Oxford: Oxford University Press, 1981), part 3.

31. In 1869, travelling from London to Yokohama took fifty-four days via the Suez Canal and thirty-three days via the Pacific Ocean. Kokaze Hidemasa, "Jō [Introduction]," in *Gurōbaruka no naka no kindai Nihon* [Modern Japan within globalization], ed. Kokaze Hidemasa and Suetake Yoshiya (Tokyo: Yūshisha, 2015), 4.

32. See S. B. Saul, *Studies in British Overseas Trade 1870–1914* (Liverpool: Liverpool University Press, 1960), and Nishimura Shizuya, "Daiichiji gurōbaruka to Ajia ni okeru eikei kokusai ginkō [The first globalization and British international banks in Asia]," in *Kokusai ginkō to Ajia* [International banks and Asia], ed. Nishimura Shizuya, Suzuki Toshio, and Akagawa Motoaki (Tokyo: Keio University Press, 2014), 3–152.

33. Jones, *Multinationals and Global Capitalism*, part 1. Harold James also points out that "economists who have tried to find a statistical basis for comparison of this first era of globalization with our own era are usually struck by the degree of similarity." See James, *The End of Globalization*, 11–12. How to measure globalization is a difficult question, but the first global economy clearly achieved stronger cohesiveness in finance and trade than before the early nineteenth century and after the Great Depression.

209

INTRODUCTION

34. Usui Shigenobu, *Kikansha no keifuzu* [A genealogy of locomotives], vol. 2 (Tokyo: Kōyūsha, 1973), 258–261.

35. Sawai, *Nihon tetsudō sharyō kōgyōshi*, 26.

36. John K. Brown, *The Baldwin Locomotive Works: 1831–1915* (Baltimore: Johns Hopkins University Press, 1995), 183–189.

37. Kōda Ryōichi, *Doitsu kōsaku kikaikōgyō seiritsu shi* [Formation of the German machine tool industry] (Tokyo: Taga Shuppansha, 1994), 251–254.

38. Tanaka Tokihiko, *Meiji ishin no seikyoku to tetsudō kensetsu* [Political conditions and railroad construction during the Meiji Restoration] (Tokyo: Yoshikawa Kōbunkan, 1963).

39. Yuzawa Takeshi, "Igirisu keizai no teitai to jōki kikansha yushutsu [Stagnation in the British economy and locomotive exports]," *Gakushūin keizai-keiei kenkyūsho nenpō* [Annual report of the Institute of Economics and Business, Gakushuin University], no. 3 (1989): 19–34; Takeshi Yuzawa, "The Transfer of Railway Technologies from Britain to Japan, with Special Reference to Locomotive Manufacture," in *International Technology Transfer: Europe, Japan and the USA, 1700–1914*, ed. David Jeremy (Aldershot, UK: Edward Elgar, 1991), 199–218.

40. Since the 1980s, the field of Japanese economic history has leaned toward critiquing Western-centric historical perspectives and searching for the causes of Japan's economic development within Asia and Japan itself. See, for example, Hamashita Takeshi and Kawakatsu Heita, eds., *Ajia kōekiken to Nihon kōgyōka, 1500–1900* [Asian trading spheres and Japanese industrialization] (Tokyo: Libroport, 1991).

41. Nakamura Naofumi, *Nihon tetsudōgyō no keisei* [The formation of Japan's railways], (Tokyo: Nihon Keizai Hyōronsha, 1998).

42. Ericson, *The Sound of the Whistle*. The same observation applies to Dan Free, *Early Japanese Railways: 1853–1914* (North Clarendon, VT: Tuttle, 2008).

43. Yuzawa, "Igirisu keizai no teitai to jōki kikansha yushutsu"; Yuzawa, "The Transfer of Railway Technologies."

44. Sawai, *Nihon tetsudō sharyō kōgyō shi*.

45. Peter J. English, *British Made: Industrial Development and Related Archaeology of Japan* (Eindhoven: De Archeologische Pers Nederland, 1982).

46. Christian Wolmar, *Blood, Iron, and Gold: How the Railways Transformed the World* (London: Atlantic Books, 2009).

47. Mizushima, *Gurōbaru historī no chōsen*.

48. Wolmar does make several interesting arguments related to Japan, including time consciousness in the early days of Japan's railroads and the *Shinkansen*'s status in world history. Wolmar, *Blood, Iron, and Gold*, 208–209, 314–317.

49. Hayashida Haruo, *Nihon no tetsudō sōsō ki* [The early days of Japan's railways] (Kyoto: Minerva Shobō, 2009).

50. Steven J. Ericson, "Importing Locomotives in Meiji Japan, International Business and Technology Transfer in the Railroad Industry," *Osiris: A Research Journal Devoted to the History of Science and Its Cultural Influences*, 2nd ser., vol. 13 (1998): 129–153; Ericson, "Taming the Iron Horse: Western Locomotive Makers and Technology Transfer in Japan, 1870–1914," in *Public Spheres, Private Lives in Modern Japan, 1600–1950*, ed. Gail Bernstein, Andrew Gordon, and Kate Nakai (Cambridge, MA: Harvard University Press, 2005), 185–217.

51. Sawai, *Nihon tetsudō sharyō kōgyō shi*.

1. COMPETITION IN THE GLOBAL LOCOMOTIVE MARKET

52. Brown defines building-type machinery industries as consisting of capital equipment builders, such as locomotives and steamships, customized for a customer's detailed requirements. Brown, *Baldwin Locomotive Works*, xxvii–xxx.
53. Aoki Eiichi, "Nihon no kansenyō jōki kikannsha no hattatsu, [The development of steam locomotives for trunk lines in Japan]," *Tetsudo shigaku* [Japan railway history review] no. 9 (1991): 7–16; Yamamoto Hirofumi, ed., *Technological Innovation and the Development of Transportation in Japan* (Tokyo: United Nations University Press, 1993).
54. Interested readers should consult Kaneda Shigehiro, *Nasmyth Wilson no kikansha* [The locomotives of Nasmyth Wilson] (Suita: Kikanshashi Kenkyūkai, 1981).
55. Usui Shigenobu, *Kikansha no keifuzu* [A genealogy of locomotives], vols. 1–4 (Tokyo: Kōyūsha, 1972–1978).
56. Ishii Kanji, *Kindai Nihon to Igirisu shihon* [Modern Japan and British capital] (Tokyo: University of Tokyo Press, 1984).
57. Ishii, *Kindai Nihon to Igirisu shihon*, 403–405.
58. Recent studies, such as Okazaki Tetsuji and Oishi Naoki, eds., *Senzen ki Nihon no sōgō shōsha* [The general trading companies in the prewar era] (Tokyo: University of Tokyo Press, 2023), detail Mitsui Bussan's internal organization and network in comparison to Mitsubishi Shōji (Mitsubishi Corporation).
59. Asajima Shōichi, *Senzen ki Mitsui Bussan no kikai torihiki* [Mitsui Bussan's machinery trade in the prewar era] (Tokyo: Nihon Keizai Hyōronsha, 2001).
60. Harald Fuess, "The Global Weapons Trade and the Meiji Restoration," in *The Meiji Restoration: Japan as a Global Nation*, ed. Robert Hellyer and Harald Fuess (Cambridge: Cambridge University Press, 2020), 83–109.
61. Hellyer, *Green with Milk and Sugar*.
62. Ueyama Kazuo, *Hokubei ni okeru sōgō shōsha no katsudō* [The activities of general trading companies in North America] (Tokyo: Nihon Keizai Hyōronsha, 2005); Ueyama Kazuo and Kikkawa Yō, eds., *Senzen ki Hokubei no Nihon shōsha* [Japanese trading companies in North America during the prewar period] (Tokyo: Nihon Keizai Hyōronsha, 2013).
63. Brown, *Baldwin Locomotive Works*, xxvi–xxix; Sawai, *Nihon tetsudō sharyō kōgyō shi*, 3–4.
64. Philip Scranton, *Endless Novelty: Specialty Production and American Industrialization, 1865–1925* (Princeton, NJ: Princeton University Press, 1997), 10–16.
65. Nakaoka Tetsurō, *Nihon kindai gijutsu no keisei* [The formation of Japanese modern technology] (Tokyo: Asahi Shinbunsha, 2006), 395–406.
66. Nakaoka, *Nihon kindai gijutsu no keisei*.

1. INTERNATIONAL COMPETITION IN THE GLOBAL LOCOMOTIVE MARKET

1. Yuzawa Takeshi, *Tetsudō no tanjō* [The birth of railroads] (Tokyo: Sōgensha, 2014), 135–138.
2. Kume Kunitake, ed., *Tokumei zenken taishi Beiō kairan jikki* [The ambassador extraordinary and plenipotentiary's observation record of Europe and the United States], vol. 2 (Tokyo: Hakubunsha, 1878; repr., Tokyo: Iwanami Shoten, 1993), 149–150. Kume published this account of the journey and the Iwakura Mission's observations of the United States and Europe in a hundred volumes.

1. COMPETITION IN THE GLOBAL LOCOMOTIVE MARKET

3. As the enforcement of unequal treaties had compelled Japan to open its doors to Western powers in the 1850s through to the 1860s, attempts to revise said treaties formed the prime imperative of Japanese foreign policy. See Iokibe Kaoru, *Renegotiating Japan's Unequal Treaties: A Window on Late Nineteenth-Century Diplomacy* (Tokyo: University of Tokyo Press, 2022).

4. On this point see Gordon, *A Modern History of Japan*, 70–75.

5. Yuzawa, *Tetsudō no tanjō*, 129.

6. See table 2 in Yuzawa, "Igirisu keizai no teitai to jōki kikansha yushutsu," 20.

7. "Railway Matters," *The Engineer*, January 16, 1903, 65.

8. See table 3 of Yuzawa, "Igirisu keizai no teitai to jōki kikansha yushutsu," 21.

9. W. Pollard Digby, "The Earning Power of British Rolling Stock from 1894–1903," *The Engineer*, September 22, 1905, 279–280; Yuzawa, "Igirisu keizai no teitai to jōki kikansha yushutsu," 19.

10. Kita Masami, "19 seiki Gurasugō jōki kikansha seizōgyō hatten shi [The historical development of steam locomotives in Glasgow during the nineteenth century]," *Sōka keizai ronshū* [Soka economic review] 22, no. 4 (1993): 51–66; James W. Lowe, *British Steam Locomotive Builders* (Cambridge: Goose and Son, 1975).

11. R. H. Campbell, "The North British Locomotive Company Between the Wars," in *Business in the Age of Depression and War*, ed. R. P. T. Davenport-Hines (London: Frank Cass, 1990): 172–205.

12. Lowe, *British Steam Locomotive Builders*, 502–505; Kita, "Gurasugō jōki kikansha seizōgyō hatten shi," 57.

13. Lowe, *British Steam Locomotive Builders*, 140–142.

14. Kita, "Gurasugō jōki kikansha seizōgyō hatten shi," 57; Lowe, *British Steam Locomotive Builders*, 579–580.

15. The IGR (Kan'setsu tetsudō) was owned and operated by the government's Railway Bureau.

16. Kita, "Gurasugō jōki kikansha seizōgyō hatten shi," 51–66.

17. Lowe, *British Steam Locomotive Builders*, 497.

18. "The firm had earned a reputation of good workmanship and materials, and from 1839 to 1939 had built 1,531 steam locomotives." Lowe, *British Steam Locomotive Builders*, 499.

19. Lowe, *British Steam Locomotive Builders*, 59–61.

20. See Brown, *Baldwin Locomotive Works*, 5–7; John White, *A Short History of American Locomotive Builders in the Steam Era* (Washington, DC: Bass, 1982), 3.

21. ALCO further merged with Rogers Locomotive Works in 1905.

22. See chapter 1 and Brown, *Baldwin Locomotive Works*, 96–101.

23. Charles H. Fitch, *Report on the Manufactures of Interchangeable Mechanism* (Washington, DC: Government Printing Office, 1888), 47–48.

24. "United States Competition in the Locomotive Export Trade," *The Engineer*, September 15, 1899, 260. See also the same column in *The Engineer*, September 29, 1899, 313.

25. Ogasawara Shigeru, "19 seiki zenhan ni okeru Doitsu kikai kōgyō no hatten [The development of the German machinery industry in the first half of the nineteenth century]," *Shōgaku ronshū* (Journal of commerce, economics and economic history, Fukushima University) 38, no. 2 (1969): 12–13.

26. "Mori Hikozō-shi (Shinbashi kōjō-chō) wo tou 3 [An interview with Mr. Mori Hikozō, head of Shinbashi factory, vol. 3]," *Tetsudō jihō* [Japan railway times], no. 254 (July 1904): 5.

1. COMPETITION IN THE GLOBAL LOCOMOTIVE MARKET

27. Yuzawa, "Igirisu keizai no teitai to jōki kikansha yushutsu."

28. Kōda, *Doitsu kōsaku kikaikōgyō seiritsu shi*, 251–254. The fitting system refers to a method for improving interchangeability in fitting machine parts by using limit gauges and fit tolerances.

29. See Ogasawara, "19 seiki zenhan ni okeru Doitsu kikai kōgyō no hatten," 31–32, and Takahashi Hideyuki, "Shoki Borujihi kigyō no seichō to kikansha seisan no tenkai [The development of the early Borsig Co. and locomotive production]," *Ōita Daigaku keizai ronshū* (Oita University economic review) 27, no. 3 (1975): 1–55.

30. See Krauss-Maffei, ed., *Krauss Maffei, 150 Years of Progress Through Technology 1838–1988* (Munich: Krauss-Maffei AG, 1988), 16–19.

31. Krauss-Maffei, *150 Years of Progress Through Technology*, 19.

32. Competition between British and American locomotive manufacturers emerged in the late 1870s and raised the latter's comparative advantages in the 1880s relative to delivery deadlines, price, and quality. See Yuzawa, "The Transfer of Railway Technologies," 199–202.

33. Sawai, *Tetsudō sharyō kōgyō shi.*

34. Yuzawa, "The Transfer of Railway Technologies," 200–201.

35. There are three ways to classify steam locomotive types by region: White system, continental European, and American. For example, a locomotive with three driving wheels and one front wheel is called a Mogul type in the United States, a 2-6-0 in the United Kingdom's White system, and a 1C in continental Europe. In this book, the locomotive type will be denoted using the White system.

36. "Tender locomotive" refers to a locomotive-coupled tender; the other type, without tender, refers to a "tank locomotive."

37. "Literature," *The Engineer*, January 27, 1899, 89.

38. "Railway Matters," *The Engineer*, March 17, 1899, 262.

39. "Railway Matters," *The Engineer*, March 31, 1899, 313. See also the same column in *The Engineer*, May 26, 1899, 517.

40. Yuzawa, "Igirisu keizai no teitai to jōki kikansha yushutsu," 19–20.

41. Charles Rous-Marten, "English and American Locomotive Building," *Engineering Magazine* 17, no. 4 (1899): 545.

42. W. Pollard Digby, "The British and American Locomotive Export Trade," *The Engineer*, December 16, 1904, 587–588.

43. Brown, *Baldwin Locomotive Works*, 46–47.

44. Digby, "The British and American Locomotive Export Trade," 587–588; table 1.5 of Nakamura, *Umi wo wataru kikansha*, 52.

45. "The Glasgow Locomotive Trade," *The Engineer*, May 8, 1896, 480.

46. Charles Rous-Marten, "English and American Locomotive Building," *Engineering Magazine* 17, no. 4 (1899): 545–561, 790–811.

47. See table 1.5 of Nakamura, *Umi wo wataru kikansha*, 52.

48. *The Engineer*, March 4, 1898, 201; Yuzawa, "The Transfer of Railway Technologies," 202–210.

49. "Indian Government Contracts," *The Engineer*, June 7, 1901, 591, 597.

50. See table 1.6 of Nakamura, *Umi wo wataru kikansha*, 53.

51. "English v. American Locomotives," *The Engineer*, January 10, 1890, 34.

52. "American Locomotives and the Edinburgh International Exhibition," *The Engineer*, February 21, 1890, 152.

1. COMPETITION IN THE GLOBAL LOCOMOTIVE MARKET

53. "English and American Locomotives," *The Engineer*, March 28, 1890, 262. This was in response to *The Engineer* asking the U.S.-based *The Engineering News* about the advantages of American locomotives over British locomotives.

54. Born 1850 in England, and the grandson of Richard Trevithick, inventor of the steam locomotive. He arrived in Japan in 1876 to serve as chief of the Kobe factory's boiler section, where he became an assistant locomotive superintendent in 1878 and the locomotive superintendent-in-residence in 1880 while also serving as its chief in Shinbashi. In 1889, he rose to the post of locomotive superintendent and was treated almost as a government official before returning to England in 1897. Railway History Society of Japan, ed., *Tetsudō jinbutsu shi jiten* [A biographical dictionary of railroad history in Japan] (Tokyo: Nihon Keizai Hyōronsha, 2013), 299.

55. Francis H. Trevithick, "English and American Locomotives in Japan," *Proceedings of Institute of Civil Engineers 1895–96*, part 3, no. 125 (1896): 335.

56. Trevithick, "English and American Locomotives in Japan," table 2, 337, table 2.

57. Trevithick, 341, table 5.

58. Trevithick, 340, table 4.

59. "Differences Between American and Foreign Locomotives," *The Engineer*, January 19, 1894, 57.

60. "Colonial Locomotives," *The Engineer*, September 28, 1894, 269.

61. "Locomotive Gates," *The Engineer*, February 14, 1896, 168.

62. The journal published only one article and one letter to the editor in 1897–1898. See table 1.6 of Nakamura, *Umi wo wataru kikansha*, 53.

63. "Railway Matters," *The Engineer*, May 26, 1899, 517.

64. Fitch, *Report on the Manufactures of Interchangeable Mechanism*, 44–59.

65. "Railway Matters," *The Engineer*, November 17, 1899, 495.

66. "English and American Locomotive Building," *Engineering Magazine* 17, no. 4 (July 1899): 560.

67. "United States Competition in the Locomotive Export Trade No. 1," *The Engineer*, September 15, 1899, 260; "United States Competition in the Locomotive Export Trade No. 2," *The Engineer*, September 29, 1899, 313; "The Locomotive Trade of Great Britain," *The Engineer*, October 13, 1899, 363.

68. "The Invasion of the American Locomotives," *The Engineer*, April 28, 1899, 419.

69. "The Invasion of the American Locomotives."

70. "English and American Locomotives," *The Engineer*, July 7, 1899, 13.

71. "American Competition," *The Engineer*, October 6, 1899, 357.

72. "English and American Railways No. 3," *The Engineer*, March 23, 1900, 298.

73. Brown, *Baldwin Locomotive Works*, 241.

74. Brown, 54–55.

75. Brown, 182–183.

76. "British Locomotive Manufacturers," *The Engineer*, July 19, 1901, 70.

77. "American Locomotives in England," *The Engineer*, June 28, 1901, 661.

78. "Government Contracts," *The Engineer*, November 1, 1901, 457.

79. "American Firms and Indian Railway Contracts," *The Engineer*, June 7, 1901, 591.

80. Locomotives not delivered on time obliged their manufacturer to compensate the customer. For example, in 1894, the contract between Neilson and Nippon Railway required the former to pay the latter a hundred pounds per locomotive per week for a late delivery. See "Quick Locomotive Building," *The Engineer*, December 28, 1894, 568.

2. TECHNOLOGICAL TRANSFER, BRITISH MONOPOLIZATION

81. Brown, *The Baldwin Locomotive Works*, 44–47.
82. "Nihon ni okeru Doitsu kikansha [German locomotives in Japan]," *Tetsudō jihō*, no. 207 (September 1903): 8; "Doku Bei kikansha no kyōsō [Competition between American and German locomotives]," *Tetsudō jihō*, no. 229 (February 1904): 5.
83. Wolmar, *Blood, Iron, and Gold*.

2. TECHNOLOGICAL TRANSFER AND BRITISH MONOPOLIZATION

1. Hazel J. Jones, *Live Machines: Hired Foreigners and Meiji Japan* (Vancouver: University of British Columbia Press, 1980), xv.
2. On the essential role of Western merchants in Japan's machinery market during the 1860s see Fuess, "The Global Weapons Trade and the Meiji Restoration," 108–109.
3. On general contracting by foreigners as the opposite of the *oyatoi* system, see Nakamura, *Nihon tetsudōgyō no keisei*, chap 1.
4. Dan Free, *Early Japanese Railways, 1853–1914* (North Clarendon, VT: Tuttle, 2008), 31–34 and 49–55.
5. See Nakamura, *Nihon tetsudōgyō no keisei*, chap. 1.
6. Hayashida, *Nihon no tetsudō sōso ki*, 38–39; Jones, *Live Machines*, 35–36.
7. Tetsudōshi Gakkai, ed., *Tetsudōshi jinbutsu jiten* [Biographical dictionary of railway history] (Tokyo: Nihon Keizai Hyōron sha, 2013), 453–454.
8. Ministry of Foreign Affairs of Japan, ed., *Dai Nihon gaikō monjo* [Documents on the Empire of Japan's foreign policy] 2–3, no. 608 (Tokyo: Diplomatic Archives of the Ministry of Foreign Affairs of Japan, 1937), 390.
9. Hayashida, *Nihon no tetsudō sōso ki*, 160–161.
10. Hayashida Haruo, *Edomondo Moreru* [Edmund Morrell] (Kyoto: Minerva Shobō, 2018).
11. Kaneda Shigehiro, *Nihon jōki kikansha shi kansetsu tetsudō hen* [A history of Japan's steam locomotives: the Imperial Government Railways] (Tokyo: Kōyūsha, 1972), 6. Morel had worked in Australia before being hired by the Japanese government.
12. Kaneda, *Nihon jōki kikansha shi kansetsu tetsudō hen*, 6.
13. Hayashida, *Nihon no tetsudō sōso ki*, 233. At the time, an agreement had been made for the Oriental Bank and Malcolm Brunker to share handling fees of 1 and 1.5 percent respectively.
14. Nakamura, *Nihon tetsudōgyō no keisei*, 26
15. See chapters 3–5 of Edmund G. Holtham, *Eight Years in Japan, 1873–1881: Work, Travel, and Recreation* (London: K. Paul, Trench, 1883), and chapter 1 of Nakamura, *Nihon tetsudōgyō no keisei*.
16. Holtham, *Eight Years in Japan*, 277–278.
17. Nakamura Naofumi, "The Training School for Railway Engineers: An Early Example of an Inter-firm Vocational School in Japan," in *Accessing Technical Education in Modern Japan*, ed. Erich Pauer and Regine Mathias, vol. 2 (Kent, UK: Renaissance Books, 2022), 217–251.
18. The ICE based its curriculum on the advanced engineering education of the time. Most of its foreign professors were British and taught classes in English, while Scottish engineer Henry Dyer served as its principal from 1873 to 1882. See Henry Dyer, *Dai Nippon: The Britain of the East* (London: Blackie, 1904).

2. TECHNOLOGICAL TRANSFER, BRITISH MONOPOLIZATION

19. Yamao returned from Britain in December 1868 with Inoue Masaru and helped establish the Ministry of Public Works in 1870; he also headed the Department of Engineering Education (Kōgakuryō) in charge of the ICE. Tetsudōshi Gakkai, *Tetsudōshi jinbutsu jiten*, 433–434.

20. Francis H. Trevithick, "History and Development of the Railway System in Japan," *Transactions of the Asiatic Society of Japan*, no. 22 (1894): 115–241.

21. Gerard Lowther, "Report on Railway of Japan [1895]," *Foreign Office 1896 Miscellaneous Series*, Consular Reports on Subjects of General and Commercial Interest, no. 390 (London: Her Majesty's Stationary Office, 1895), 20.

22. Dübs & Co., *General Particulars of Engines, Tenders No. 1*, Dübs & Co. records, 3/1/1, Glasgow University Archives. See table 2.3 of Nakamura, *Umi wo wataru kikansha*, 81.

23. B2 and A8 classes were the locomotive classification categories of the Railway Operation Bureau and IGR.

24. Sharp Stewart & Co., *Order Book*, Sharp Stewart records, NBL/1/1, National Railway Museum, UK. See table 2.4 of Nakamura, *Umi wo wataru kikansha*, 82.

25. Usui, *Kikansha no keifuzu*, 1:14.

26. A tender-type locomotive was hauled by a steam locomotive containing fuel and water, which made it suitable for long-distance operation as it could carry more of these supplies and was larger than a tank-type locomotive.

27. Neilson Co., *Engine Orders*, NBL/2/1/1, National Railway Museum; table 2.5 of Nakamura, *Umi wo wataru kikansha*, 83.

28. In terms of conditions, it was agreed, for example, that a penalty of a hundred pounds per locomotive would be incurred for every week of late delivery.

29. Richard L. Hills, "Some Contributions to Locomotive Development by Beyer, Peacock & Co.," *Newcomen Society Transactions*, no. 40 (1968): 95–109; table 2.7 of Nakamura, *Umi wo wataru kikansha*, 85.

30. Nippon Tetsudō, ed., *Meiji 34-nen nenpō* [1901 annual report] (Tokyo: Nippon Railway Co., 1902), 99–101.

31. "Nippon Tetsudō kaishachō no enzetsu [Speech by the president of Nippon Railway Co.]," *Tetsudō jihō*, no. 179 (February 1903): 9.

32. Negotiated contracts provided a direct channel between supplier and customer without competitive bidding. Many private railroads in this era managed price, delivery time, and quality by using both negotiated contracts and competitive bidding for procurement.

33. "Nippon Tetsudō kaishachō no enzetsu," 8; Nippon Tetsudō, ed., *Meiji 36-nen nenpō* [1903 annual report] (Tokyo: Nippon Railway Co., 1904), 65.

34. The Usui Pass used the ABT system, one of the major rack rail systems.

35. Usui, *Kikansha no keifuzu*, 2:269.

36. Nasmyth Papers, *Loco Specifications 1867–1922*, Salford Local History Library; table 2.8 of Nakamura, *Umi wo wataru kikansha*, 86.

37. Usui, *Kikansha no keifuzu*, 1:50–53.

38. Nasmyth Papers, *Loco Specifications 1867–1922* and *Reference Book 2*; table 2.9 of Nakamura, *Umi wo wataru kikansha*, 87.

39. Usui, *Kikansha no keifuzu*, 1:50.

40. Ian Nish, *Collected Writings of Ian Nish: Part 2* (Richmond: Japan Library, 2001), 53.

2. TECHNOLOGICAL TRANSFER, BRITISH MONOPOLIZATION

41. Hayashida, *Nihon no tetsudō sōsō ki*, 277–278.

42. Shervinton arrived in Japan in 1873 as a civil engineer, becoming a deputy engineer and subsequently principal engineer of the Kobe Section in 1875. In the same year, he served as an instructor at the Kōgisei Yōseisho (TSRE). After returning to England in 1881, he served as an adviser and preliminary inspector in London for the IGR until 1897. Tetsudōshi Gakkai, *Tetsudōshi jinbutsu jiten*, 233–234; *Teishinshō kōbunsho tetsudōbu kigu buppin 6 Meiji 30* [Official archives of the Ministry of Communications and Transportation, railway section, goods 6, 1897] (Tokyo: Teishinshō, 1897).

43. Shervinton's remuneration included an annual fee of two hundred pounds for his advisory work and a handling fee equal to 1 percent of the price of the goods he purchased as preliminary inspector. "Dai ichiji kensain Shāvinton kaishoku narabi kōninsha sentei no ken [Firing primary inspector Shervinton and selecting his successor]," *Teishinshō kōbunsho tetsudōbu kigu buppin*.

44. "Modern Japan 17: The Railways," *The Engineer*, March 4, 1898, 201.

45. A. R. Brown worked as an *oyatoi* in shipbuilding; after serving as general manager for the Nippon Yusen shipping company, he returned to Glasgow in 1889, where the Japanese government appointed him an honorary consul general and he established A. R. Brown & Co. The company played an important role in procuring materials and importing technology for the Japanese shipbuilding industry. Nakaoka, *Nihon kindai gijutsu no keisei*, 396–398; Lewis W. Bush, *The Life and Times of the Illustrious Captain Brawn* (Rutland, VT: C.E. Tuttle, 1969).

46. See table 2.4 of Nakamura, *Umi wo wataru kikansha*, 82.

47. Dübs & Co., *General Particulars of Engines, Tenders No. 1*; table 2.3 of Nakamura, *Umi wo wataru kikansha*, 81.

48. Neilson Co., *Engine Orders 1899*; table 2.5 of Nakamura, *Umi wo wataru kikansha*, 83.

49. Neilson, *Engine Orders*; table 2.5 of Nakamura, *Umi wo wataru kikansha*, 83.

50. See chapters 3 and 4 of Nakamura, *Nihon tetsudōgyō no keisei*.

51. Excepting Kyushu Railway, which procured technology from Germany for diplomatic and political reasons, and Hokkaido Colliery and Railway, which had procured materials from the United States since the Kaitakushi era.

52. Murakami Kyōichi, *Dai tetsudōka Minami Kiyoshi-kun no keireki* [The biography of Mr. Minami Kiyoshi, venerable railroad engineer and manager] (Tokyo: Japan Railway Times, 1904), 8.

53. Andrew Gordon, *A Modern History of Japan*, 3rd ed. (Oxford: Oxford University Press, 2014), 57–58; Alexander McKay, *Scottish Samurai: Thomas Blake Glover, 1839–1911* (Edinburgh: Canongate Press, 1993), chap. 10.

54. Sugiyama Shinya, *Meiji ishin to Igirisu shōnin* [The Meiji Restoration and British merchants] (Tokyo: Iwanami Shoten, 1993), 194–197.

55. Ishii Kanji, *Kindai Nihon to Igirisu shihon*, 7–11; Ishii Mayako, *Kindai Chūgoku to Igirisu shihon* [Modern China and British capital] (Tokyo: University of Tokyo Press, 1998), 36–38.

56. See table 2.12 of Nakamura, *Umi wo wataru kikansha*, 90.

57. Jardine Matheson & Co., *Letter Book, Yokohama to Hong Kong*, September 13, 1889, Jardine Matheson & Co. records B27/4 (Cambridge University Library).

58. See table 2.12 of Nakamura, *Umi wo wataru kikansha*, 90.

59. Dübs & Co., *General Particulars of Engines, Tenders No. 1*, Dübs & Co. records, 3/1/1 (Glasgow University Archives), 360, 391.

2. TECHNOLOGICAL TRANSFER, BRITISH MONOPOLIZATION

60. Dübs & Co., *General Particulars of Engines, Tenders No. 1*; table 2.3 of Nakamura, *Umi wo wataru kikansha*, 81.

61. Köll, *Railroads and the Transformation of China*; Chiba Masashi, *Kindai kōtsū taikei to Shin teikoku no henbō* [Modern transportation systems and the transformation of the Qing Dynasty] (Tokyo: Nihon Keizai Hyōronsha, 2006).

3. JAPAN'S INDUSTRIAL REVOLUTION AND AMERICAN LOCOMOTIVES

1. Fukao Kyōji and Settsu Tokihiko, "Seichō to makuro keizai [Growth and the macro-economy]," in *Iwanami kōza Nihon keizai no rekishi 3* [Iwanami lecture series on Japanese economic history, vol. 3], ed. Fukao Kyōji, Nakamura Naofumi, and Nakabayashi Masaki (Tokyo: Iwanami Shoten, 2017), 4–5. Japan's growth rate at the time matched that of the United Kingdom and Germany and far exceeded the United Kingdom's during the Industrial Revolution. See Saitō Osamu, "Eikoku sangyō kakumei ron no genzai [The British Industrial Revolution: A historiographical essay]," *Nihon Gakushiin kiyō* [Proceedings of the Japan Academy] 76, no. 2 (2021): 208–211.

2. Fukao and Settsu, "Seichō to makuro keizai," 5. The primary sector's share of labor force composition declined from 71 percent in 1874 to 62 percent in 1890 and 58 percent in 1913.

3. Nakamura Naofumi, *Chihō karano sangyō kakumei* [Local perspectives on Japan's Industrial Revolution] (Nagoya: Nagoya University Press, 2010), chap. 2.

4. Nakamura, *Chihō karano sangyō kakumei*, chap. 2.

5. Noda Masaho, *Nihon shōken shijō seiritsu shi* [A history of the formation of the securities markets in Japan] (Tokyo: Yūhikaku, 1980).

6. Minami Ryōshin, *Chōki keizai tōkei 12: Tetsudō to denryoku* [Long-term Economic statistics 12: Railways and electricity] (Tokyo: Tōyō Keizai, 1979), tables 11 and 12; Nakamura Naofumi, "Shisan tokushusei to kigyō no kyōkai [Asset specificity and firms' boundaries]," in *Kigyō no keizaigaku* [Economics of the firm: Structure and dynamics], ed. Nakabayashi Masaki and Ishiguro Shingo (Tokyo: Yūhikaku, 2014), 101–119.

7. Nakamura, *Nihon tetsudōgyō no keisei*, chaps. 3 and 4.

8. Gordon, *Fabricating Consumers*, introd.; Robert Bruce Davies, *Peacefully Working to Conquer the World: Singer Sewing Machines in Foreign Markets, 1854–1920* (New York: Arno Press, 1976).

9. The Tōkaidō line spanned six hundred kilometers between Shinbashi in Tokyo to Kobe and connected Tokyo, Kyoto, and Osaka, the three biggest cities in Japan.

10. "Report on the Foreign Trade of Japan for the Year 1893," *Diplomatic and Consular Reports*, July 16, 1894, 9.

11. Gerard Lowther, "Report on the Railways of Japan [1895]," *Foreign Office 1896 Miscellaneous Series, Consular Reports on Subjects of General and Commercial Interest*, no. 390 (London: Her Majesty's Stationary Office, 1895).

12. Gerard Lowther, "Report on the Railways of Japan [1897]," *Foreign Office 1897 Miscellaneous Series, Consular Reports on Subjects of General and Commercial Interest*, no. 427 (London: Her Majesty's Stationary Office, 1897).

13. Lowther, "Report on the Railways [1897]."

3. JAPAN'S INDUSTRIAL REVOLUTION

14. Lowther, "Report on the Railways [1895]," 20.

15. In 1874, there were twenty-nine foreign engineers, and after 1883, only five remained. See Nakamura, *Umi wo wataru kikansha*, 94.

16. Harada Katsumasa, "Technological Independence and Progress of Standardization in the Japanese Railways," *Developing Economies* 18, no. 3 (1980): 314–315.

17. Charles A. W. Pownall arrived in Japan in 1882 to serve as a chief engineer in Kobe, where he was in charge of designing bridges, and moved to Tokyo in 1889. Railway History Society of Japan, *Tetsudō shi jinbutsu jiten*, 370.

18. Mori Hikozō recollects that Trevithick, on becoming director of the government railway's Kobe factory, was among the last to leave and had already begun serving as a "retired" consultant. Nihon Kokuyū Tetsudō, ed., *Tetsudō gijutsu hattatsu shi VI dai 4-hen sharyō to kikai 2* [History of railway technology development VI, vol. 4: Rolling stock and machines 2] (Tokyo: Japan National Railways, 1958; repr., Tokyo: Kress Shuppan, 1990), 1212–1213.

19. Lowther, "Report on the Railways [1895]," 20."

20. See part 1 of Nakamura, *Nihon tetsudōgyō no keisei*.

21. Born in England in 1845, R. F. Trevithick arrived in Japan in 1888 to become a train superintendent in Kobe, where he built and maintained locomotives until 1904. As later discussed, he designed and helped build Japan's first locomotive in 1893 and trained many Japanese engineers. Railway History Society of Japan, *Tetsudō shi jinbutsu jiten*, 299–300.

22. The new Railway Bureau oversaw all railroad business (the IGR and private railways), while the Railway Operations Bureau managed the IGR's operations.

23. Teisinshō, ed., *Teisinshō shokuin roku* [List of personnel at the Ministry of Communications and Transportation] (Tokyo: Teisinshō, 1894–1896); Insatsu-kyoku, ed., *Shokuin roku* [List of personnel] (Tokyo: Insatsu kyoku, 1897–1909); Tetsudō-kyoku, ed., *Tetsudō-kyoku nenpō* [Annual Report of Railway Bureau] (Tokyo: Tetsudō-kyoku, 1894–1906).

24. See table 3.2 of Nakamura, *Umi wo wataru kikansha*, 154.

25. This stood in marked contrast to the achievement of independence in railway construction technology during the 1880s, when the first cohort of students studying abroad and graduates of the Training School for Railway Engineers (Kōgisei Yōseisho) played leading roles while civil engineers from ICE contributed only peripherally. See Nakamura Naofumi, "Tetsudō gijutsusha shūdan no keisei to Kōbu-daigakko [The development of Japanese railway engineers and the Imperial College of Engineering]," in *Kōbusho to sono jidai* [The Ministry of Public Works and its era], ed. Suzuki Jun (Tokyo: Yamakawa Shuppansha, 2002), 95–116.

26. Nakaoka, *Nihon kindai gijutsu no keisei*, 402.

27. Harada, "Technological Independence and Progress of Standardization," 316.

28. Usui, *Kikansha no keifuzu*, 3:298–307.

29. Usui, *Kikansha no keifuzu*, 3:298–307. Mori graduated from the Department of Mechanical Engineering of the College of Engineering at Tokyo Imperial University in 1891 and became deputy director of the Kobe factory in 1896.

30. Teishinshō, ed., *Meiji 35-nen Teishinshō shokuinroku* [List of personnel at the Ministry of Communications and Transportation, 1902] (Tokyo: Teishinshō, 1902), 41.

31. See table 3.1 of Nakamura, *Umi wo wataru kikansha*, 153.

32. Teishinshō, *Meiji 35-nen Teishinshō shokuinroku*, 9–10.

33. Railway History Society of Japan, *Tetsudō shi jinbutsu jiten*, 228–229; table 3.1 of Nakamura, *Umi wo wataru kikansha*, 153.

3. JAPAN'S INDUSTRIAL REVOLUTION

34. Kinoshita Seiya, Satō Naoyoshi, Matsumoto Naoya, and Ashida Yoshinori, "Kaikei hō niokeru kōkyō kōji nyūsatsu seido no rekishiteki kōsatsu [A historical study on the public works procurement system under the Public Accounting Act]," *Doboku gakkai ronbun shū* [Journal of the Japan Society of Civil Engineers] F4, vol. 66, no. 1 (2010): 169–171. This was a new type of law already introduced in France, Italy, and Belgium; Germany, the United Kingdom, and the United States had no integrated accounting acts, and Japan's efforts to develop a modern legal system led it to swiftly adopt the most advanced global laws in this era.

35. The "Railway Bureau Regulations on the Trade of Goods" stipulated a format of sales contract required when importing locomotives and bridge materials from overseas that covered seventeen articles: contract deposits (article 1); delivery date and delivery location (article 2); specifications (article 3); inspections—first inspection in country of manufacture, second inspection at payment location—(articles 4–9); contract cancellation due to nonfulfillment or breach of contract (articles 10 and 11); delinquent account charge or contract cancellation in cases of delayed delivery (article 12); procedure upon delivery of goods (articles 13–16); and payments in Japanese yen based on exchange rates of the Yokohama Specie Bank (article 17). "Sales Contract for Trade of Foreign Goods," *Teishinshō Kōbunshō tetsudōbu kigubuppin 6 Meiji 30-nen* [Official archives of the Ministry of Communications and Transportation, railway section, apparatus and goods 6, June 17, 1896].

36. "Kikansha no nyūsatsu [Locomotive tenders]," *Kogyō zasshi* [Industrial magazine], no. 131 (September 1897): 34.

37. Unless otherwise stated, all dollar figures used in this book refer to U.S. dollars.

38. "Beikoku e chūmon no kikansha [Locomotives ordered from the United States]," *Kōgyō zasshi*, no. 135 (November 1897): 35.

39. "A Letter from Shervinton to Aldrich," *Teishinshō kōbunsho, tetsudōbu, kigubuppin 6 Meiji 30-nen*, November 6, 1896.

40. "Tetsudō-kyoku kōbai kakarichō gushin [Report of the Railway Bureau Purchasing Section chief]," *Teishinshō kōbunsho, tetsudōbu, kigubuppin 6 Meiji 30-nen*, December 25, 1896.

41. "Sales Contract for Trade of Foreign Goods," *Teishinshō kōbunsho, tetsudōbu, kigubuppin 6 Meiji 30-nen*, June 17, 1896. This contract was also used for the purchase of bridge materials; as they were mass-printed forms, they were likely also used to purchase locomotives.

42. "Tetsudō-kyoku kōbai kakarichō gushin [Report of the Railway Bureau Purchasing Section chief]," *Teishinshō kōbunsho, tetsudōbu, kigubuppin 6 Meiji 30-nen*, March 21, 1897. Unfortunately, source limitations prevent us from knowing the final outcome of this case.

43. The private tender is one of the competitive bidding systems. Takeda Haruhito, *Dangō no keizaigaku* [The economics of collusion] (Tokyo: Shūeisha, 1994), 148.

44. The locomotive tender by the Hokkaido government's Railway Division described below occurred during this period.

45. Kinoshita Ritsuan, ed., *Teikoku tetsudō yōkan dai 1 han* [Companion to imperial Japan's railways, vol. 1] (Tokyo: Tetsudō Jihōkyoku, 1900); Nihon Kokuyū Tetsudō, *Tetsudo Gijyutsu Hattatsu shi*, vols. 5 and 6; table 3.4 of Nakamura, *Umi wo wataru kikansha*, 155–156.

46. Uchida Hoshimi, "Meiji kōki minkan kigyō no gijutsusha bunpu [Distribution of engineers in private companies in the late Meiji era]," *Kei'ei shigaku* (Japan business history

3. JAPAN'S INDUSTRIAL REVOLUTION

review) 14, no. 2 (1979): 1–30; Uchida Hoshimi, "Shoki kōkōsotsu gijutsusha no katsudō bunya, shūkei kekka [Fields of activity and aggregate results for founding-era Higher Technical School engineer graduates]," *Tokyo kei-daigaku kaishi* [Journal of Tokyo Keizai University], no. 108 (1978): 139–182.

47. The process of copying another manufacturer's product by seeing how it is made through repairing it.

48. Nihon Kokuyū Tetsudō, ed., *Nihon kokuyū tetsudō 100-nen shi dai 4-kan* [A hundred-year history of the Japan National Railways, vol. 4] (Tokyo: Japan National Railways, 1972), 106.

49. Usui, *Kikansha no keifuzu*, 3:314. The Omiya factory later produced six originally designed 0-3-0-type tank locomotives.

50. See Nakamura, "Diversification and Convergence," 50–52.

51. Usui, *Kikansha no keifuzu*, 3:310–312.

52. Murakami, *Minami Kiyoshi-kun no keireki*, 8–10.

53. Sanyo Tetsudō Sōmuka, ed., *Kisoku ruishō* [Collected rules] (Kobe: Sanyo Railway, July 1, 1907), 223–225.

54. Article 3 explained the designated competitive bidding procedure to procure goods: "at least five appropriate dealers shall be specified and, upon approval from the executive director, shall be notified of all necessary conditions including the name, number or amount, delivery date, delivery location, specification documents, and blueprints for the goods to be procured at least five days ahead of the start of the bidding period."

55. Baldwin Locomotive Works, *Orders for Engines*, 1890–1892 and 1893–1897, Smithsonian Institution Archives, Baldwin Locomotive Works Collection #157.

56. "Provisional Regulations for the Trade of Goods," in *Nippon Tetsudō Kabushiki Kaisha reiki shūsan* [Collection of Nippon Railway regulations], ed. Nippon Tetsudō Shōmuka (Tokyo: Nippon Railway, October 1903), 823–826.

57. As per article 11: "The two methods for procuring goods are competitive bidding and negotiated contract." And article 12: "There are two methods of competitive bidding: regular competitive bidding and designated competitive bidding. A regular competitive bidding procedure is used when it is desirable to have a broad range of relevant agents compete. A designated competitive bidding procedure is used in cases when it is necessary to limit the scope of bidders due to the quality, etc. of a good." See "Provisional Regulations for the Trade of Goods."

58. "Provisional Regulations for the Trade of Goods."

59. "Nippon tetsudō kaishachō no enzetsu," *Tetsudō jihō*, no. 179 (February 1903): 8.

60. "Nippon tetsudō kaishachō no enzetsu."

61. Ericson, "Importing Locomotives in Meiji Japan," 146–147.

62. In Nippon's case, Tanaka Shōhei, the Train Section director, controversially held apparent loyalty to Beyer Peacock; this eventually led to the company president having to defend Tanaka at a stockholders meeting. "Nippon tetsudō kaishachō no enzetsu."

63. A commission established in 1869 to develop Hokkaido that invited foreign employees from the United States with extensive experience in frontier settlement to advise its activities.

64. Nihon Kokuyū Tetsudō Hokkaido Sōkyoku, ed., *Hokkaido tetsudō hyakunen-shi jō* [A century of Hokkaido railways, part 1] (Sapporo: Nihon Kokuyū Tetsudō, 1976), 748–749.

65. Tetsudōshi Gakkai, *Tetsudōshi jinbutsu jiten*, 179–180.

3. JAPAN'S INDUSTRIAL REVOLUTION

66. David Shavit, *The United States in Asia: A Historical Dictionary* (Westport, CT: Greenwood Press, 1990), 113.

67. This line connected Sapporo, the capital of Hokkaido, with Otaru, its outer port.

68. "Zai Bei kensain Kurōfōrudo yori kensa tesūryō seikyū no ken [Inspection fee request from J. U. Crawford, an inspector in the United States]," *Teishinshō kōbunsho, tetsudō no bu, kiki-buppin 6, Meiji 30-nen* [Official archives of the Ministry of Communications and Transportation, railway section, apparatus and goods, no. 6, 1897].

69. See Nakamura Naofumi, "The First Global Economy and the US-Japan Locomotive Trade: A Case Study on Baldwin Locomotive Works and Frazar & Co," *Japanese Research in Business History* 40 (2023): 11–13.

70. Brown, *Baldwin Locomotive Works*, 171–183.

71. Except for the fitting strips of boilers. See Fitch, *Report on the Manufactures of Interchangeable Mechanism*, 48.

72. See table 6.2 of Brown, *Baldwin Locomotive Works*, 181.

73. Brown, *Baldwin Locomotive Works*, 183–189; Fitch, *Report on the Manufactures of Interchangeable Mechanism*, 51–59.

74. David A. Hounshell, *From the American System to Mass Production, 1800–1932: The Development of Manufacturing Technology in the United States* (Baltimore: Johns Hopkins University Press, 1985); Hashimoto Takehiko, *Monozukuri no kagaku shi* [A scientific history of manufacturing] (Tokyo: Kōdansha, 2013).

75. Brown, *Baldwin Locomotive Works*, 182.

76. Brown, 44–46.

77. Baldwin Locomotive Works, *Orders for Engines*, 1887; table 3.6 of Nakamura, *Umi wo wataru kikansha*, 158.

78. Philip Scranton's analysis of the order books of the American machine tool manufacturer G. A. Gray Co. explains that discounts awarded by manufacturers to dealers were used as a means of paying the latter sales commissions; see Scranton, *Endless Novelty*, 200. In the case of Baldwin, however, either commissions or discounts were used depending on the dealer. Based on the fact that orders where dealers received commissions were aggregated under the category of "ordered through agency," in this book I distinguish commissions from the typical brokerage fees paid to dealers, interpreting them as intermediary brokerage fees paid to manufacturer's agents. See Baldwin Locomotive Works, *Orders for Engines*, 1890–1892, and table 3.1.

79. Baldwin Locomotive Works, *Orders for Engines*, 1890; table 3.6 of Nakamura, *Umi wo wataru kikansha*, 158.

80. Minami served as a consulting engineer for these railways, advising them on railway construction and procurement of railway materials. See Murakami, *Minami Kiyoshi-kun no keireki*, 12–19.

81. Nakamura Naofumi, "Seiki tenkanki ni okeru kikansha seizō gyō no kokusai kyōsō [International competition in the locomotive manufacturing industry during the turn of the century]," in *Kokusai kyōsōryoku no keieishi* [A business history of international competitiveness], ed. Yuzawa Takeshi, Suzuki Tsuneo, Kikkawa Takeo, and Sasaki Satoshi (Tokyo: Yūhikaku, 2009), 45–47.

82. See Nakamura, "The First Global Economy and the US-Japan Locomotive Trade," 14–17.

83. Mitsui Bussan honten kikaibu chōsakakari, *Chōsa shūhō higo hantaishō no kinkyō dai 2* [Classified research reports on competitors' recent situations, no. 2], ca. 1920, 43–46;

3. JAPAN'S INDUSTRIAL REVOLUTION

Morita Chūkichi, *Yokohama seikō meiyō kagami* [Who's who in Yokohama] (Yokohama: Yokohama Shōkyō Shinpōsha, 1910), 831–832; W. Feldwick, ed., *Present-Day Impressions of Japan,* (Yokohama: Globe Encyclopedia Co., 1919), 215; Yokohama Kaikō Shiryōkan, ed., *Zusetsu Yokohama gaikokujin kyoryūchi* [Illustration of the Yokohama Foreign Settlement] (Yokohama: Yokohama City, 1998), 90; Samuel Matthew Vauclain Jr., *Japan Diary 1904,* Southern Methodist University, DeGolyer Library, Samuel Matthews Vauclain Jr. Papers, 1896–1929, #2011.0020; Samuel Matthew Vauclain Jr., *Japan and Australia Diary 1904,* Southern Methodist University, DeGolyer Library, Samuel Matthews Vauclain, Jr. Papers, 1896–1929, #A2011.0020; Hino, *Yokohama bōeki shōkei*; Yokohama Seimeiroku Hakkōsho, ed., *Yokohama seimeiroku zen* [Complete directory of Yokohama] (Yokohama: Yokohama Seimeiroku Hakkōsho, 1898), 72.

84. Everett Frazar (1834–1901) also served as the consul general for Korea in New York from 1883 to 1900.

85. Yokohama Seimeiroku Hakkōsho, *Yokohama seimeiroku*, 72.

86. See table 3.8 of Nakamura, *Umi wo wataru kikansha*, 160.

87. Mitsui Bussan honten kikaibu chōsakakari, *Chōsa shūhō higō hantaishō no kinkyō dai 2,* 45–46.

88. Mitsui Bussan honten kikaibu chōsakakari, 45–46.

89. Nakamura, *Umi wo wataru kikansha*, 159.

90. Nakamura, 161.

91. "A Letter from Yamada Majirō to the Tokyo Head Office, Overseas Department (August 13, 1901)," *Tokio Letter No. 1 (1901–1902)*, 21–24. RG131/A1/Entry-124/Box-856 Okura, NARA at College Park.

92. See Nakamura, "The First Global Economy and the US-Japan Locomotive Trade," 17–21.

93. British Consulate in Japan, *Diplomatic and Consular Reports on Trade and Finance*, no. 1695 (February 22, 1896), 44.

94. "Kikansha kyōkyū no kyōsō [Locomotive supply competition]," *Kōgyō zasshi*, no. 133 (November 1897): 23.

95. On Tyler's promotion of locomotive sales in East Asia, see Ericson, "Importing Locomotives in Meiji Japan," 144–149; Nakamura Naofumi, "Reconsidering the US-Japan Trade in Railroad Equipment: An American Sales Representative in Early 20th-Century Japan," *ISS Discussion Paper Series*, F-199 (2024), https://www.iss.u-tokyo.ac.jp /publishments/dpf/index.html.

96. W. C. Tyler, Notebook, October 1901, courtesy of Professor Ellen B. Widmer.

97. Glenn Porter and Harold C. Livesay, *Merchants and Manufacturers* (Baltimore: Johns Hopkins University Press, 1971).

98. I express my deepest gratitude to Prof. Ellen B. Widmer of Wellesley College, Tyler's great-granddaughter, for her invaluable assistance in obtaining access to documents related to him, and to her sons, for their guidance in learning about his career.

99. Nakamura, "Reconsidering the US-Japan Trade in Railroad Equipment," 15–30.

100. In contrast, traditional salesmen lacked expertise and technological knowledge and were not subject to managerial control, which made controlling their egotistical behavior a crucial problem in early sales management. See Kazuo Usui, *The Development of Marketing Management: The Case of the USA, c. 1910–1940* (Burlington, VT: Ashgate Publishing, 2008).

3. JAPAN'S INDUSTRIAL REVOLUTION

101. Burnham, Williams & Co., *Baldwin Locomotive Works Narrow Gauge Locomotives, Japanese Edition, Frazar & Co. of Japan Agents, Yokohama* (Philadelphia: J. B. Lippincott Co., 1897).

102. Not to be confused with Joseph Ury Crawford, the former Kaitakushi consulting engineer introduced in this chapter who had returned to the United States and was living in Philadelphia as of 1901. As of 1898, W. H. Crawford was stationed in Frazar's Yokohama office as a sales engineer for Baldwin, where he marketed the company's locomotives in Japan. Ericson, "Taming the Iron Horse," 203; Yokohama Seimeiroku Hakkōsho, *Yokohama seimeiroku*, 72.

103. Ericson, "Taming the Iron Horse," 202–203.

104. Samuel M. Vauclain and Earl Chapin May, *Steaming Up! The Autobiography of Samuel M. Vauclain* (New York: Brewer and Warren, 1930), 194–200; "Vauclain Family Papers and Genealogical Research Material," Historical Society of Pennsylvania, Collection 3666.

105. Samuel Matthew Vauclain Jr., *Japan Diary 1904*, and *Japan and Australia Diary 1904*.

106. Including Barnby, E. W. Frazar, Inuzaki, and Idzumi; see table 3.8 of Nakamura, *Umi wo wataru kikansha*, 160.

107. Vauclain Jr., "Japan and Australia Diary 1904," entry for October 15, 1904. He noted that Hiraoka "had agreed [a] scheme for the development of Manchuria and the supplying of locomotives to enter into an agreement with some English or American builders."

108. Vauclain Jr. "Japan Diary 1904," October 28, 1904.

109. Vauclain Jr. "Japan Diary 1904," November 25, 1904.

4. THE RISE OF JAPANESE TRADING COMPANIES

1. Nakamura Naofumi and Ōshima Hisayuki, "Kōtsū kakumei to Meiji no shōgyō [The transport revolution and commerce in the Meiji era]," in Fukao, Nakamura, and Nakabayashi, *Iwanami kōza Nihon keizai no rekishi*, 244–245.

2. Nakamura Naofumi, "Trading Locomotives Between the USA and Japan: Okura & Co. at the Beginning of the Twentieth Century," *Journal of the Royal Asiatic Society* 34, no. 3 (2024): 522.

3. Nippon Yusen, established in 1885 as one of the Mitsubishi Group's core companies, is the largest steamship company in Japan. See William D. Wray, *Mitsubishi and the N.Y.K., 1870–1914* (Cambridge, MA: Harvard University Press, 1984).

4. Toyo Kisen, established in 1896 by Asano Sōichirō, was Japan's third-largest steamship company during the pre–World War II period.

5. International telegrams were fast but very expensive compared to international mail. Overseas offices often used a combination of both methods; for example, Ōkura Gumi's New York branch would first send a brief outline of its business to the Tokyo head office by telegram and then a detailed report by postal mail.

6. Zai nyūyoku sōryōji [Consulate general of Japan in New York], "Hōkoku: Nyūyoku kō to nisshin ryōkoku sonota tōyō shokō tono kōun jōko [Report from the consulate general of Japan in New York on the shipping situation between New York and East Asian ports including Japan and China] (November 29, 1907)," *Tsushō isan Meiji 41 nen* [Collected trade reports 1908], no. 4, 103.

4. THE RISE OF JAPANESE TRADING COMPANIES

7. See Nakagawa Kiyoshi, "Meiji Taishōki niokeru heikishōsha Takata Shōkai [Takata Shōkai, a weapons trading company in the Meiji-Taisho era]," *Hakuō hōgaku* [Hakuoh review of law and politics] 1 (1994): 203–208; Nakagawa Kiyoshi, "Meiji Taishōki no daihyōteki kikai shōsha Takata shōkai (jō) [Takata Shōkai, a representative machinery trading company during the Meiji-Taisho era]," *Hakuō daigaku ronshū* [Hakuoh University review] 9, no. 2 (1995): 68–73; Nagura Bunji, *Nihon gunji kanren sangyō shi* [A history of Japan's military-linked industries] (Tokyo: Nihon Keizai Hyōronsha, 2013), 74–78.

8. Takata Shōkai became a sole proprietorship after Takata bought out Ahrens's and James's shares after their passings in 1885 and 1888 respectively.

9. Baldwin Locomotive Works, *Register of Engines Made by Burnham William & Co.*, Baldwin Locomotive Works Collection #157, Smithsonian Institution Archives.

10. Dübs & Co., *General Particulars of Engines, Tenders, 1898*; table 2.3 of Nakamura, *Umi wo wataru kikansha*, 81.

11. Nasmyth Papers, *Loco Specifications, 1902*; table 2.8 of Nakamura, *Umi wo wataru kikansha*, 86.

12. Nakagawa, "Meiji Taishōki niokeru heikishōsha Takata Shōkai," 210; Kasai Masanao, "Takata Shōkai to Uesutinguhausyusha [Takata Shōkai and the Westinghouse Electric and Manufacturing Co.]," *Shōgaku ronshū* (Journal of commerce, economics and economic history, Fukushima University) 59, no. 4 (1991): 187–199.

13. Kasai, "Takata shōkai to Uesutinguhausyusha," 191.

14. Kiyama Minoru, *Kindai Nihon to Mitsui Bussan* [Mitsui Bussan and modern Japan], (Kyoto: Minerva Shobō, 2009). On Mitsui's railway trade see Ueyama, *Hokubei niokeru sōgō shōsha no katsudō*, and Asajima, *Senzenki Mitsui Bussan no kikai torihiki*.

15. Asajima, *Senzenki Mitsui Bussan no kikai torihiki*, 15.

16. Vulcan Foundry, "Specification Book 6," National Museums Liverpool.

17. Hills, "Some Contributions to Locomotive Development by Beyer, Peacock & Co.;" Nasmyth Papers, *Loco Specifications 1903–1904*; tables 2.7 and 2.8 of Nakamura, *Umi wo wataru kikansha*, 85–86.

18. Mitsui Bussan, *Meiji 30-nendo shimohanki jikyō hōkokusho* [Business report for the second half of FY1897], 32.

19. Mitsui Bussan later became the local agent for ALCO.

20. See Nakamura, *Umi wo wataru kikansha*, 163.

21. Ueyama, *Hokubei niokeru sōgō shōsya no katsudō*, 36.

22. Asajima, *Senzenki Mitsui Bussan no kikai torihiki*, 41. See table 3.12 of Nakamura, *Umi wo wataru kikansha*, 164. From 1897 to 1899, the London branch's shipments totaled 9.07 million yen, while those of the New York branch were 6.36 million yen.

23. Between 1893 and 1911, the company formed into a general partnership. See Watanabe Sei, *Ōkura zaibatsu no kaiko* [A retrospective of the Ōkura zaibatsu] (Tokyo: self-pub., 2002), 109–113.

24. Tetsudōshi Gakkai, *Tetsudōshi jinbutsu jiten*, 142–143.

25. Nakamura, "Trading Locomotives Between the USA and Japan," 2–3.

26. Dübs & Co., *General Particulars of Engines, Tenders*; table 2.3 of Nakamura, *Umi wo wataru kikansha*, 81.

27. Nasmyth Papers, *Loco Specifications*; table 2.8 of Nakamura, *Umi wo wataru kikansha*, 86.

28. The papers from Ōkura Gumi's New York office used as historical records in this chapter come from a collection of documents, held in NARA at College Park, that the U.S.

4. THE RISE OF JAPANESE TRADING COMPANIES

government appears to have confiscated from Japanese companies active within its borders right after Pearl Harbor. See Kawabe Nobuo, "Japanese Business in the United States Before World War II: The Case of Mitsubishi Shoji Kaisha, the San Francisco and Seattle Branches" (PhD diss., Ohio State University, 1980), 10, 242.

29. Yamada, born 1870 in Wakayama Prefecture, was as of December 1917 Ōkura Gumi's vice president for business affairs and later its president as well as a member of its board of directors. Kōjunsha, *Nihon shinshiroku Shōwa 16-nen han* [Who's who in Japan 1941] (Tokyo: Kōjunsha, 1941), "ya" column III.

30. See Ōkura & Co., *No. 1 Domestic Letters 1900–1901*, 17, RG131/A1/Entry-123/Box-838 Ōkura, NARA at College Park.

31. The major studies on Ōkura Gumi are Ōkura Zaibatsu Kenkyūkai, ed., *Ōkura zaibatsu no kenkyū* [A study of the Ōkura zaibatsu] (Tokyo: Kondo Shuppan, 1982) and Nakamura Seishi, "Taishō Shōwa shoki no Ōkura zaibatsu [The Ōkura zaibatsu from the Taisho to the early Showa eras], *Keiei shigaku* (Japan business history review) 15, no. 3 (1980): 48–74. While these make no mention of the activities of the company's U.S. offices, a basic analysis can be found in Watanabe Sei, "Hadaka ni sareta sōgō shōsha [A general trading company laid bare]," *Enerugī shi kenkyū* [Energy history review] 26 (2011): 1–67.

32. See Nakamura, "Trading Locomotives Between the USA and Japan," 5–15.

33. "A Letter from Yamada to Uchiyama Yorikichi (April 20, 1901)," *No. 1 Domestic Letters*, 32.

34. "A Letter from Yamada to the Tokyo Head Office, Overseas Department (June 10, 1901)," *No. 1 Domestic Letters*, 193–194.

35. "A Letter from Yamada to the Tokyo Head Office, Overseas Department (February 5, 1902)," *Tokio Letter No. 2* (1902), 103–104, RG131/A1/Entry–124/Box–856 Okura.

36. Nakamura, "Ōkura–gumi New York shiten no shidō to tetsudō yōhin torihiki," 209.

37. *Kanpō* [Official gazette], no. 5379 (June 10, 1901): 183.

38. "A Letter from Yamada to the Tokyo Head Office, Overseas Department (July 23, 1901)," *No. 1 Domestic Letters*, 421–425.

39. Japan's biggest general trading company before World War II and later an agent for ALCO.

40. "A Letter from Yamada to the Tokyo Head Office, Overseas Department (July 23, 1901)," *No. 1 Domestic Letters*, 421–425.

41. "A Letter from Yamada to the Tokyo Head Office, Overseas Department (July 23, 1901)."

42. "A Letter from Yamada to the Tokyo Head Office, Overseas Department (July 23, 1901)."

43. "A Letter from Yamada to the Tokyo Head Office, Overseas Department (July 23, 1901)."

44. "A Copy of a Telegraph to Rogers (July 25, 1901)," *No. 1 Domestic Letters*, 436; "A Letter from Yamada to the Tokyo Head Office, Overseas Department (July 28, 1901)," *No. 1 Domestic Letters*, 442–445.

45. "A Letter from Yamada to Kadono Chōkurō (August 4, 1901)," *No. 1 Domestic Letters*, 458–460.

46. *Tokio Letter No. 1*, 16.

47. "A Letter from Yamada to the Tokyo Head Office, Overseas Department (October 1, 1901)," *Tokio Letter No. 1*, 170–174.

48. As of 1898, Frazar's brokerage fee for Baldwin locomotives was 5 percent. Baldwin Locomotive Works, *Engine Orders, 1898–1900*.

49. *Tokio Letter No. 1*, 17–18.

4. THE RISE OF JAPANESE TRADING COMPANIES

50. "A Telegraph to Kadono (August 10, 1901)," *Tokio Letter No. 1*, 13.

51. "A Letter from Yamada to the Tokyo Head Office, Overseas Department (August 30, 1901)," *Tokio Letter No. 1*, 62–66; "A Letter from Yamada to the Tokyo Head Office, Overseas Department (September 20, 1901)," *Tokio Letter No. 1*, 151–154.

52. Nakamura Naofumi, *Chihō karano sangyō kakumei* [Reconsidering Japan's Industrial Revolution from a local perspective] (Nagoya: Nagoya University Press, 2010), 72–73.

53. "A Letter from Yamada to Tokyo Head Office (August 13, 1901)," 21–24.

54. The firebox size determines the locomotive's output; the track wheel center, which bears a heavy load, requires a material of high strength and durability.

55. Crawford became a consulting engineer for Ōkura Gumi by September 5, 1901. "A Letter from Yamada to Tokyo Head Office, Overseas Department (September 5, 1901)," *Tokio Letter No. 1*, 115–116.

56. "A Letter from Yamada to Tokyo Head Office, Overseas Department (August 22, 1901)."

57. "A Letter from Yamada to the Tokyo Head Office, Overseas Department (November 5, 1901)," *Tokio Letter No. 1*, 284–286.

58. "A Letter from Yamada to Tokyo Head Office, Overseas Department (October 17, 1901)," *Tokio Letter No. 1*, 228–231.

59. A number of companies manufactured locomotives for industrial use, including the Lima Locomotive Works (which supplied the forest industry), Porter (small locomotives), and the Vulcan Iron Works.

60. Mitsui Bussan, *Mitsui Bussan shitenchō kaigiroku 1 Meiji 35-nen* [Minutes of the Mitsui Bussan branch managers' meeting 1], no. 4 (1902): 18–19.

61. Mitsui Bussan, *Mitsui Bussan shitenchō kaigiroku 1*, 16–17.

62. Mitsui Bussan, 21.

63. Mitsui Bussan, 17–18.

64. Willard C. Tyler, "Notebook, 1901–1902," August 26, 1902. With appreciation to Prof. Ellen Widmer for sharing the W. C. Tyler records in her possession.

65. "A Letter from Yamada to Tokyo Head Office, Overseas Department (July 23, 1901)," *No. 1 Domestic Letters 1900–1901*, 421–425.

66. "Because of its strong business presence in South America, ALCO does not have the courage to simply cut all ties with American Trading Co." Mitsui Bussan, *Mitsui Bussan shitenchō kaigiroku 1*, 18–19.

67. In this regard, Iwahara Kenzō commented, "ALCO has made American Trading Co. its agent in South America and is considering entrusting us with its business in Japan." Mitsui Bussan, *Mitsui Bussan shitenchō kaigiroku 1*, 18–19.

68. "Agency Contract No. 5, American Locomotive Sales Co.," in *Kyū Bussan keiyaku shorui* [Former Mitsui Bussan contract documents], Mitsui Archives, Bussan 2367–4.

69. "Agency Contract No. 5, American Locomotive Sales Co."

70. "A Letter from Yamada to Tokyo Head Office, Overseas Department (September 14, 1901)," *Tokio Letter No. 1*, 139–143.

71. He again raised this point to the head office as follows: "With regard to the locomotives for Chosen Keifu Railway, about which we received an inquiry from the head office, although we initially requested price quotes from ALCO and Baldwin, we were refused on both counts. Given these circumstances, I believe that it is absolutely necessary for our company to form a special relationship with Rogers." In "A Letter from Yamada to Tokyo Head Office, Overseas Department (January 25, 1902)," *Tokio Letter No. 2*, 61–62.

4. THE RISE OF JAPANESE TRADING COMPANIES

72. "A Letter from Yamada to Tokyo Head Office, Overseas Department (January 25, 1902)," 61–62.
73. "A Letter from Yamada to Tokyo Head Office, Overseas Department (February 15, 1902)," *Tokio Letter No. 2*, 129.
74. "A Letter from Yamada to Tokyo Head Office, Overseas Department (March 8, 1902)," *Tokio Letter No. 2*, 210.
75. "A Letter from Yamada to Tokyo Head Office, Overseas Department (March 24, 1902)," *Tokio Letter No. 2*, 238.
76. "A Letter from Yamada to Tokyo Head Office, Overseas Department (May 28, 1902)," *Tokio Letter No. 2*, 466.
77. "A Letter from Yamada to Tokyo Head Office, Overseas Department (June 10, 1902)," *Tokio Letter No. 3*, 6.
78. See chapter 1 of Nakamura, *Nihon tetsudōgyō no keisei*, and Hayashida, *Nihon no tetsudō sōsō ki*.

5. WAR, EMPIRE BUILDING, AND THE LOCOMOTIVE TRADE

1. Chiba Isao, "Nisshin-Nichiro sensō" [The Sino-Japanese and Russo-Japanese Wars], in *Iwanami koza Nihon rekishi* [Iwanami series on Japanese history], vol. 16 (Tokyo: Iwanami Shoten, 2014), 113–146.
2. Also known as the Itsubi Incident, during which the Japanese legation garrison led the killing of the queen who had been the consort of Gojong, the last king of the Joseon Dynasty.
3. The main line of the Chinese Eastern Railway (Manzhouli–Suifenhe) was a loan railroad built by Russia as a short-circuit line for the Trans-Siberian Railway and opened in 1901.
4. See Felix Patrikeeff and Harold Shukman, *Railways and the Russo-Japanese War: Transporting War* (Abingdon, UK: Routledge, 2007).
5. Chiba, "Nisshin-Nichiro sensō," 140–141.
6. The Yongsan–Sinuiju line went into service in April 1905 as a military railroad.
7. Steven J. Ericson, "Riding the Rails: The Japanese Railways Meet the Challenge of War," in *The Russo-Japanese War in Global Perspective: World War Zero*, vol. 2, ed. John Steinberg et al. (Leiden: Brill, 2007), 225–237.
8. The Japanese standard gauge is three feet six inches, while the Russian is five feet.
9. Ericson, "Riding the Rails," 244–247.
10. Christian Wolmar, *Engines of War: How Wars Were Won and Lost on the Railways* (London: Atlantic Books, 2010), chap. 5.
11. See Nakamura, *Umi wo wataru kikansha*, 166. In 1905, the market share of British rolling stock in Japan was around 40 percent.
12. Tetsudōshi Gakkai, *Tetsudōōshi jinbutsu jiten*, 188–189.
13. Tetsudōshi Gakkai, 328–330.
14. Taiwan Sōtokufu tetsudōbu, ed., *Taiwan tetsudō shi* [A history of Taiwan's railways] (Taipei: Taiwan Sōtokufu, 1911).
15. Five of the twelve cars added to the fleet in 1908 were B6-class tank locomotives (0-6-2) imported by the Japanese government in large numbers for wartime transportation during the Russo-Japanese War and later transferred to Taiwan.

5. WAR, EMPIRE BUILDING, AND THE LOCOMOTIVE TRADE

16. Sawai, *Nihon tetsudō sharyō kōgyō shi*, 49–50.

17. Takahashi Yasutaka, *Nihon shokuminchi tetsudō shiron* [A history of Japanese colonial railroads] (Tokyo: Nihon Keizai Hyōronsha, 1995), 57–68. The Keifu and Keinin Railways merged in 1903.

18. Takahashi, *Nihon shokuminchi tetsudō shiron*, 75.

19. Chōsen Sōtokufu Tetsudō-kyoku, ed., *Chōsen tetsudō shi* [A history of Korea's railways] (Seoul: Chōsen Sōtokufu, 1915).

20. Kunizawa joined Kyushu Railway after graduating from the Civil Engineering Department of Tokyo Imperial University in 1889 (as part of the third generation of Japanese engineers who graduated from the university after its 1886 establishment). He moved to the IGR in 1893 and served as the Kanazawa section manager. On the SMR's establishment, he became a director, and in 1908, its vice president; he then chaired the company's board of directors from 1917 to 1919. See Tetsudōshi Gakkai, *Tetsudōshi jinbutsu jiten*, 171.

21. Of the seven technical executives in the railroad division as of March 1909, six were from the IGR, four of whom had experience in the Field Railway HQ. Minami Manshū tetsudō kabushiki kaisha, ed., *Minami Manshū tetsudō kabushiki kaisha jūnenshi* [The tenth anniversary of the SMR] (Dalian: South Manchuria Railway, 1919); Minami Manshū tetsudō kabushiki kaisha, ed., *Shokuinroku* [Employee directory] (Dalian: South Manchuria Railway, 1908).

22. The narrow-gauge locomotives requisitioned during the Russo-Japanese War were gradually returned to the domestic railroads that had supplied them.

23. Lim Chaisung, *Higashi Ajia no naka no Mantetsu* [The SMR in East Asia] (Nagoya: Nagoya University Press, 2021), 103–110.

24. Karafuto-chō [Karafuto Agency], ed., *Karafuto yōran* [Karafuto handbook] (Toyohara: Karafuto-chō, 1914), 217.

25. *Review of the Locomotive Industry*, 1909–1911, UGD109/2/5, Glasgow University Archives; table 4.1 of Nakamura, *Umi wo wataru kikansha*, 185.

26. "While the falling off in numbers as compared with the previous year is considerable, it is seen to be very serious indeed when compared with three years ago, and it is still more pronounced when it is considered that even the fewer number in 1910 were for the most part on short time." *Review of the Locomotive Industry*, 1910, 2–3.

27. Kita, "19-seiki Gurasugō jōki kikansha seizō hatten shi," 55.

28. R. H. Campbell, "The North British Locomotive Company Between the Wars," in *Business in the Age of Depression and War*, ed. R. P. T. Davenport-Hines (London: Frank Cass, 1990), 172–205, tables VII, VIII, IX.

29. Digby, "The Earning Power of British Rolling Stock from 1894 to 1903," 279–280; table 1.1 of Nakamura, *Umi wo wataru kikansha*, 47.

30. North British Locomotive Co., *Order Book 1*, GC/152/NBL, NBL Collection, Mitchell Library in Glasgow; table 4.3 of Nakamura, *Umi wo wataru kikansha*, 187.

31. Whittall was a British trading company established in 1875 by James Whittall (1827–1893), a Jardine Matheson partner and Shanghai branch manager. See George B. Endacott, *A Biographical Sketch-Book of Early Hong Kong* (Hong Kong: Hong Kong University Press, 1962), 161; Ishii, *Kindai Nihon to Igirisu shihon*, 7.

32. Yamashita Masaaki, "Dai ichiji taisen zen no sharyō kikansha sangyō to setsubi shintaku kin'yū [Rolling stock, locomotive industry and equipment trust financing before World War I]," *Shōken kenkyū* [Securities research review], no. 60 (1980): 229–306; Brown,

5. WAR, EMPIRE BUILDING, AND THE LOCOMOTIVE TRADE

Baldwin Locomotive Works; order books of Baldwin, ALCO, and Rogers. See table 4.4 of Nakamura, *Umi wo wataru kikansha*, 188.

33. Established in August 1888 with the Moji–Yatsushiro line, the Tosu–Nagasaki line, and the Kokura–Yukuhashi line. Maschinenfabrik Esslingen also delivered four rack locomotives to the IGR in 1892 that were used to cross the Usui Pass.

34. Yuzawa, "Igirisu keizai no teitai to jōki kikansha yushutsu."

35. Nakamura, *Nihon testudōgyō no keisei*, 302.

36. See part 2 of Nakamura, *Nihon tetsudōgyō no keisei*.

37. Hubert Kiesewetter, *Industrielle Revolution in Deutschland* (Eichstatt: Franz Steiner Verlag, 2004), chaps. 12 and 14.

38. The Krauss tank locomotive (25.5 tons) was GBP 920, whereas Nasmyth Wilson's (21.34 tons) was GBP 1,030. See Nasmyth Papers, *Specifications and Reference Book 2*, Salford Local History Library; Krauss-Maffei, *Krauss Auftragsbuch* [Order book, Bayerisches Wirtschaftsarchiv].

39. "Locomotive Engines for India" and "Indian Locomotive Engine Contracts," *The Engineer*, October 25, 1901, 433–435; "Foreign Trade and Commercial Espionage," *The Engineer*, June 14, 1912, 625.

40. "Nihon Tetsudō kaishachō no enzetsu," 8.

41. "Nihon niokeru Doitsu kikansha [German locomotives in Japan]," *Tetsudō jihō*, no. 207 (September 1903): 8.

42. *Tetsudō jihō*, no. 205 (August 1903): 8.

43. See table 4.6 of Nakamura, *Umi wo wataru kikansha*, 190.

44. "Doku Bei kikansha no kyōsō [Competition between German and American locomotives]," *Tetsudō jihō*, no. 229 (February 1904): 5.

45. Kōda, *Doitsu kōsaku kikai kōgyō seiritsu shi*, 253–255.

46. "Nihon Tetsudō kaishachō no enzetsu," 8.

47. "Shima Yasujirō shi wo tou 1 [An interview with Mr. Shima Yasujiro 1]," *Tetsudō jihō*, no. 265 (October 1904): 5.

48. "Shima Yasujirō shi wo tou 1," 6.

49. Technically Sale & Frazar from 1904 onward. Charles Sale, the partner in Frazar's new name, notably supplied Japan with leather, food, and machinery during the Russo-Japanese War and provided railroad materials for Keifu, Keigi, and the SMR after the war. Morita, *Yokohama seikō meiyo kagami*, 832.

50. Baldwin Locomotive Works, *Engine Specifications 1904*, MSS 0061-61x, Series 2, Southern Methodist University, DeGolyer Library; table 4.7 of Nakamura, *Umi wo wataru kikansha*, 191.

51. *Tetsudō jihō*, no. 262 (September 1904): 10.

52. *Tetsudō jihō*, no. 263 (October 1904): 12; *Tetsudō jihō*, no. 264 (October 1904): 9.

53. Saitō Akira, *Jōki kikansha 200-nen shi* [200 years of steam locomotives] (Tokyo: NTT Press, 2007), 220. Here Saitō mentions 171 British, 166 American, and 75 German locomotives. However, the 30 German locomotives delivered in 1904 were ordered in August 1903, not during the Russo-Japanese War.

54. Vauclain, *Japan and Australia Diary 1904* (October 15, 1904), A2011/0020.

55. Mitsui Bussan, *Kikai tetsudō kanamono kaigi gijiroku Meiji 39-nen* [Proceedings of a meeting on machinery, railroads, and metal, 1906], 41–42, Bussan 206.

56. Mitsui Bussan, *Kikai tetsudō kanamono kaigi gijiroku*, 41.

6. LOCALIZING LOCOMOTIVE PRODUCTION IN JAPAN

57. See table 3.11 of Nakamura, *Umi wo wataru kikansha*, 163.

58. Mitsui Bussan, *Meiji 37-nendo jigyō hōkoku* [FY 1904 business report] (Tokyo: Maruzen, 2007 reprint), 9.

59. ALCO, *Register of Contracts, 1906–1907*, Ledgers, Syracuse University; table 4.8 of Nakamura, *Umi wo wataru kikansha*, 192–193.

60. Incidentally, Crawford was the production inspector for the Kansei Railway's locomotives manufactured by the Pittsburgh factory.

61. The *Tetsudō jihō* reported that the SMR ordered from the United States "180 locomotives, 60 passenger cars, and 2,000 freight cars currently being manufactured. Of these, seven locomotives are scheduled to arrive in Dalian as early as late June [1907]. Passenger and freight cars are also expected to gradually arrive and to be put into service around the same time." *Tetsudō jihō*, no. 399 (May 1907): 8.

62. Table 4.8 of Nakamura, *Umi wo wataru kikansha*, 192–193.

63. Table 4.9 of Nakamura, 194. The volume of railroad material transacted by Mitsui Bussan was valued at 4,881,000 yen in the second half of 1907 and at 10,406,000 yen in the first half of 1908.

64. Mitsui Bussan, *Kikaibu kaigi gijiroku Meiji 40-nen* [Proceedings of a meeting on the machinery department, 1907], 7.

65. Mitsui Bussan, *Kikaibu kaigi gijiroku*, 7–8.

66. Table 4.9 of Nakamura, *Umi wo wataru kikansha*, 194.

67. Mitsui Bussan, *Jigyō hōkokusho*, no. 5, 30–31, and no. 6, 37–38. Imports and sales of railroad materials for the first half of 1912 totaled 2.22 million yen for Mitsui and 64.75 million yen for Japan as a whole.

68. Table 4.10 of Nakamura, *Umi wo wataru kikansha*, 195.

69. Ogawa Shigen, *Nan Shin tetsudō senro chōsa kiji* [Report on the survey of railroads in the Southern Qing China] (December 1899–April 1900), 7.

70. Yoshikawa Sanjirō, *Shin-koku Fukken Sekkō ryōshō nai tetsudō senro chōsa hōkokusho* [Report on the railroad survey in Qing China's Fujian and Zhejiang provinces], 1900.

71. ALCO, *Register of Contracts 1907*; table 4.8 of Nakamura, *Umi wo wataru kikansha*, 192.

72. Mitsui Bussan, *Kikaibu kaigi gijiroku Meiji 40-nen*, 20.

73. Mitsui Bussan, 15.

74. Mitsui Bussan, *Meiji 42-nen shimohanki jigyō hōkokusho* [FY 1909 second half business report] (Tokyo: Maruzen, 2007 reprint), 26.

6. LOCALIZING LOCOMOTIVE PRODUCTION IN JAPAN

1. Andrew Gordon, *The Evolution of Labor Relations in Japan: Heavy Industry, 1853–1955* (Cambridge, MA: Harvard University Press), chap. 2.

2. John P. Tang, "Railroad Expansion and Industrialization: Evidence from Meiji Japan," *Journal of Economic History* 74, no. 3 (2014): 863–886.

3. This formula resulted from negotiations between the Japanese government and railroad company stakeholders, with the average profit ratio duration and the coefficient for its multiplication as points of contention. See Nakamura Naofumi, "Gurōbaru ka to Meiji no tetsudō hatten [Railroad development and globalization in the Meiji era]," in *Meiji to iu isan* [The Meiji era as heritage], ed. Takii Kazuhiro (Kyoto: Minerva Shobō, 2020), 509–525.

6. LOCALIZING LOCOMOTIVE PRODUCTION IN JAPAN

4. Six of Baldwin's twenty locomotives were intended for the Korean Peninsula.
5. "Tetsudōin jimu bunshō kitei dai 14-jō [Article 14 of Railway Agency rules on task divisions]," *Shin tetsudō hōreishū zen* [New complete laws on railroads] (March 1909), 15.
6. "Tetsudō kanrikyoku bunka kitei dai 6-jō [Article 6 of administrative rules on railroad divisions]," *Shin tetsudō hōreishū zen*, 23.
7. In 1913, the manufacturing sections of the railroad administration bureaus were centralized in the Manufacturing Division of the Railway Agency, while said agency directly oversaw the factories. But the Manufacturing Department's establishment in 1915 returned manufacturing sections to the railroad administration bureaus, which also reclaimed their factories. Nihon Kokuyū Tetsudō, ed., *Tetsudō gijutsu hattatsu shi V dai 4-hen sharyō to kikai 1* [A history of railroad technology development V, part 4: rolling stock and machines 1] (Tokyo: Nihon Kokuyū Tetsudō, 1958), 2–3.
8. See table 5.1 of Nakamura, *Umi wo wataru kikansha*, 222.
9. The Kobe factory stopped repairing locomotives in 1911 and closed in 1916. Nihon Kokuyū Tetsudō, *Tetsudō gijutsu hattatsu shi V*, 1191.
10. Asakura Kiichi, "Shima Yasujirō-sensei no jigyō [Mr. Shima Yasujiro's tasks]," *Journal of the Society of Mechanical Engineers* 51, no. 352 (1947): 20.
11. Akiyama Shōhachi had experience designing and producing the original C tank locomotive at Nippon's Omiya factory in 1904. See Usui, *Kikansha no keifuzu*, 3:315.
12. Ōta Yoshimatsu learned to draw and design locomotives from R. F. Trevithick and Mori Hikozō at the IGR Kobe factory after 1888. In 1904, he moved to Shinbashi factory with Mori, where he oversaw locomotive design. During his time at Shinbashi, he and Mori designed the Japanese original lightweight passenger locomotive. In 1910, he left the IGR to head Kawasaki Dockyard's locomotive design section, and in 1913 he designed the JNR 9600-class tender locomotive, Japan's first original standard freight locomotive. Tetsudōshi Gakkai, *Tetsudō shi jinbutsu jiten*, 94.
13. However, the Railway Agency did not maintain the capacity to manufacture new rolling stock. In 1910, it divided up the manufacture and repair of rolling stock and ordered new stock from private manufacturers in Japan; thereafter, its factories concentrated on repairs. See Daito Eisuke, "Railways and Scientific Management in Japan, 1907–30," *Business History* 31, no. 1 (1989): 9–10.
14. Asakura, "Shima Yasujirō-sensei no jigyō," 20. As explained in chapter 5, these locomotives had been converted to the narrow gauge used by domestic Japanese railroads, so the Railway Agency did not have to retrofit them. Most of them ran on government and private railroads, with a few moved to the Taiwan Sōtokufu.
15. Sawai, *Nihon tetsudō sharyō kōgyō shi*, 56–57.
16. Takamura Naosuke, "Dokusen soshiki no keisei [Formation of monopoly structures]," in *Nichi-Ro sengo no Nihon keizai* [The Japanese economy after the Russo-Japanese war], ed. Takamura Naosuke (Tokyo: Hanawa Shobō, 1988), 171.
17. Oikawa Yoshinobu, *Inoue Masaru* (Kyoto: Minerva Shobō, 2013), 221–239.
18. Usui, *Kikansha no keifuzu*, 3:340–347.
19. Hattori learned locomotive technology as a technical trainee (*gijutsu kenshūsei*) at IGR in 1874 and became an engineer at IGR's Kobe factory until 1896. See table 3.1 of Nakamura, *Umi wo wataru kikansha*, 153.
20. Sawai, *Nihon tetsudō sharyō kōgyō shi*, 46–53.

6. LOCALIZING LOCOMOTIVE PRODUCTION IN JAPAN

21. Sawai, 57.

22. Harada Katsumasa, *Nihon tetsudō shi* [Japan's railroad history] (Tokyo: Tosui Shobō, 2001), 85–95.

23. Sawai, *Nihon tetsudō sharyō kōgyō shi*, 58–59.

24. "Superheating in the Past," *The Engineer*, November 18, 1910, 546.

25. J. F. Gairns, *Superheating on Locomotives* (London: Locomotive Publishing, 1912), 38–55.

26. "The Paris Exhibition: Borsig Locomotive with Superheater," *The Engineer*, September 7, 1900, 233.

27. "The Paris Exhibition," 233.

28. "Superheating Locomotives," *The Engineer*, April 8, 1904, 361.

29. "International Exhibition at St. Louis," *The Engineer*, March 17, 1905, 258.

30. "American Engineering News: Locomotive and Rolling Stock in the United States," *The Engineer*, April 26, 1907, 430.

31. The Schenectady superheater was invented by F. C. Cole, ALCO's chief engineer. See Robert Garbe, *The Application of Highly Superheated Steam to Locomotives* (New York: Norman W. Henley, 1908), 34–35.

32. "Railway Matters," *The Engineer*, May 11, 1906, 474.

33. "Railway Matters," *The Engineer*, January 24, 1908, 89.

34. Robert Garbe, "The Application of Highly Superheated Steam to Locomotives, No. 1," *The Engineer*, October 25, 1907, 407. This article was serialized seven times and published in New York in 1908. See Garbe, *The Application of Highly Superheated Steam*.

35. George Hughes, "Railway Matters," *The Engineer*, January 24, 1908, 89.

36. "Superheating," *The Engineer*, February 6, 1903, 149.

37. "Superheating Locomotives," *The Engineer*, February 26, 1904, 211.

38. "The Work of Superheater and Compound Locomotives," *The Engineer*, December 30, 1908, 662.

39. "Compounding and Superheating in Horwich Locomotives No. 1," *The Engineer*, March 18, 1910, 287. Subsequently serialized thrice until April 1910.

40. "Locomotive Engines in 1911," *The Engineer*, January 5, 1912. See also the same column in the January 16 issue from the same year.

41. "Compounding and Superheating, Lancashire and Yorkshire Railway" and "Railway Matters," *The Engineer*, January 20, 1911, 61 and 67.

42. "A Question of Superheating," *The Engineer*, November 24, 1911, 542.

43. Aoki Eiichi, "Kōtsū, un'yu taikei no tōgō II tetsudō [Integration of traffic and transportation networks II: Railways]," in *Kōtsū, un'yu no hattatsu to gijutsu kakushin* [Technological innovation and development of traffic and transportation], ed. Yamamoto Hirofumi (Tokyo: United Nations University Press, 1986), 91–92.

44. Nihon Kokuyū Tetsudō, *Tetsudō gijutsu hattatsu shi V*, 14; Usui, *Kikansha no keifuzu*, 4:475–477.

45. Aoki Eiichi, "Kōtsu un'yu gijutsu no jiritsu [The independence of transformation technology]," in Yamamoto, *Kōtsu, un'yu no hattatsu to gijutsu kakushin*, 92; Harada Katsumasa, *Nihon tetsudō shi* [A history of Japan's railroads] (Tokyo: Tosui Shobō, 2001), 84–99.

46. Usui, *Kikansha no keifuzu*, 4:458–465.

47. However, when Mallet-type compound locomotives were deployed in 1912, their specifications changed to the superheated steam type. Usui, *Kikansha no keifuzu*, 4:450–455.

6. LOCALIZING LOCOMOTIVE PRODUCTION IN JAPAN

48. Asakura graduated from the Tokyo Imperial University's School of Mechanical Engineering in 1908 and became an engineer with the Manufacturing Section.

49. Asakura, "Shima Yasujirō sensei no jigyō," 20.

50. On March 22, 1910, Shiba Gonzaburō was appointed head of the Manufacturing Section. See *Kanpō*, March 22, 1910. In 1911, upon returning to Japan, Shima reclaimed the same post.

51. The tender had been publicly announced at least before September; a letter from the London branch of Ōkura Gumi to its Tokyo head office, dated October 14, 1911, bears a reference to an earlier letter from Tokyo dated September 20, titled "I. G. R. NEW REQUIREMENTS." Ōkura Gumi New York Branch, *London to Tokyo 1910–1926*, RG131/A1/Entry-129/Box-949, NARA at College Park.

52. "A Letter from Claude M. MacDonald (British Embassy, Tokyo) to Sir Edward Grey," January 21, 1911, *Foreign Office Files for Japan, 1911*, FO371/1141/4357, UK National Archives.

53. "A Letter from the London Branch of Ōkura Gumi to the Tokyo Head Office (October 11, 1910)," *London to Tokyo 1910–1926*.

54. "A Letter from the London Branch of Ōkura Gumi to the Tokyo Head Office (November 5, 1910)," *London to Tokyo 1910–1926*.

55. "A Letter from the London Branch of Ōkura Gumi to the Tokyo Head Office (November 12, 1910)," *London to Tokyo 1910–1926*.

56. "A Letter from the London Branch of Ōkura Gumi to the Tokyo Head Office (December 10, 1910)," *London to Tokyo 1910–1926*. This clarifies that the London branch was unaware of the extension of the tender results.

57. "A Letter from the London Branch of Ōkura Gumi to the Tokyo Head Office (December 17, 1910)," *London to Tokyo 1910–1926*.

58. While the wheel arrangement ALCO proposed was 4-6-2, the original specifications required a 4-6-0.

59. At this time, Shima, who had drafted the specifications for the model locomotives, opined that both ALCO and NBL should be rejected. See Usui, *Kikansha no keifuzu*, 4:461.

60. North British Locomotive, *Engine Orders*, 39–40. This appears in NBL's catalog introducing the locomotives to be shown at the 1910 Railway and Land Transport Exhibition in Buenos Aires. See North British Locomotive, *The Locomotives of Argentina* (Glasgow: NBL, 1909).

61. "A Letter from the London Branch of Ōkura Gumi to the Tokyo Head Office (December 31, 1910)," *London to Tokyo 1910–1926*.

62. "Tenders for Locomotives for Japan: North British Locomotive Co. Request Assistance of FO in Obtaining Tenders (December 24, 1910)," FO371/925/46506.

63. "A Telegram from Springburn [NBL] to London [FO] (at 9:41 a.m., December 24, 1910)," FO371/925/46798.

64. "A Letter from NBL [Glasgow] to Secretary of State for Foreign Affairs [London] (December 24, 1910)," FO371/925/46798. The Foreign Office received this on December 28.

65. "A Telegram from FO to Sir C. MacDonald, Tokyo, Telegram No. 39 (at 1:15 p.m., December 24, 1910)," FO371/925/46798.

66. "A Letter from Claude MacDonald to Edward Grey (January 21, 1911)," FO371/1141/4357.

6. LOCALIZING LOCOMOTIVE PRODUCTION IN JAPAN

67. After receiving the letter dated January 21, the British Foreign Office informed the NBL of this information on February 10, 1911. See "A Letter from FO Chief Clerk [London] to NBL [Glasgow] (February 10, 1911)," FO371/1141/4357.

68. Sawai, *Nihon tetsudō sharyō kōgyō shi*, 60–61.

69. The Brooks factory locomotives were shipped between March 14 and 25 and the Schenectady ones between March 25 and 28. American Locomotive Company, *Register of Contracts No. 11*, Ledgers, ALCO Records, in Syracuse University Library.

70. According to Asakura, "The order was placed around February (1911), but the delivery date was exceptionally short." Asakura Kiichi, *Gijutsu seikatsu 50-nen* [50 years of engineer life] (Tokyo: Nikkan Kōgyō Shinbunsha, 1958), 9.

71. Usui, *Kikansha no keifuzu*, 4:464.

72. "A Letter from NBL to Secretary of State for Foreign Affairs (February 12, 1911)," FO371/1141/5525.

73. Ishii, *Kindai Chūgoku to Igirisu shihon*, 30–33.

74. Sawai, *Nihon tetsudō sharyō kōgyō shi*, 58–61; Usui, *Kikansha no keifuzu*, 4:464–465; ALCO, *Register of Contracts Vols. 11–12* (1910–1912).

75. Usui, *Kikansha no keifuzu*, 4:442.

76. Shima returned in 1912. See Asakura, *Gijutsu seikatsu 50-nen*, 20.

77. See Nakamura, "Diversification and Convergence," 60–62, for the following section.

78. Asakura, *Gijutsu seikatsu 50-nen*, 10–11.

79. Asakura, 11.

80. In February 1912, Asakura moved to Munich, where he served as the inspector for four steep-grade superheated tanks made by Maffei and grew his knowledge of German locomotive manufacturing practices. Asakura, *Gijutsu seikatsu 50-nen*, 15.

81. Nakaoka, *Nihon kindai gijutsu no keisei*, 352–354.

82. Usui, *Kikansha no keifuzu*, 4:465.

83. Sawai, *Nihon tetsudō sharyō kōgyō shi*, 59.

84. Usui, *Kikansha no keifuzu*, 4:479–487.

85. Sawai, *Nihon tetsudō sharyō kōgyō shi*, 59.

86. Asakura Kiichi, "9600-kei no sekkei no omoide [Memories of designing the JNR class 9600]," *Tetsudō pikutoriaru* [Railway pictorial], no. 175 (1965): 4–6.

87. Asakura, *Gijutsu seikatsu 50-nen*, 15.

88. Usui, *Kikansha no keifuzu*, 4:448.

89. To overcome the severe limitations and fragility of narrow-gauge railroad tracks, Shima and other mechanical engineers at the Railway Agency advocated reconstructing them to standard gauge in the late 1910s. This was opposed by the Ministry of Finance, who worried about financial difficulties, and political parties, especially the Seiyūkai, who wanted to construct new nationwide lines that would appeal to local voters. In the late 1930s, the Ministry of Railways tried to construct a new standard gauge line and develop a bullet train (*dangan ressha*) system; both failed due to World War II. As a result, the introduction of standard gauge in Japan was postponed until the 1964 construction of the Shinkansen.

90. A future task is to understand the development of locomotive technology by investigating the accumulation of skilled workers in this manufacturing industry.

91. Sawai, *Nihon tetsudō sharyō kōgyō shi*, 60–61. Kawasaki Dockyard's 8850-class locomotive, built in 1912, copied the same type that Borsig manufactured in 1911.

6. LOCALIZING LOCOMOTIVE PRODUCTION IN JAPAN

92. As discussed below, Japan continues to import small German and U.S. locomotives.

93. Abel, *Dream Super-Express*, chap. 5.

94. Mitsui Bussan Kikaibu, *Kikai shōbai to naichi kōgyō kai no sūsei* [Trends in domestic industries and machinery trading] (Tokyo: Mitsui Bussan, 1919), 3.

95. Mitsui Bussan Kikaibu, *Kikai shōbai to naichi kōgyō*, 6. Following its final order for twenty-four Mallet-type compound steep-grade locomotives from ALCO in 1912, Mitsui shifted to supplying rolling stock materials to domestic locomotive manufacturers.

96. Table 4.11 of Nakamura, *Umi wo wataru kikansha*, 196.

97. Table 5.3 of Nakamura, 224.

98. See "Shina no tetsudō [Railroads in China]" in Mitsui Bussan Kikaibu, *Kikai shōbai to naichi kōgyō*, 35–36.

99. Akasaka Yoshihiro, "Kansen kokuyūkago no shitetsu yusō shijō [The transport market for private railroads after railroad nationalization]," in *Shijō to keiei no rekishi* [History of markets and management], ed. Andō Seiichi and Fujita Teiichirō (Osaka: Seibundō Shuppan, 1996), 239–242.

100. Akasaka, "Kansen kokuyūkago," 248–251.

101. See table 5.4 of Nakamura, *Umi wo wataru kikansha*, 220, and 224n81.

102. Established in 1907 by Amenomiya Keijirō and reorganized as the Dai-Nippon Kidō Ironworks in 1911. Nakagawa Kōichi, Imashiro Mitsuhide, Kato Shinichi, and Seko Tatsuo, *Keiben ōkoku Amenomiya* [Amenomiya's light railroad kingdom] (Tokyo: Tanzawa Shinsha, 1972), 66–67.

103. Nakamura, *Umi wo wataru kikansha*, 224.

104. Other medium-sized manufacturers such as Nippon Sharyo, Ishikawa Ironworks, Mita Ironworks, Kusunoki Machinery, and Fukagawa Shipyard also made small steam locomotives. Sawai, *Nihon tetsudō sharyō kōgyō shi*, 94.

105. Usui, *Kikansha no keifuzu*, 1:94–95.

106. Between 1911 and 1913, Orenstein & Koppel introduced and standardized interchangeable parts under the guidance of G. Schlesinger, who played a key role in propagating the American system in Germany. Kōda, *Doitsu kōsaku kikai kōgyō seiritsu shi*, 265.

107. Usui, *Kikansha no keifuzu*, 2:232. World War I disrupted imports from German manufacturers; small and medium-sized Japanese manufacturers took advantage of this opportunity to increase their production. Nakagawa et al., *Keiben ōkoku Amenomiya*, 67; Sawai, *Nihon tetsudō sharyō kōgyō shi*, 96–98.

108. Usui, *Kikansha no keifuzu*, 4:234–235.

109. Inoue, "Nihon kindai gijutsushi no ichi kenkyū," 87–89; Nakaoka, *Nihon kindai gijutsu no keisei*, 322–406.

110. Inoue, "Nihon kindai gijutsushi no ichi kenkyū," 88.

111. Sawai, *Nihon tetsudō sharyō kōgyō shi*, 132–133, 175–179.

112. Of the total locomotive imports for the period 1929–1933, Japanese products accounted for 93.8 percent in Taiwan, 95.9 percent in Korea, and 74.3 percent in the SMR. Sawai, *Nihon tetsudō sharyō kōgyō shi*, chaps. 3 and 4.

113. See the introduction to Onozuka Tomoji, ed., *Dai 1-ji sekai taisen kaisen gen'in no saikentō* [Reconsidering the causes of World War I's outbreak] (Tokyo: Iwanami Shoten, 2014), 1–37.

114. See Sawai, *Nihon tetsudō sharyō kōgyō shi*, chaps. 3 and 4.

115. Sawai, chap. 4.

CONCLUSION

1. See part 2 of Nakamura, *Nihon tetsudōgyō no keisei*; Nakamura Naofumi, "Meijiki tetsudōgyō ni okeru kigyō tōchi to kigyō kin'yū [Railroad industry corporate governance and financing in Meiji Japan]," in *Kindai Nihon no enerugī to kigō katsudō* [Energy and corporate activities in modern Japan], ed. Ogino Yoshihiro (Tokyo: Nihon Keizai Hyōronsha, 2010), 119–136.
2. Suzuki Toshio, *Japanese Government Loan Issues on the London Capital Market, 1870–1913* (London: Athlone Press, 1994); Suzuki Toshio, "Dai ichiji sekai taisen zen no Rondon kin'yū shijō to Nihon kigyō [Japanese firms in the London financial market before World War I]," in *Sangyō kakumei to kigyō keiei* [Business administration and the Industrial Revolution], ed. Abe Takeshi and Nakamura Naofumi (Kyoto: Minerva Shobō, 2010), 281–258.
3. Nakaoka, *Nihon kindai gijutsu no keisei*, 455–460.
4. See Nakamura, "Diversification and Convergence," 46–55.
5. In 1903, there were 30 locomotives in Taiwan and 19 in Korea, including the 13 at Keifu Railway (then under construction); both totals were far below Japan's 1,604 locomotives. Taiwan Sōtokufu Kōtsū-kyoku Tetsudōbu, ed., *Taiwan tetsudō shi ge* [A history of Taiwan Railways, vol. 2] (Taipei: Taiwan Sōtokufu, 1911), 108–109, table 4.7.
6. Porter and Livesay, *Merchants and Manufacturers*, 142–143; Nakamura, "Reconsidering the US-Japan Trade in Railroad Equipment."
7. In particular, the Tientsin–Pukow Railway was a significant customer for American manufacturers. On its construction and management, see chapters 1 and 2 of Köll, *Railroads and the Transformation of China*.
8. Manufacturers and customers faced prohibitive search and transaction costs in this emerging market; multinational trading companies possessed information that lowered these costs and increased overall profits. See Nakamura Naofumi, "The First Global Economy and the US-Japanese Locomotive Trade," *Japanese Research in Business History*, no. 40 (2023): 6–23.
9. Sawai, *Nihon Tetsudō sharyō kōgyō shi*, chap. 4.
10. The SMR under Japanese influence was an exception to this.
11. Köll, *Railroads and the Transformation of China*, 83–85.
12. Köll, 169–180.
13. Jones, *Multinationals and Global Capitalism*, chap. 2.
14. Siemens, Alstom, and Bombardier until the 2010s; in 2015, China's CSR and CNR merged to form CRRC, the world's largest rolling stock manufacturer, leading to counter-M&A movements among the former "big three." As a result, Alstom purchased Bombardier Transportation and became the world's second-largest rolling stock maker in 2021.
15. See chapter 6.

BIBLIOGRAPHY

Abel, Jessamyn R. *Dream Super-Express: A Cultural History of the World's First Bullet Train*. Stanford, CA: Stanford University Press, 2022.

Akasaka Yoshihiro. "Kansen kokuyūka go no shitetsu yusō shijō" [Transport market for private railways after the railway nationalization]. In *Shijō to keiei no rekishi* [History of markets and management], edited by Andō Seiichi and Fujita Teiichirō, 237–264. Osaka: Seibundō shuppan, 1996.

Akita Shigeru. "Ajia kokusai chitsujyo to Igirisu teikoku, hegemoni" [International order in Asia, British Empire, and hegemony]. In *Globalu Historī no chōsen* [Challenges of global history], edited by Mizushima Tsukasa, 102–125. Tokyo: Yamakawa shuppan sha, 2008.

American Locomotive Company. *First Annual Report to the Stockholders*. New York: ALCO, 1902.

Aoki Eiichi. "Kōtsu unyu gijyutsu no jiritsu" [Independence of transformation technology]. In *Kōtsu un'yu no hattatsu to gijutsu kakushin* [Technological innovation and development of transportation], edited by Yamamoto Hirofumi, 88–98. Tokyo: University of United Nation Press, 1986.

——. "Kōtsū, un'yu taikei no tōgō II tetsudō" [Integration of the traffic and transportation networks II railways]. In *Kōtsū, un'yu no hattatsu to gijyutsu kakushin* [Technological innovation and development of the traffic and transportation], edited by Yamamoto Hirofumi, 214–141. Tokyo: United Nations University Press, 1986.

——. "Nihon no kansenyō jōki kikannsha no hattatsu" [Development of steam locomotives for trunk line in Japan]. *Tetsudo shigaku* [Japan railway history review], no. 9 (1991): 7–16.

Asajima Shōichi. *Senzen ki Mitsui bussan no kikai torihiki* [Mitsui Bussan's machinery trade in the prewar era]. Tokyo: Nihon keizai hyōron sha, 2001.

BIBLIOGRAPHY

Asakura Kiichi. *Jijutsu seikatsu 50 nen* [50 years of life as an engineer]. Tokyo: Nikan kōgyō shinbun sha, 1958.

——. "9600 kei no sekkei no omoide" [Memories of designing the JNR class 9600]. *Tetsudō pikutoriaru* [Railway pictorial], no. 175 (1965): 4–6.

——. "Shima Yasujirō-sensei no jigyō" [Activities of Mr. Shima Yasujiro]. *Nihon kikai gakkai shi* [Journal of the Society of Mechanical Engineers] 51, no. 352 (1947): 20–23.

British Consulate in Japan. *Diplomatic and Consular Reports on Trade and Finance*, no. 1695 (February 22, 1896).

Brown, John K. *The Baldwin Locomotive Works: 1831–1915*. Baltimore: John Hopkins University Press, 1995.

Burnham, Williams & Co. *Baldwin Locomotive Works Narrow Gauge Locomotives, Japanese Edition, Frazar & Co. of Japan Agents, Yokohama*. Philadelphia: J. B. Lippincott Co., 1897.

Campbell, R. H. "The North British Locomotive Company Between the Wars." In *Business in the Age of Depression and War*, edited by R. P. T. Davenport-Hines, 172–205. London: Frank Cass, 1990.

Carter, S. B., Gartner, S. S., Haines, M. R., Olmstead, A. L., Sutch, R., and Wright, G., eds. *Historical Statistics of the United States, Millennial Edition Online*. Cambridge: Cambridge University Press, 2006. https://hsus.cambridge.org/HSUSWeb/HSUSEntryServlet.

Chiba Isao. "Nissin-Nichiro sensō" [Sino-Japanese War and Russo-Japanese War]. In *Iwanami koza Nihon rekishi* (Iwanami series of Japanese history), vol. 16, edited by Otsu Tōru, Sakurai Eiji, Fujii Jōji, Yoshida Yutaka, and Lee Sungsi, 113–146. Tokyo: Iwanami Shoten, 2014.

Chiba Masashi. *Kindai kōtsū taikei to Shin Teikoku no henbō* [Modern transportation systems and the transformation of the Qing Dynasty. Tokyo: Nihon Keizai Hyōron sha, 2006.

Chōsen Sōtokufu Tetsudō kyoku, ed. *Chōsen tetsudō shi* [A history of Korean railways]. Seoul: Chōsen Sōtokufu, 1915.

Crouzet, François. "Essor, déclin et renaissance de l'industrie française des locomotives." *Revue d'Histoire Economique et Sociale* 55, nos. 1–2 (1977): 112–210.

Daito Eisuke. "Railways and Scientific Management in Japan, 1907–30." *Business History* 31, no. 1 (1989): 1–28.

Dajyō kan, ed. *Meiji 14 nen bun gaikokujin shirabe* [Report of foreign employees in 1881]. Tokyo: Dajyō kan, 1881.

Davies, Robert Bruce. *Peacefully Working to Conquer the World: Singer Sewing Machines in Foreign Markets, 1854–1920*. New York: Arno Press, 1976.

Digby, W. Pollard. "The British and American Locomotive Export Trade." *The Engineer*, December 16, 1904, 587–588.

——. "The Earning Power of British Rolling Stock from 1894–1903." *The Engineer*, September 22, 1905, 279–280.

Dyer, Henry. *Dai Nippon: The Britain of the East*. London: Blackie, 1904.

Eisenbahnjahr Ausstellungsgesellschaft, ed. *Zug der Zeit, Zeit der Zuge: Deutsche Eisenbahn 1835–1985*. Berlin: Siedler, 1985.

Endacott, George. B. *A Biographical Sketch-Book of Early Hong Kong*. Hong Kong: Hong Kong University Press, 1962.

English, Peter J. *British Made: Industrial Development and Related Archaeology of Japan*. Eindhoven: De Archeologische Pers Nederland, 1982.

240

BIBLIOGRAPHY

Ericson, Steven J. "Importing Locomotives in Meiji Japan, International Business and Technology Transfer in the Railroad Industry." *Osiris: A Research Journal Devoted to the History of Science and Its Cultural Influences*, 2nd ser., no. 13 (1998): 129–153.

——. "Riding the Rails: The Japanese Railways Meet the Challenge of War." In *The Russo-Japanese War in Global Perspective: World War Zero*, vol. 2, edited by John Steinberg, David Wolff, Steve Marks, Bruce Menning, David Schimmelpenninck van der Oye, and Shinji Yokote, 225–237. Leiden: E. J. Brill, 2007.

——. *The Sound of the Whistle: Railroads and the State in Meiji Japan*. Cambridge, MA: Harvard University Press, 1996.

——. "Taming the Iron Horse: Western Locomotive Makers and Technology Transfer in Japan, 1870–1914." In *Public Spheres, Private Lives in Modern Japan, 1600–1950*, edited by Gail Bernstein, Andrew Gordon, and Kete Nakai, 185–217. Cambridge, MA: Harvard University Press, 2005.

Feldwick, W., ed. *Present-Day Impression of Japan*. Yokohama: Globe Encyclopedia Co., 1919.

Fitch, Charles H. *Report on the Manufactures of Interchangeable Mechanism*. Washington, DC: Government Printing Office, 1888.

Free, Dan. *Early Japanese Railways, 1853–1914: Engineering Triumphs That Transformed Meiji-Era Japan*. North Clarendon, VT: Tuttle, 2008.

Fremdling, R., Federspiel, R., and Kunz, A. eds. *Statistik der Eisenbahnen in Deutsceland 1835–1989*. St. Katharinen: Scripta Mercaturae Verlag, 1995.

Fuess, Harald. "The Global Weapons Trade and Meiji Restoration." In *The Meiji Restoration: Japan as a Global Nation*, edited by Robert Hellyer and Harald Fuss, 83–109. Cambridge: Cambridge University Press, 2020.

Fukao Kyōji and Settsu Tokihiko. "Seichō to makuro Keizai" [Growth and macroeconomy]. In *Iwanami kōza Nihon Keizai no rekishi 3* [Iwanami series of Japanese economic history vol. 3], edited by Fukao Kyōji, Nakamura Naofumi, and Nakabayashi Masaki, 2–22. Tokyo: Iwanami shoten, 2017.

Gairns, J. F. *Superheating on Locomotive*. London: Locomotive Publishing, 1912.

Garbe, Robert. "The Application of Highly Superheated Steam to Locomotives, No. 1." *The Engineer*, October 25, 1907, 407–408.

——. *The Application of Highly Superheated Steam*. New York: Norman W. Henley, 1908.

Gerschenkron, Alexander. *Economic Backwardness in Historical Perspective*. Cambridge, MA: Belknap Press of Harvard University, 1962.

Gordon, Andrew. *The Evolution of Labor Relations in Japan: Heavy Industry, 1853–1955*. Cambridge, MA: Harvard University Press, 1985.

——. *Fabricating Consumers: The Sewing Machine in Modern Japan*. Berkeley: University of California Press, 2011.

——. *A Modern History of Japan: From Tokugawa Times to the Present*. 3rd ed. Oxford: Oxford University Press, 2014.

Hamashita Takeshi and Kawakatsu Heita, eds. *Ajia kōekiken to Nihon kōgyōka, 1500–1900* [Asian trading sphere and Japanese industrialization] Tokyo: Libroport, 1991.

Harada Katsumasa. *Nihon tetsudō shi* [A history of Japan's railways]. Tokyo: Tosui shobō, 2001.

Hashimoto Takehiko. *Monozukuri no kagaku shi* [A scientific history of manufacturing]. Tokyo: Kōdan sha, 2013.

Hayashida Haruo. *Edomondo Moreru* [Edmund Morrell]. Kyoto: Mireruva Shobō, 2018.

BIBLIOGRAPHY

——. *Nihon no Tetsudō Sōsō ki* [The early days of Japan's railways]. Kyoto: Minerva Shobō, 2009.

Headrick, Daniel R. *The Tools of Empire: Technology and European Imperialism in the Nineteenth Century*. Oxford: Oxford University Press, 1981.

Hellyer, Robert. *Green with Milk and Sugar: When Japan Filled America's Tea Cups*. New York: Columbia University Press, 2021.

Hellyer, Robert, and Harald Fuess, eds. *The Meiji Restoration: Japan as a Global Nation*. Cambridge: Cambridge University Press, 2020.

Helmholtz, R., and Staby W., eds. *Die Entwicklung der Lokomotive 1 Band*. Munich: Georg D. W. Callwey, 1981.

Hills, Richard L. "Some Contributions to Locomotive Development by Beyer Peacock & Co." *Newcomen Society Transactions*, no. 40 (1968): 75–123.

Hokkaidō testudō bu, ed. *Hokkaidō testudō bu nenpō* [Annual report of the Hokkaido Department of Railways]. Sapporo: Hokkaido Department of Railways, 1896–1900.

——, ed. *Tetsudō bupō* [Report of the Railway Department], no. 151. September 30, 1902.

Holtham, Edmund G. *Eight Years in Japan, 1873–1881: Work, Travel, and Recreation*. London: K. Paul, Trench, 1883.

Hopkins, Terence K., and Immanuel M. Wallerstein. "Commodity Chains in the World-Economy Prior to 1800." *Review* (Fernand Braudel Center) 10, no. 1 (1986): 157–170.

Hounshell, David A. *From the American System to Mass Production, 1800–1932: The Development of Manufacturing Technology in the United States*. Baltimore: Johns Hopkins University Press, 1985.

Inoue Yōichirō. "Nihon kindai gijutsushi no ichi kenkyū" [A historical study of Japan's modern technology]. *Keizai ronsō* [Economic review, Kyoto University] 99, no. 1 (1967): 82–98.

Insatsu kyoku, ed. *Shokuin roku* [List of personnel]. Tokyo: Insatsu kyoku, 1897–1909.

Iokibe Kaoru. *Renegotiating Japan's Unequal Treaties: A Window on Late Nineteenth-Century Diplomacy*. Tokyo: University of Tokyo Press, 2022.

Irisu, ed. *Irisu 150 nen: Reimei no kioku* [150 year anniversary of Illies & Co.: Memories of the beginning era] Tokyo: K. K. Irisu, 2009.

Ishii Kanji. *Kindai Nihon to Igirisu shihon* [Modern Japan and the British capital]. Tokyo: University of Tokyo Press, 1984.

Ishii Mayako. *Kindai Chūgoku to Igirisu shihon* [Modern China and British capital]. Tokyo: University of Tokyo Press, 1998.

James, Harold. *The End of Globalization: Lessons from the Great Depression*. Cambridge, MA: Harvard University Press, 2002.

Jones, Geoffrey. *Merchants to Multinationals: British Trading Companies in the Nineteenth and Twentieth Centuries*. Oxford: Oxford University Press, 2000.

——. *Multinationals and Global Capitalism: From the Nineteenth to the Twenty First Century*. Oxford: Oxford University Press, 2005.

Jones, Hazel. J. *Live Machines: Hired Foreigners and Meiji Japan*. Vancouver: University of British Columbia Press, 1980.

Kaneda Shigehiro. *Nasmyth Wilson no kikansha* [Locomotives of Nasmyth Wilson]. Suita: Kikansha shi kenkū-kai, 1981.

——. *Nihon jōki kikansha shi, Kansetsu tetsudō hen* [A history of Japan's steam locomotives, a part of the Imperial Government Railways]. Tokyo: Kōyū sha, 1972.

Karafuto chō, ed. *Karafuto yōran* [Karafuto handbook]. Toyohara: Karafuto chō, 1914.

BIBLIOGRAPHY

Kasai Masanao. "Takata shōkai to Uesutinguhaususha" [Takata & Co. and Westinghouse Electric & Manufacturing Co.]. *Shōgaku ronshū* [Journal of commerce, economics and economic history, Fukushima University] 59, no. 4 (1991): 183–210.

Kasuya Makoto. *Gōshō no Meiji* [A wealthy merchant in the Meiji period; the case of the house of Mitsui]. Nagoya: Nagoya University Press, 2002.

Kawabe Nobuo. "Japanese Business in the United States Before World War II: The Case of Mitsubishi Shoji Kaisha, the San Francisco and Seattle Branches." PhD diss., Ohio State University, 1980.

Kawasaki Takeshi, Mochida Toshihiko, and Yamaguchi Takashi. "Ōshū tetsudō muke sharyō gijutsu" [Technology on railway vehicles for Europe]. *Hitachi hyōron* 89, no. 11 (2007): 66–69.

Kiesewetter, Hubert. *Industrielle Revolution in Deutschland.* Eichstatt: Franz Steiner Verlag, 2004.

Kita Masami. "19 Seiki Gurasugō jōki kikansha seizōgyō hatten shi" [Developmental history of the steam locomotives at Glasgow in the 19th century]. *Sōka keizai ronshu* [Soka economic review] 22, no. 4 (1993).

Kinoshita Ritsuan, ed. *Teikoku tetsudō yōkan dai 1 han* [Companion of railways in imperial Japan vol. 1]. Tokyo: Tetsudō jihō kyoku, 1900.

——, ed. *Teikoku tetsudō yōkan dai 3 han* [Companion of railways in imperial Japan vol. 3]. Tokyo: Tetsudō jihō kyoku, 1906.

Kinoshita Seiya, Sato Naoyoshi, Matsumoto Naoya, and Ashida Yoshinori. "Kaikei hō niokeru kōkyō kōji nyūsatsu seido no rekishiteki kōsatsu" [Historical study on the public works procurement system set under the Public Accounting Act]. *Doboku gakkai ronbun shū F4* [Journal of Japan Society of Civil Engineers, ser. F4] 66, no. 1 (2010): 169–180.

Kiyama Minoru. *Kindai Nihon to Mitsui bussan* [Mitsui & Co. and modern Japan]. Kyoto: Minerva shobō, 2009.

Kōda Ryōichi. *Doitsu kōsaku kikaikōgyō seiritsu shi* [Formation of German machine tool industry]. Tokyo: Taga shuppan sha, 1994.

Kokaze Hidemasa. "Jyo" [Introduction]. In *Gulobalu-ka no nakano kindai Nihon* [Modern Japan and globalization], edited by Kokaze Hidemasa and Suetake Yoshiya, 1–10. Tokyo: Yushi sha, 2015.

Köll, Elisabeth. *Railroads and the Transformation of China.* Cambridge, MA: Harvard University Press, 2019.

Krauss-Maffei, ed. *Krauss Maffei: 150 Years of Progress Through Technology, 1838–1988.* Munich: Krauss-Maffei AG, 1988.

Kume Kunitake, ed. *Tokumei zenken taishi Beiō kairan jikki* [Ambassador extraordinary and plenipotentiary, observation record of Europe and the United States], vol. 2. Tokyo: Hakubunsha, 1878. Reprint, Tokyo: Iwanami Shoten, 1993.

League of Nations Economic and Financial Section, ed. *International Statistical Year-Book 1926.* Geneva: League of Nations, 1927.

Lean, Eugenia. *Vernacular Industrialism in China: Local Innovation and Translated Technologies in the Making of a Cosmetics Empire, 1900–1940.* New York: Columbia University Press, 2020.

Lim Chaisung. *Higashi Ajia no nakano Mantetsu* [South Manchuria Railway in East Asia]. Nagoya: Nagoya University Press, 2021.

Lowe, James W. *British Steam Locomotive Builders.* Cambridge: Goose and Son, 1975.

BIBLIOGRAPHY

Lowther, Gerard. "Report on the Railways of Japan [1895]." *Foreign Office 1896 Miscellaneous Series, Consular Reports on Subjects of General and Commercial Interest*, no. 390. London: Her Majesty's Stationary Office, 1896.

——. "Report on the Railways of Japan [1897]." *Foreign Office 1897 Miscellaneous Series, Consular Reports on Subjects of General and Commercial Interest*, no. 427. London: Her Majesty's Stationary Office, 1897.

Maddison, Angus, *Contours of the World Economy, 1–2030 AD*. Oxford: Oxford University Press, 2007.

Matsusaka, Yoshihisa T. *The Making of Japanese Manchuria, 1904–1932*. Cambridge, MA: Harvard University Asia Center, 2003.

McKay, Alexander. *Scottish Samurai: Thomas Blake Glover 1839–1911*. Edinburgh: Canongate Press, 1993.

Messerschmidt, Wolfgang. *Taschenbuch Deutsche Lokomotivfabriken*. Stuttgart: Franckh, 1977.

Minami Manshū tetsudō kabushikikaisha, ed. *Minami Manshū tetsudō kabushikikaisha jūnenshi* [Ten-year anniversary of South Manchuria Railway]. Dalian: South Manchuria Railway, 1919.

Minami Manshū tetsudō kabushikikaisha, ed. *Shokuin roku* [Company directory]. Dalian: South Manchuria Railway, 1908.

Minami Ryōshin. *Chōki keizai tōkei 12: Tetsudō to denryoku* [Long-term Economic statistics 12: Railway and electricity]. Tokyo: Tōyō Keizai, 1979.

——. *The Economic Development of Japan*. 2nd ed. London: Macmillan, 1994.

Ministry of Foreign Affairs of Japan, ed. *Dai Nihon gaikō monjo* [Documents on Japanese foreign policy], vol. 2, no. 3, p. 608. Tokyo: Diplomatic Archives of the Ministry of Foreign Affairs of Japan, 1937.

Mitsui bussan. *Kikai tetsudō kanamono kaigi gijiroku Meiji 39 nen* [Proceedings of a meeting about machinery, railways, and metal]. 1906.

——. *Meiji 37 nendo jigyō hōkokusho* [Business report in 1904 FY]. Tokyo: Maruzen, 2007 reprint.

——. *Meiji 42 nen shimohanki jigyō hōkokusho* [Business report in the second half of 1909 FY]. Tokyo: Maruzen, 2007 reprint.

——. *Mitsui bussan shitenchō kaigiroku 1 Meiji 35 nen* [Minutes of the Mitsui & Co. branch managers' meeting 1], no. 4. 1902.

Mitsui bussan honten kikaibu chōsakakari. *Chōsa shūhō higō hantaishō no kinkyō dai 2* [Research reports, secret, competitor's recent situation, no. 2). N.d. [1920?].

Mitsui bussan kikaibu. *Kikai shōbai to naichi kōgyō kai no sūsei* [Trends in domestic industries and machinery trading]. Tokyo: Mitsui & Co., 1919.

Mizushima Tsukasa, ed. *Globalu Historī no chōsen* [Challenges of global history]. Tokyo: Yamakawa shuppan sha, 2008.

Morita Chukichi. *Yokohama seikō meiyo kagami* [Who's who in Yokohama]. Yokohama: Yokohama Shōkyō shinpōsha, 1910.

Murakami Kyōichi. *Dai tetsudō ka Minami Kiyoshi kun no keireki* [Biography of Mr. Minami Kiyoshi, a great railway engineer and manager]. Tokyo: Tesudō jihō kyoku, 1904.

Nagura Bunji. *Nihon gunji kanren sangyō shi* [A history of Japan's weapons-related industries]. Tokyo: Nihon keizai hyōron sha, 2013.

Nakagawa Kiyoshi. "Meiji Taishōki niokeru heikishōsha Takata Shōkai" [Takata & Co., a weapons-trading company in the Meiji-Taisho era]. *Hakuō hōgaku* [Hakuo review of law and politics], no. 1 (1994): 193–240.

BIBLIOGRAPHY

———. "Meiji Taishōki no daihyōteki kikai shōsha Takata shōkai (jō)" [Takata & Co., a representative machinery trading company during the Meiji-Taisho era]. *Hakuō daigaku ronshū* [Hakuo university review] 9, no. 2 (1995): 51–108.

Nakagawa Kōichi, Imashiro Mitsuhide, Katō Shinichi, and Seko Tatsuo. *Keiben ōkoku Amenomiya* [Amenomiya's light railway kingdom]. Tokyo: Tanzawa shinsha, 1972.

Nakamura Naofumi. *Chihō karano sangyō kakumei* [Reconsidering Japan's Industrial Revolution from a local perspective]. Nagoya: Nagoya University Press, 2010.

———. "Diversification and Convergence." In *The Development of Railway Technology in East Asia in Comparative Perspective*, edited by Sawai Minoru, 41–65. Singapore: Springer, 2017.

———. "The First Global Economy and the US-Japanese Locomotive Trade." *Japanese Research in Business History*, no. 40 (2023): 6–23.

———. "Gurōbaru ka to Meiji no tetsudō hatten" [Railway development and globalization in the Meiji era]. In *Meiji toyū isan* [Meiji era as a heritage], edited by Takii Kazuhiro. Kyoto: Minerva shobō, 2020.

———. "Meiji ki tetsudōgyō ni okeru kigyō tōchi to kigyō kin'yū" [Corporate governance and financing in railway industry in Meiji Japan]. In *Kindai nihon no enerugī to kigō katsudō* [Energy and corporate activities in modern Japan], edited by Ogino Yoshihiro, 119–136. Tokyo: Nihon keizai hyōron sha, 2010.

———. *Nihon tetsudōgyō no keisei* [The formation of the Japan's railways]. Tokyo: Nihon Keizai hyōron sha, 1998.

———. "Reconsidering the US-Japan Trade in Railroad Equipment: An American Sales Representative in Early 20th-Century Japan." *ISS Discussion Paper Series*, F-199 (2024). https://www.iss.u-tokyo.ac.jp/publishments/dpf/index.html.

———. "Seiki tenkanki niokeru kikansha seizōgyō no kokusai kyōsō" [International competition in the locomotive manufacturing industry during the turn of nineteenth and twentieth centuries]. In *Kokusai kyosōryoku no keieishi* [Business history of international competitiveness], edited by Yuzawa Takeshi, Suzuki Tsuneo, Kikkawa Takeo, and Sasaki Satoshi, 35–58. Tokyo: Yūhikaku, 2009.

———. "Shisan tokushu-sei to kigyō no kyōkai" [Asset specificity and boundary of firms]. In *Kigyō no keizaigaku* [Economics of the firm: Structure and dynamics], edited by Nakabayashi Masaki and Ishiguro Shingo, 101–119. Tokyo: Yūhikaku, 2014.

———. "Tetsudō gijutsusha shūdan no keisei to Kōbu daigakko" [Development of Japanese railway engineers and the Imperial College of Engineering]. In *Kōbu sho to sono jidai* [Ministry of Public Works and the times), edited by Suzuki Jun, 95–116. Tokyo: Yamakawa shuppan sha, 2002.

———. "Trading Locomotives Between the USA and Japan: Okura & Co. at the Beginning of the Twentieth Century." *Journal of the Royal Asiatic Society* 34, no. 3 (2024): 519–534.

———. "The Training School for Railway Engineers: An Early Example of an Inter-firm Vocational School in Japan." In *Accessing Technical Education in Modern Japan*, vol. 2, edited by Erich Pauer and Regine Mathias, 217–251. Kent, UK: Renaissance Books, 2022.

———. *Umi wo wataru kikansha* [Locomotives from across the sea]. Tokyo: Yoshikawa kōbunkan, 2016.

Nakamura Naofumi and Ōshima Hisayuki. "Kōtsū kakumei to Meiji no shōgyō" [Transport revolution and commerce in the Meiji era]. In *Iwanami kōza Nihon keizai no rekishi, 3* [Iwanami series of Japanese economic history vol. 3], edited by Fukao Kyōji, Nakamura Naofumi, and Nakabayashi Masaki, 232–272. Tokyo: Iwanami shoten, 2017.

BIBLIOGRAPHY

Nakamura Seishi. "Taishō Shōwashoki no Okura zaibatsu" [Okura zaibatsu during from Taisho era to early Showa era]. *Keiei shikaku* [Japan business history review] 15, no. 3 (1980): 48–74.

Nakaoka Tetsurō, ed. *Gijyutsu-keisei no kokusai hiraku: Kougyou ka no shakai teki nōryoku* [International comparison in the technological formation: The abilities of a society for industrialization]. Tokyo: Chikuma shobō, 1990.

——. *Nihon kindai gijutsu no keisei* [Formation of modern technology in Japan]. Tokyo: Asahi shinbun sha, 2006.

National Railway Museum [United Kingdom]. *Records of North British Locomotive Company Ltd & Constituent Companies, Locomotive Builders*. York: National Railway Museum, 2003.

Nihon kokuyū tetsudō, ed. *Nihon kokuyū tetsudō 100nen shi dai 1 kan* [One-hundred-year history of Japan National Railways vol. 1]. Tokyo: Japan National Railways, 1969.

——, ed. *Nihon kokuyū tetsudō 100nen shi, dai 4 kan* [One-hundred-year history of the Japan National Railways vol. 4]. Tokyo: Japan National Railways, 1972.

——, ed., *Nihon kokuyū tetsudō hyakunenshi, shashinshi* [One-hundred-year history of Japan National Railways, photo history]. Tokyo: Japan National Railways, 1972.

——, ed. *Tetsudō gijutsu hattatsu shi V dai 4 hen sharyō to kikai 1* [History of the development of railway technology *V* part 4 rolling stock and machines 1]. 1958; reprint published by Kress Shuppan in 1990.

——, ed., *Tetsudō gijutsu hattatsu shi VI dai 4 hen sharyō to kikai 2* [History of the development of railway technology VI part 4 rolling stock and machines 2]. Tokyo: Japan National Railways, 1958. Reprint, Tokyo: Kress Shuppan, 1990.

Nihon kokuyū tetsudō Hokkaido sōkyoku, ed. *Hokkaido tetsudō hyakunen-shi jō* [One-hundred-year history of Hokkaido Railways part 1]. Sapporo: Japan National Railways, Hokkaido Head Office, 1976.

Nippon tetsudō, ed. *Meiji 34 nen nenpō* [Annual report in 1901]. Tokyo: Nippon Railway Co., 1902.

——, ed. *Meiji 36 nen nenpō* [Annual report in 1903]. Tokyo: Nippon Railway Co., 1904.

Nippon tetsudō shomuka, ed. *Nippon tetsudō kabushiki kaisha reiki shūsan* [Rules collection]. Tokyo: Nippon Railway, October 1903.

Nish, Ian. *Collected Writings of Ian Nish*. Part 2, *Japanese Political History—Japan and East Asia*. Richmond, UK: Japan Library, 2001.

Nishimura Shizuya. "Daiichiji gulōbaluka to Ajia niokeru Ei kei Kokusai ginkō" [The first globalization and British international banks in Asia]. In *Kokusai ginkō to Ajia* [International banks and Asia], edited by Nishimura Shizuya, Suzuki Toshio, and Akagawa Motoaki, 3–152. Tokyo: Keio University Press, 2014.

Noda Masaho. *Nihon shōken shijō seiritsu shi* [A history of the formation of the securities markets in Japan]. Tokyo: Yūhikaku, 1980.

Noda Masaho, Harada Katsumasa, Aoki Eiichi, and Oikawa Yoshinobu, eds. *Nihon no tetsudō* [A history of Japan's railways]. Tokyo: Nihon keizai hyōron sha, 1986.

North British Locomotive. *The Locomotives of Argentina*. Glasgow: North British Locomotive Co., 1909.

Ogasawara Shigeru. "19 Seiki-zenhan niokeru Doitsu kikai kōgyō no hatten" [The development of German machinery industry in the first half of the nineteenth century]. *Shōgaku ronshū* [Journal of commerce, economics and economic history, Fukushima University] 38, no. 2 (1969): 1–55.

Oikawa Yoshinobu. *Inoue Masaru* [A biography of Inoue Masaru]. Kyoto: Minerva shobō, 2013.

BIBLIOGRAPHY

Okazaki Tetsuji and Oishi Naoki, eds. *Senzen ki Nihon no sōgō shōsha* [The general trading companies in the prewar era]. Tokyo: University of Tokyo Press, 2023.

Okura zaibatsu kenkyūkai, ed. *Okura zaibatsu no kenkyū* [A study of the Okura zaibatsu]. Tokyo: Kondo Shuppan, 1982.

Onozuka Tomoji, ed. *Dai 1 ji sekaitaisen kaisen geiin no saikentō* [Reconsidering causes of the outbreak of World War I]. Tokyo: Iwanami shoten, 2014.

Oshima Hisayuki. "Mitsui bussan niokeru yusō gyōmu to yōsen shijō" [Mitsui & Co.'s transportation business and the chartered vessel market in Japan]. In *Shōhin ryūtsū no kindaishi* [A modern history of goods distribution], edited by Nakanishi Satoru and Nakamura Naofumi, 211–246. Tokyo: Nihon keizai hyōron sha, 2003.

Patrikeeff, Felix, and Harold Shukman. *Railways and the Russo-Japanese War: Transporting War.* Abingdon, UK: Routledge, 2007.

Porter, Glenn, and Harold C. Livesay. *Merchants and Manufacturers: Studies in the Changing Structure of Nineteenth-Century Marketing.* Baltimore: Johns Hopkins University Press, 1971.

Rous-Marten, Charles. "English and American Locomotive Building." *Engineering Magazine,* 17, no. 4 (1899): 545–561.

Saitō Akira, *Jōki kikansha 200-nen shi* [200 years of steam locomotives]. Tokyo: NTT Press, 2007.

Saitō Osamu. "Eikoku sangyōkakumei ron no genzai" [The British Industrial Revolution: A historiographical essay]. *Nihon Gakushiin kiyō* [Proceedings of the Japan Academy] 76, no. 2 (2021): 203–234.

Sanyo tetsudō sōmuka, ed. *Kisoku ruishō* [Rules collection]. Kobe: Sanyo Railway, July 1, 1907.

Saul, S. B. *Studies in British Overseas Trade: 1870–1914.* Liverpool: Liverpool University Press, 1960.

Sawai Minoru. *Nihon tetsudō sharyō kōgyō shi* [A history of Japan's railcar industry]. Tokyo: Nihon keizai hyōron sha, 1998.

Scranton, Philip. *Endless Novelty: Specialty Production and American Industrialization, 1865–1925.* Princeton, NJ: Princeton University Press, 1997.

Shavit, David. *The United States in Asia: A Historical Dictionary.* Westport, CT: Greenwood Press, 1990.

Suehiro Akira. *Catch-Up Industrialization.* Singapore: NUS Press, 2008.

Sugiyama Shinya. *Meiji ishin to Igirisu shōnin* [The Meiji Restoration and British merchants]. Tokyo: Iwanami shoten, 1993.

Suzuki Toshio. "Dai ichiji sekai taisen zen no Rondon kin'yū shijō to Nihon kigyō" [Japanese firms in the financial market of London before World War I]. In *Sangyō kakumei to kigyō keiei* [Business administrations and the Industrial Revolution], edited by Abe Takeshi and Nakamura Naofumi, 279–289. Kyoto: Minerva shobō, 2010.

——. *Japanese Government Loan Issue in the London Capital Market 1870–1913.* London: Athlone Press, 1994.

Taiwan sōtokufu kotsūkyoku tetsudō bu, ed. *Taiwan tetsudō shi* [A history of Taiwan railways]. Taipei: Taiwan sōtokufu, 1911.

Takahashi Hideyuki. "Shoki Borujihi kigyō no seichō to kikansha seisan no tenkai" [The development of early Borsig Co. and locomotive products]. *Ōita Daigaku keizai ronshū* [Oita University economic review] 27, no. 6 (1975): 1–38.

Takahashi Yasutaka. *Nihon shokuminchi tetsudō shiron* [A history of Japanese colonial railroads]. Tokyo: Nihon Keizai Hyōronsha, 1995.

BIBLIOGRAPHY

Takamura Naosuke. "Dokusen soshiki no keisei" [Formation of a monopoly structure]. In *Nichiro sengo no Nihon keizai* [The Japanese economy after the Russo-Japanese War], edited by Takamura Naosuke, 159–202. Tokyo: Hanawa shobō, 1988.

Takeda Haruhito. *Dangō no keizaigaku* [Economics of collusion]. Tokyo: Shūei sha, 1994.

Tanaka Tokihiko. *Meiji ishin no seikyoku to tetsudō kensetsu* [The political situation and construction of railways during the Meiji Restoration]. Tokyo: Yoshikawa Kōbunkan, 1963.

Tang, John P. "Railroad Expansion and Industrialization: Evidence from Meiji Japan." *Journal of Economic History* 74, no. 3 (2014): 863–886.

Tanimoto Masayuki and Sawai Minoru. *Nihon Keizai shi* [Japanese economic history]. Tokyo: Yūhikaku, 2016.

Teishinshō, ed. *Meiji 35 nen Teishinshō shokuinroku* [List of personnel at the Ministry of Communications and Transportation, 1902]. Tokyo: Teishinshō, 1902.

Teisinshō, ed. *Teisinshō shokuin roku* [List of personnel at the Ministry of Communications and Transportation]. Tokyo: Teisinshō, 1894–1896.

Tetsudō jihō kyoku, ed. *Shin tetsudō hōrei shū zen* [New railway laws and regulations, whole]. Tokyo: Tetsudō jihō kyoku, 1907.

Tetsudō kyoku, ed. *Meiji 40 nendo Tetsudō kyoku nenpō* [Annual report of the Railway Bureau in 1907 FY]. Tokyo: Tetsudō kyoku, 1909.

Tetsudō kyoku, ed. *Tetsudō-kyoku nenpō* [Annual report of Railway Bureau]. Tokyo: Tetsudō-kyoku, 1894–1906.

Tetsudōshi Gakkai [Railway History Society of Japan], ed. *Tetsudō jinbutsu shi jiten* [Biographical dictionary of railway history in Japan]. Tokyo: Nihon Keizai Hyōron sha, 2013.

Tetsudō shō, ed. *Nihon tesudō shi chūhen* [A history of Japan, vol. 2]. Tokyo: Tetsudō shō, 1921.

Tetsudō shō, ed. *Nihon tesudō shi gehen* [A history of Japan, vol. 3]. Tokyo: Tetsudō shō, 1921.

Trevithick, Francis H. "English and American Locomotives in Japan." *Proceedings of Institute of Civil Engineers 1895–1896*, pt. 3, no. 125 (1896): 335–346.

——. "History and Development of the Railway System in Japan." *Transactions of the Asiatic Society of Japan*, no. 22 (1894): 115–241.

Uchida Hoshimi. "Meiji-kōki minkan kigyō no gijutsusha bunpu" [Distribution of engineers in private companies in the late Meiji era] *Keiei shigaku* [Japan business history review] 14, no. 2 (1979): 1–30.

——. "Shoki kōkōsotsu gijutsusha no katsudōbunya, shūkeikekka" [Field of activity of engineers who graduated from the Higher Technical School during its founding era, aggregate results]. *Tokyo kei-daigaku kaishi* [Journal of Tokyo Keizai University], no. 108 (1978): 139–182.

Ueyama Kazuo. *Hoku Bei niokeru sōgō shōsha no katsudō* [The activities of a general trading company in North America]. Tokyo: Nihon keizai hyōron sha, 2005.

Ueyama Kazuo and Kikkawa Yō, eds. *Senzen ki Hoku Bei no Nihon shōsha* [Japanese trading companies in North America during the prewar period]. Tokyo: Nihon keizai hyoron sha, 2013.

Usui Kazuo. *The Development of Marketing Management: The Case of the USA, c. 1910–1940.* Burlington, VT: Ashgate Publishing, 2008.

Usui Shigenobu. *Kikansha no keifu-zu* [Genealogy of locomotives]. 4 vols. Tokyo: Kōyū sha, 1972–78.

Vauclain, Samuel M., and Earl Chapin May. *Steaming Up! The Autobiography of Samuel M. Vauclain.* New York: Brewer and Warren, 1930.

BIBLIOGRAPHY

Watanabe Sei. "Hadaka nisareta sōgō shōsha" [A general trading company laid bare]. *Enerugī shi kenkyū* [Energy history review], no. 26 (2011).

——. *Okura zaibatsu no kaiko* [Retrospective of Okura zaibatsu]. Tokyo: privately printed, 2002.

Westwood, John. *The Historical Atlas of World Railroads*. London: Cartographica Press, 2008.

White, John. *A Short History of American Locomotive Builders in the Steam Era*. Washington, DC: Bass, 1982.

Wolmar, Christian. *Blood, Iron, and Gold: How the Railways Transformed the World*. London: Atlantic Books, 2009.

——. *Engines of War: How Wars Were Won and Lost on the Railways*. London: Atlantic Books, 2010.

Yamamoto Hirofumi, ed. *Technological Innovation and the Development of Transportation in Japan*. Tokyo: United Nations University Press, 1993.

Yamashita Masaaki. "Dai ichiji taisen zen no sharyō kikansha sangyō to setsubi shintaku kinyū" [The rolling stock and locomotive industry and equipment trust financing before World War I]. *Shōken kenkyū* [Securities research review], no. 60 (1980): 229–306.

Yokohama kaikō shiryōkan, ed. *Zusetsu Yokohama gaikokujin kyoryūchi* [Illustration of the Yokohama Foreign Settlement]. Yokohama: Yokohama City, 1998.

Yokohama seimei roku hakkō sho, ed. *Yokohama seimei roku zen* [Directory of Yokohama, whole]. Yokohama: Yokohama seimei roku hakkō sho, 1898.

Yokohama shishi hensankakari, ed. *Yokohama Shiryō* [Yokohama historical materials]. Yokohama: Yokohama City, 1928.

Yuzawa Takeshi. "Igirisu keizai no teitai to jōki kikansha yushutsu" [Stagnation of British economy and locomotive export]. *Gahushuin keizai-keiei kenkyusho nenpō* [Annual report of Institute of Economics and Business, Gakushuin University], no. 3 (1989).

——. *Tetsudō no tanjō* [The birth of railways]. Tokyo: Sōgen sha, 2014.

——. "The Transfer of Railway Technologies from Britain to Japan, with special Reference to the Locomotive Manufacture." In *International Technology Transfer, Europe, Japan and the USA, 1700–1914*, edited by David Jeremy, 199–218. Aldershot, UK: Edward Elgar, 1991.

INDEX

Abel, Jessamyn, 7, 189

Accounting Act (1889, Japan), 86

Akiyama Shōhachi, 170

A. L. Hohenzollern (manufacturer), 37, 152

Albert R. Brown & Co., 66, 71

Aldrich, Arthur S., 60, 70, 71, 82, 89, 200

Alstom (manufacturer), 205

Amenomiya Ironworks (Dai-Nihon kidō Tekkō-bu), 192

American Bridge Co., 129

American Locomotive Co. (ALCO), 34, 35, 123, 127–132, 175, 202; export of, 79, 147, 149, 151, 163, 168, 177, 178, 180–182, 190–191; marketing activities of, 106–109; Mitsui Bussan and, 108, 123, 130, 131, 155, 158–162, 181

American system of locomotive production, 15, 16, 20, 26, 38, 44, 51, 52, 99, 149, 154, 158; competitive advantage of, 36, 48, 198

American Trading Co., 130, 132

Anglo-Japanese Alliance, 138, 180, 182

Anglo-Japanese Treaty of Commerce and Navigation, 141

Anpō line (Antung-Mukden Light Railway), 139, 146

Aoki Eiichi, 18

Aoyama Yoichi, 85, 170

Asajima Shōichi, 18

Asakura Kiichi, 177, 179, 181, 183–188

Atlantic Mutual Insurance Co., 104

Avonside Engine Co., 63

Baldwin Locomotive Works, 16, 22, 23, 32–36, 41, 44–47, 50, 63, 91, 92, 94, 128, 130, 175, 202; export of, 42, 79, 100–105, 118, 131, 140, 146–150, 163, 168, 177, 182; Frazar and, 123, 155, 156, 158, 159; marketing activities of, 109–113; productivity of, 49, 66, 67, 99, 156, 157; publications of, 36, 102, 151

Baldwin, Matthias, 35, 36

Bantan Railway, 94, 103

Barry Dock and Railway, 46

INDEX

Bavarian State Railways, 39

Behr & Co., 118

Beijing-Zhangjiakou (Jingzhang) Railway, 190

Beyer Peacock & Co., 27–29, 32, 45, 47, 63, 64, 69, 89, 95, 103, 119, 148, 177, 178; export of, 33, 66, 68

Beyer, Charles F., 33

Borsig Lokomotiv Werke, 36–39, 116, 132, 173, 177–179, 181, 183–185, 189; export of, 146, 153–155

Borsig, Johann Friedrich August, 39

Brooks Locomotive Works (later part of ALCO), 34, 35, 88, 130, 181

Brown, John K., 20, 101

Buenos Aires and Pacific Railway, 178

Canadian Pacific Railway, 175, 176

Chicago and Southern Railroad, 160

Chikuho Railway, 94, 100, 102, 103

China Japan Trading Co., 132

Chinese Civil War, 205

Chinese Eastern Railway, 101, 137–140, 146

Climax Manufacturing Co., 34

Cooke Locomotive and Machine Works (later part of ALCO), 34, 35, 160

Crawford, Joseph U., 96–98, 124, 126, 127, 133, 134

Crawford, William H., 104, 109

Crewe Works of London and Northwestern Railway, 26, 27

Crouzet, Francois, 11

CRRC (manufacturer), 205

Dai-ichi Bank, 171

Decauville rails, 119

Dickson Manufacturing Co. (later part of ALCO), 34, 35

Digby, W. Pollard, 12, 43

Dübs & Co. (later part of NBL), 27–31, 33, 63–66, 71, 74, 91, 95, 118, 121, 129, 157

Dübs, Henry, 30, 31

E. Kessler (manufacturer, later Maschinenbau-Gesellschaft Karlsruhe), 37

Eisengießerei und Maschinenfabrik von L. Schwartzkopff (later Berliner Maschinenbau AG), 37, 38, 95, 129, 153, 155, 177, 178, 181, 183, 185–187

Endō Kinsuke, 56

English, Peter J., 17, 63

Ericson, Steven J., 6, 17, 140

Federspiel, R., 11, 37

Field Railway Headquarters (Japan), 140, 146, 147

First World War, 2–4, 146, 155, 159, 163, 187, 190, 193–195, 203; Second, 204, 205

Foreign Office (UK), 180–182

Frazar & Co. (later Sale Frazar & Co.), 95, 100, 102–105, 109, 118, 123, 129, 131, 149, 150, 155, 156, 161, 182, 200

Frazar, Everett W., 104

Frazar, Everett, 103, 104

Frazar, George, 103

Fremdling, R., 11, 37

Fuess, Harald, 18

Fukao Kyōji, 77

Fukushima Nuijirō, 85

F. Wöhlert'sche Maschinenbau-Anstalt AG., 37

Garbe, Robert, 174, 175

Gaskell, Holbrook, 32

Gerschenkron, Alexander, 9

global economy, 2–5, 76, 142; First, 10, 13, 18, 19, 24, 25, 52, 54, 116, 132, 184, 195, 197, 198; Second, 205

globalization, 2–4, 6, 7, 22–24, 77, 166, 197, 201, 206

Glover, Thomas B., 73, 74

Gordon, Andrew, 6

INDEX

Gotō Shinpei, 143, 144, 169–171, 173, 181
Grant Locomotive Works (New Jersey), 34
Great Central Railway, 41
Great Northern Railroad (U.S.), 117, 160
Great Northern Railway, 41
Great Western Railway, 33
Guomindang government (China), 75

H. Ahrens Co., 117, 118
H. K. Porter Co., 34, 35, 96, 98, 130, 193
Hakatawan Railway, 112
Hankai Railway, 86, 152
Hankaku Railway, 159
Hannoversche Maschinenbau AG
    (Hanomag), 36, 37, 95, 129, 153, 155, 175
Haraguchi Kaname, 83
Hartmann, Richard, 37
Hasegawa Kinsuke, 143, 145, 147
Hasegawa Shōgo, 171
Hata Seikichirō, 83, 85
Hattori Tsutomu, 172
Hawthorn Leslie & Co., 28, 29
Hayashida Haruo, 17
Hellyer, Robert, 6, 19
Helmholtz, R., 11, 37
Henschel & Sohn, 36, 37, 39, 95, 155, 157, 182
Hills, Richard, 63
Hinkley Locomotive Works, 34
Hirai Seijirō, 83, 97, 98
Hiraoka Hiroshi, 111, 158, 171
Hitachi Ltd., 1, 205
Hitachi Maru, 194
Hokkaido Colliery and Railway, 72, 91, 100,
    111, 118, 159, 170; Iwamizawa factory, 111,
    112; Temiya factory, 91, 112
Hokkaido Government Railways, 91, 111,
    122–127, 131, 133
Horonai Railway, 96, 97, 100
Hoshu Railway, 103

Iida Giichi, 129
Ikeda Masahiko, 170

Illies & Co., 152, 153, 161, 181
imitation production, 7, 167, 184, 185, 194, 204,
    206; imitating locomotives, 166, 188, 201
Imperial College of Engineering (ICE,
    Kōbu daigakkō), 60, 61, 79, 83, 84, 86,
    90, 91
Imperial Diet, 167
Imperial Government Railways (IGR), 8,
    32, 91, 93–95, 98, 120, 127, 131, 136,
    140–143, 145, 146, 153, 202; after
    nationalization, 161, 163, 165–168, 171, 184,
    194, 229; Kobe factory, 83–85, 170, 172;
    locomotive procurement for, 64–66,
    74–76, 100, 103, 105, 106, 108, 109, 118, 121,
    148, 157, 160; procurement system of,
    68–72, 86–90, 129; Shinbashi factory, 36,
    85, 170, 176; technological development
    of, 56–61, 78–85, 113
Imperial Naval Shipyard, 183
Imperial Railway Office (Teikoku
    tetsudō-chō), 168
Industrial Revolution, 2; Japanese, 2, 4, 5, 22,
    77, 78, 113, 114, 116, 141, 143, 165, 201
Inoue Kaoru, 56, 171
Inoue Masaru, 56–59, 142, 171
interchangeable parts, 15, 35, 38, 99, 149, 193,
    198; production, 46, 48, 49, 51, 99, 154, 155
Ishii Kanji, 18
Isono Shōkai, 95
Itō Hirobumi, 27, 56
Iwahara Kenzō, 128, 129, 160
Iwakura mission, 27
Iwasaki Hikomatsu, 91, 92, 112, 170
Iwasaki Hisaya, 171

J.A. Maffei (manufacturer), 36, 37, 39, 40,
    182, 186
Japan-Korea Protocol, 138
Jardine Matheson & Co., 18, 64, 72–74, 76,
    95, 118, 119, 132, 148
Jiangsu Railway, 162
Jiaotong University, 204

INDEX

John Birch & Co., 64, 66, 69–71, 95, 118

Jones, Geoffrey, 2

Kadono, Chōkurō, 121, 124, 126, 133

Kaitakushi (Hokkaido Development Commision), 35, 96–98, 126

Kaminishi Toshimasa, 88–90

Kansei Railway, 64, 72–74, 86, 87, 91, 106, 112, 148, 159

Karafuto Agency (Karafuto-chō), 147

Katsura Tarō, 171

Kawasaki, Dockyard Co., 171, 172, 177, 184–186, 188–190, 202; Heavy Industries, 1, 205

Kawasaki Shōzō, 172

Keifu Railway (Seoul-Busan line), 138, 145, 146, 156, 158, 167, 202

Keigi Railway (Seoul-Shinuiju line), 138, 140, 146, 156

Keinin Railway (Seoul-Incheon line), 145

Kido Takayoshi, 27

Kisha Seizō Co., 111, 112, 142, 145, 156, 158, 165, 171, 172, 184, 185, 187, 190, 202

Kitson & Co., 27–29, 63, 148

Kobu Railway, 70, 112, 118

Kodama Gentarō, 143

Krupp AG, 118

Kume Kunitake, 27

Kunizawa Shinbei, 146

Kunz, A., 11, 37

Kyoto Imperial University, 112

Kyoto Railway, 119

Kyushu Railway, 62, 66, 72, 90, 91, 112, 113, 126, 127, 152, 159, 170; Kokura factory, 112

Lay, Horatio Nelson, 55, 56

Light Railway Act (Keiben tstsudō hō), 192

Light Railway Subsidy Act (Keiben tstsudō hojo-hō), 192, 193

Lima Locomotive Works, 34

Lindsley, John, 103, 104

Liverpool and Manchester Railway, 31, 32

localization, 2, 3, 6, 7, 21, 24, 166, 195, 197, 199, 201

Locomotivfabrik Krauss & Co., 37–40, 152

Lorimer, William, 31

Lowther, Gerald, 62, 81, 82

Ludwig Loewe & Co., 154

MacDonald, Claude M., 181

Malcolm Brunker & Co., 56, 60, 64, 66, 68–72, 74

Mallet compound locomotive, 112, 177, 178, 181, 190

Manchester Locomotive Works (later part of ALCO), 34, 35

Maschinenbau G. Vulkan (Vulcan Works in Stettin), 37, 175

Maschinenbauanstalt Übigau, 36

Maschinenfabrik Esslingen, 37, 39

Mason Machine Works, 34

Masudaya Kahei, 73

Matsukata Kōjirō, 172

Matsukata Masayoshi, 172

Matsumoto Sōichirō, 83, 97, 98, 126, 127

Messerschmidt, Wolfgang, 37

Midland Railway, 41, 50

Minami Kiyoshi, 93, 94, 103

Ministry of Civil Affairs (Minbu-shō), 56

Ministry of Communications and Transportation (Teishin-shō), 19, 86, 168

Ministry of Railways (Tetsudō-shō), 195

Ministry of Railways in the Republic of China, 204

Minnesota Land and Construction, 160

Mitchell, James, 30

Mitsubishi Gōshi (Mitsubishi LP), 73, 78, 171; Nagasaki shipyard,165, 194

Mitsui Bussan (Mitsui & Co.), 18, 23, 68, 95, 104, 109, 114–116, 130–133, 149, 153, 181, 182, 199, 200, 203; documents of, 20; in China, 149, 158–162, 189–190, 195; Machinery and

254

INDEX

Railway Units of, 107, 119, 158, 161; New York branch of, 119, 120, 128–130

Miyazaki Kōji, 83

Morel, Edmund, 56, 57, 60, 79

Mori Hikozō, 36, 38, 84, 170, 176

M. Raspe & Co., 68, 95, 153

Nakano Railway Battalion of Imperial Japanese Army, 112

Nakaoka Tetsurō, 21, 83

Nankai Railway, 129

Nara Railway, 15, 118

Narashino Horse Tramway, 111

Narita Railway, 70

Nasmyth Wilson & Co., 28, 29, 32, 45, 68, 69, 71, 74, 103, 118, 119, 121; export of, 33, 63, 64, 66

Nasmyth, James, 32

nationalization, railroad, 13, 18, 23, 66, 136, 146, 159, 160, 166–168, 189, 192, 201, 202; before, 18, 149, 169; after, 15, 93, 161, 163, 165, 172, 177, 195

Neilson, Reid & Co. (later part of NBL), 27–31, 33, 63–69, 71, 72, 91–93, 95, 129

Neilson, Walter, 30

New York & National Board of Marine Underwriters, 103

New York (Rome) Locomotive Works, 34

New York Oriental Steamship Co., 124

Newport Engine & Ship Building Co., 104

Niles Tool Works Co., 104

Nippon Railway, 61, 72, 74, 109, 111, 112, 126, 154; engineers of, 90, 91, 145, 170–171; locomotive purchasing by, 64, 66, 68, 69, 103, 105, 119, 159; Omiya factory, 91, 170; procurement system of, 94–96

Nippon Sharyō Ltd., 1, 171, 172, 190, 202

Nippon Yusen Kaishia (NYK Line), 117

Nogami Yaeji, 170

Norris Locomotive Works, 33, 34

North British Locomotive Company (NBL), 24, 30–32, 116, 132, 167, 177–182, 184, 189; export of, 29, 33, 63, 64, 66–68, 140, 148, 157

Norton Megaw & Co., 105

Ogasawara Shigeru, 37

Ogawa Shigen, 161

Ōkubo Toshimichi, 27

Ōkura Gumi (Ōkura & Co.), 20, 23, 24, 64, 88, 105, 114–116, 120–129, 148, 153, 199, 200; NBL and, 159, 178, 179, 181; Rogers and, 131–133

Ōkura Kihachirō, 120

Orenstein & Koppel AG, 193

Oriental Bank, 56, 60, 70

Osaka Electric Railway, 112

Osaka English School, 143

Osaka Railway, 64, 72–74, 118, 119

Ōsakayama Tunnel, 82

Ōta Yoshimatsu, 84, 170, 172, 176, 184

oyatoi, 5, 71, 82, 84, 86, 93, 113, 124, 194, 199, 200; system of, 22, 53–55, 60, 61, 70, 75, 134, 203

Parkes, Harry S., 55

Patrikeeff, Felix, 138

Peacock, Richard, 33

Pennsylvania Railroad, 98, 121

Pittsburgh Locomotive and Car Works (later part of ALCO), 34, 35, 159

Portland Locomotive Works, 34

Pownall, Charles A.W., 82

Provisional Military Railway Inspectorate (Japan), 138, 146, 156

Prussian State Railways, 39, 173–175

Qing Dynasty, 55, 136, 137, 142, 143

rack locomotive, 68

Railway Agency (Tetsudō-in), 24, 143, 144, 161, 165–172, 177–187, 189, 190, 192, 195, 196, 201, 202; Manufacturing Section, 86, 87, 154, 166, 169–172, 177, 182, 184

INDEX

Railway Bureau (Tetsudō-kyoku), 19, 57, 58, 60, 70, 71, 82, 86, 127, 134, 142, 143, 171; of Ministry of Communications and Transportation, 83, 87, 112, 131, 154, 168

Railway Bureau in the Office of the Governor-General in Korea, 146

Railway Construction Act, 141

Railway Department (Tetsudō-ryō), 56

Railway Operations Bureau (Tetsudō sagyō-kyoku), 83–85, 89, 156, 170

Rensselaer Polytechnic Institute, 83, 97

Rhode Island Locomotive Works (later part of ALCO), 34, 35, 160

Richmond Locomotive Works (later part of ALCO), 34, 35, 160

Robert Stephenson & Co., 27, 35

Rogers Locomotive Works (later part of ALCO), 33, 34, 116, 123–129, 131–133, 159, 160

Russo-Japanese War, 23, 66, 112, 130, 136, 138, 140, 148, 155–157, 160, 161, 202, 203; after, 135, 139, 141–143, 146, 147, 149, 159, 162, 163, 165, 171, 195

sales engineer, 5, 19, 23, 79, 104, 105, 109, 110, 113, 158, 202

sales representative, 5, 19, 23, 79, 105–109, 113, 198, 202

Samuel Samuel & Co., 148

Sangu Railway, 70

Sanyo Railway, 62, 66, 72, 74, 91–96, 103, 109, 112, 121, 170; Hyōgo factory, 91, 92; procurement system of, 94; Takatori factory, 170

Sawai Minoru, 14, 15, 17, 18

Schenectady Locomotive Works (later part of ALCO), 33–35, 88, 92, 119, 120, 123, 126–128, 159, 181

Schenectady-type superheater, 175

Schichau (manufacturer), 37

Schmidt, Wilhelm, 173, 174

Schmidt-type superheater, 155, 174, 175, 184

Scott, James, 118

Scott, Robert, 118

Sengoku Mitsugu, 83, 112

Settsu Tokihiko, 77

Shandong Railway, 190

Sharp Stewart & Co. (later part of NBL), 27, 30–32, 56, 63, 64, 66, 68, 71, 95, 129

Shervinton, Thomas R., 71, 89, 134

Shiba Gontarō, 85, 170, 177

Shibusawa Eiichi, 171

Shima Yasujirō, 86, 87, 91, 154, 155, 166, 170, 171, 173, 175–177, 179, 181–188

Shin Keita, 182

Shinkansen, 2, 7, 189, 205

Shukman, Harold, 138

Siberian Railway, 105, 138

Siemens (manufacturer), 205

Simon J. Gordon & Co., 105

Sino-Japanese War, First, 23, 80, 119, 135–138, 141–143, 163, 171, 200, 202; Second, 205

Sobu Railway, 69, 70

South Manchuria Railway (SMR), 101, 131, 139, 143, 147, 163, 173, 194, 202–204; locomotive purchasing by, 146, 149, 158, 160–162, 168, 190, 195

Southern Pacific Rrilroad, 117

Staby, W., 11, 37

Stephenson, George, 27

Suez Canal, 12, 117, 124, 160

superheated steam locomotive, 16, 24, 39, 50–52, 155, 166, 167, 173–189, 198

Suzuki Ikuyata, 85

Suzuki Sōjirō, 112

Taiwan Sōtokufu (the Office of the Governor General in Taipei), 121, 142–145; Civil Affairs Bureau, 143

Takasu Seiji, 170

Takata Shōkai, 64, 88, 95, 116–120, 148, 182, 199

Takata Shinzō, 117

INDEX

Tanaka Tokihiko, 16

Taunton Locomotive Manufacturing Co., 34

Tenyō Maru, 194

Tianjin-Pukou (Jinpu) Railway, 190

Tokyo Electric Railway, 111, 112, 159

Tokyo Higher Commercial School, 121

Tokyo Technical School (later Tokyo Higher Technical School), 83, 90, 91

Tokyo Imperial University, 83, 90, 194, 200, 201; Department of Civil Engineering, 121; Department of Mechanical Engineering, 84, 86, 87, 170, 187

Toyo Kisen Kaisha, 117

Training School for Railway Engineers (Kōgisei yōseisho), 60, 143

Trans-Taiwan Railways, 143–145

Treaty of Portsmouth, 140, 146

Treaty of Shimonoseki, 136

Trevithick, Francis H., 45, 46, 69, 71, 72, 82, 83, 103, 200

Trevithick, Richard Francis, 83- 85, 177

Tyler, Willard C., 79, 106–109, 128, 129, 202

Uchiyama Yorikichi, 124

uniform system of standard locomotives, 35

Union-Giesserei Lokomotivfabrik, 37

Usui Shigenobu, 18, 31, 59, 63, 69, 180, 193

Utsunomiya Kanichi, 131, 132

Vauclain compound locomotive, 92, 102, 109, 112

Vauclain Jr., Samuel M., 79, 109–113, 158, 202

Vauclain, Samuel M., 102, 109, 113

Vulcan Foundry Limited, 28, 29, 59, 63, 91, 119

Vulcan Iron Works, 34

Walter, W. B., 73

Watanabe Hidejirō, 158

Westinghouse Electric & Manufacturing Co., 104, 118

White, George P., 56

White, John, 34, 191

Whittall & Co., 148

William Duff & Son, 89

Wolmar, Christian, 17

working plan, 84, 92, 183, 201

Xinhai Revolution, 75

Yamada Majirō, 105, 121–127, 131–133

Yamamoto Koshirō, 107, 161, 162

Yamao Yōzō, 56, 60

Yano T., 73, 74

Yawata Steel Works, 111, 165

Yokohama Railway, 160

Yokohama Specie Bank, 100, 117, 125, 133

Yorkshire Engine Co., 63

Yoshikawa Sanjirō, 161, 162

Yoshino Matashirō, 85

Yue-Han Railway, 162

Yuzawa Takeshi, 17, 152

Zhejiang Railway, 163

Zushi Tamiyoshi, 83